Planning
a Family
Garden

Planning
—a Family—
Garden

GEORGE SEDDON

MACDONALD & CO
LONDON & SYDNEY

Copyright © George Seddon 1982

First published in Great Britain in 1982
by Macdonald & Co (Publishers) Ltd
London & Sydney

Holywell House
Worship Street
London EC2A 2EN

Design: *Anne Davison*
Illustration: *Andrew Farmer (pp. x–xi, 68–9,
    142–3 and 178) and Lorna Turpin*

ISBN 0 356 08539 2

Filmset by SX Composing Ltd
Rayleigh, Essex

Printed in Great Britain by
Hazell, Watson & Viney Ltd
Aylesbury, Bucks

Contents

Part One   A 'growing up' garden   9

What is a 'growing up' garden?   12
Where to start   14
An important digression on fertility   17
How to make paths and a patio   20
How to make lawns   28
How to build a raised bed   42
How to build a raised pool   52
Plants and fish for a small pool   61
The summerhouse   66

Part Two   A garden for a young family to grow up in   67

Children come first   70
The garden as a playground   72
How to make a sandpit   77
Somewhere to hide   79
The summerhouse as refuge   82
Which pets to choose   83
A child's own garden   90
Exit children   92

Part Three   How to garden in spite of the children   93

Up the wall   96
The front garden from a new angle   105
Planting a one-colour garden   108
Colour for autumn   129
The scented garden   131
Back to ferns   137
Insect life   139

Part Four   The garden in middle age   141

Time for change   144
A pick of the plants for ground cover   145
Put out more flags   157
Plants for tubs   160
With an eye to the future   165

Investing in a greenhouse   167
Making a hobby of alpines   172

Part Five   The garden in old age

Reducing the drudgery   179
Sitting comfortably   181
Gardening indoors   182

Epilogue   183

Index   185

Planning
a Family
Garden

A 'growing up' garden

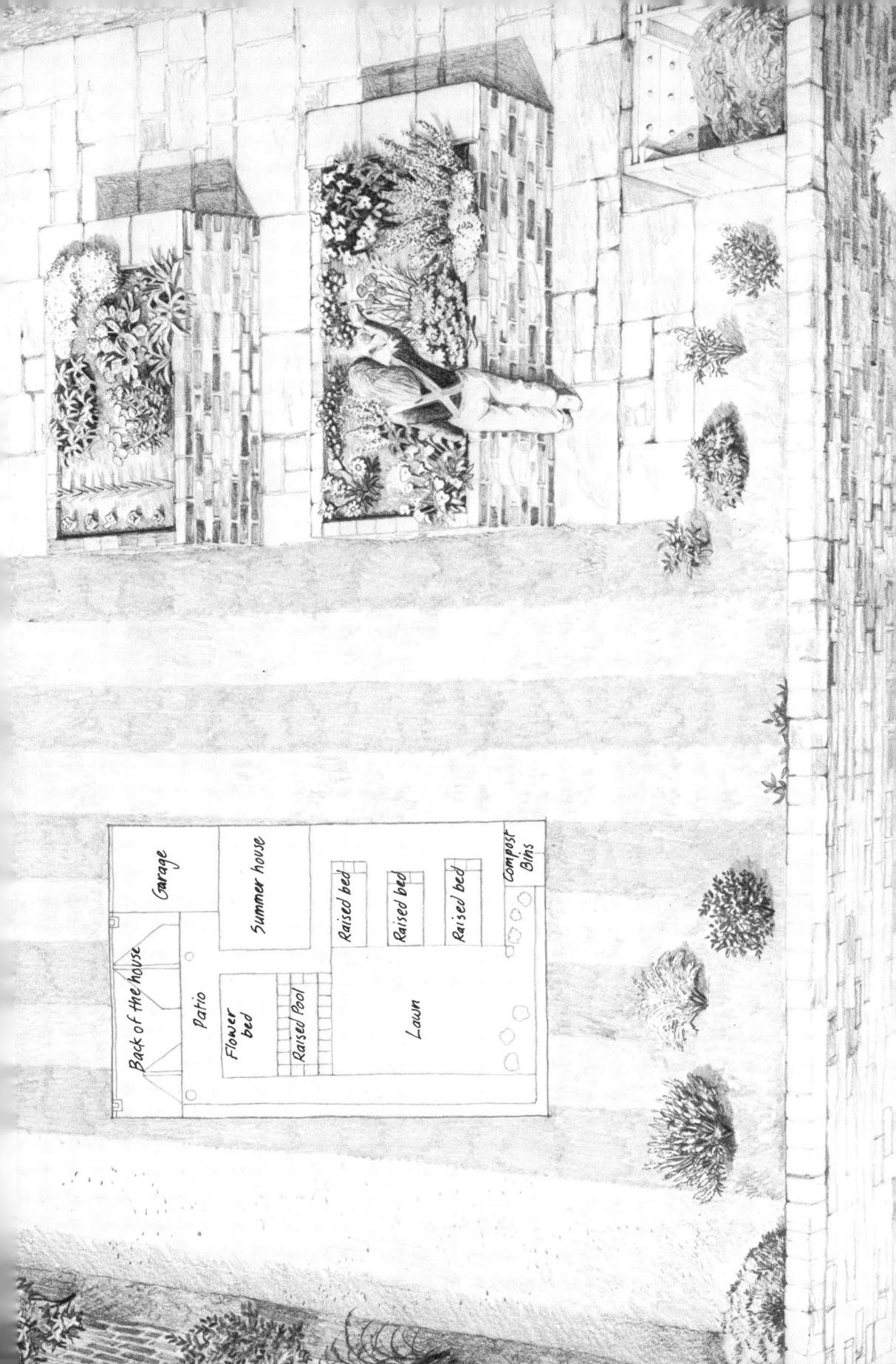

What is a 'growing up' garden?

People, not plants, are the important part of a garden. Admittedly you do not get this impression from glossy gardening books with their acres of well-groomed photographs and not a human being in sight. But a real garden is not a ghetto set aside for plants to grow in; like the house itself it is a place for people to grow up in happily and eventually to grow old in happily – to be enjoyed from the cradle to the grave.

How much enjoyment you get from a garden depends on putting it to the right use at different stages of life. If it is to be the rearing ground of a young family the roles it can play change rapidly over comparatively few years.

Even if you have no children the part that a garden – and looking after it – plays in your life must gradually change because of the physical fact of growing old. When you are twenty it is impossible to appreciate what your body will feel like at forty or seventy, a very fortunate safeguard for preserving the sanity of the young. But whatever else happens to you, you will grow older as long as you stay alive, and it is foolish to let the practical consequences of that take you by surprise, in gardening as in everything else. You probably already realize that when you are ninety you might not be able to bend down to weed, even though you can have no idea what it actually feels like to be ninety and not to be able to bend down to weed. Sensibly, long before that, you will have planned your garden so that it does not become a wilderness of weed constantly reminding you of your lost strength.

A 'growing up' garden must therefore be designed to anticipate, and adapt to, varying needs and, ultimately, to diminishing physical vigour. Such a garden would develop over the years, each change as far as possible incorporating what has gone before, thus saving both hard work and money. Without forethought you will constantly be tearing apart what you have created and starting again, or giving up in frustration.

Obviously the planning of a garden for a lifetime will largely be determined by whether there are children, in existence or projected, or whether there is none and will be none. Without children planning a garden is a far simpler affair. All you have to decide is whether, while you are still young, you want to do as much gardening as possible, or as little as you can get away with. If you are a keen gardener there are thousands of other books to egg you on and teach you how. If you are a reluctant gardener the sensible thing is to settle for old-age, minimum-work gardening right from the start; this book will help to show you how.

The book does not set out to be a blueprint for any one garden, let alone for all gardens. It tries to show that to get the best out of the modest patch which is the average modern garden it should be planned against the real background of the owner's life and not according to the extravagances of garden designers. Its aim is a flexible, developing, multi-purpose garden.

Even if you do not stay in the same garden all your life (and more people do than is generally imagined), each new garden you may have to tackle should be planned for the years ahead, so anticipating the later stages of life. This is even more vital if you start a new garden in middle age, otherwise you may leave planning your old-age garden too late and sadly find that you have not the energy or strength to carry out your plans.

Where to start

The majority of people are not seriously interested in gardening until they have a garden of their own. They are then seduced into creating the kind of garden which is entirely unsuited to their needs, present or potential. They have at the back of their minds, however it may have got there, an image of a dream garden, the kind of garden in which no one hangs out any washing.

The starting point of a garden more in touch with reality is to establish a basic framework at the start which can be used unchanged, or adapted, for a whole lifetime. This basic plan includes paths and a paved area; raised beds (and a raised pool if you wish); and a summerhouse. With proper care and maintenance they will last your lifetime and beyond. If you have a vast garden and money to match you may add tennis courts and swimming pools, but what I have in mind is a far less ambitious garden, but used ambitiously.

Paths

Every garden needs paths; and if the existing ones do not fit in with your overall plan you may have to tear them up and start again. As far as you can, and even farther, avoid building steps. Garden designers are obsessed with creating gardens on different levels 'to add interest'. This involves building steps, which add much more than interest – hazards for children and old people and obstacles for anyone with a barrow. Sloping paths are better than steps if the garden is not level. Children can use them in all kinds of play, barrows can face them, and old people can walk up and down them with less fear. (How to make paths and a patio, page 20.)

Paved areas

As well as paths every garden needs a paved area for sitting out – call it a patio if you must. The important thing about it is that it is a hard surface which will stand harder wear than a lawn, and dry out faster. The nearer the house the better, so that the child's pram can be watched from the house, or drinks and meals easily wheeled or carried out to it. If there is a choice, pick a site which is not exposed to the overhead summer sun and where the evening sun is not glaring straight in your eyes. If need be, partial shade may be achieved by giving it a living roof of climbing plants growing up a wooden framework. As you grow older other paved areas can be laid elsewhere in the garden to save labour. (How to make paths and a patio, page 20; Put out more flags, page 157.)

Raised beds

Some of my ideas for a family garden are based on hindsight, but other people's hindsight is not to be despised; turn it into your own foresight. I now know that the older you get the further away the ground seems to be and the harder it is to reach it. I did not appreciate that when I was young – if I had done so I would have been building raised beds to keep the ground within easy reach. An enormous amount of research is carried out to decide the proper height of working surfaces in the kitchen and in offices to prevent backache, but research into back-breaking gardening has been curiously neglected. Once you have realized that raised beds will be a must in old age it seems foolish not to take advantage of them for all your gardening life.

Raised beds have other and more immediate advantages besides this regard for old age. They create the garden designer's change of levels without the use of steps. They will feature largely in young children's imaginative play. Because the beds are small not many plants are needed to fill them, and those few plants make far more impact than they would have done at ground level. Moreover, the plants will be in no danger of being trampled on in the search for lost balls, and they are also reasonably safe from dogs. (How to build a raised bed, page 42.)

Raised pool

If you have a longing for a pool – an ornamental pool, not a swimming pool – it is sensible to make it a raised pool. Your children are less likely to fall into it and drown when they are young and you are less likely to stumble into it when you are old. As with raised beds you might as well have one right from the start so that you can enjoy it for as many years as you can. (How to build a raised pool, page 52.)

Summerhouse

Above all, at this early stage in house ownership I would build – or have built – a summerhouse. My first home after my marriage was a huge Victorian house in which a doctor and his wife had lived for forty years, bringing up three sons. Not counting vast cellars the house had eighteen rooms, only two of which, in those postwar years, we could sparsely furnish. In the garden there was an old, but perfectly sound, wooden summerhouse. It was this, and the uses we and our young son found for it – as our predecessors and their children had obviously done – that made me realize the infinite virtues of a well-designed summerhouse. It is potentially the most useful feature of any garden, especially a family garden.

An increasing number of house owners decide at some time in their life to embark on a home extension, often not until the house is bursting at the seams. The family has grown but the house has not. Then a prefabricated unit is tacked on, or a room blending with the architecture of the house is added, or living space is carved out of the attic.

But instead of waiting years to spread, is it not more sensible to do this as soon as possible? You will have use of the extra space for so much longer and, in these inflationary times, it will cost you far less.

Services

Such thinking ahead is a vital ingredient in planning a garden for a lifetime. One important aspect is making provision for such essential services as water and electricity. These are far easier and cheaper to install when the framework of the garden is being built. Having decided where you want the raised beds and the pool (and, eventually, the greenhouse) lay water pipes to them before putting down paths. The summerhouse and the greenhouse will also need electricity; lay the cables, enclosed in plastic pipes, right at the start. This will avoid an enormous amount of labour and disturbance later, and extra expense. There is no need, however, to buy at the start all of the electrical and automatic watering equipment you may want later. Better to spread the cost as much as you can.

Plants

Paths, paved areas, raised beds, a pool and a summerhouse do not make a garden, but only the skeleton of one. It then has to be fleshed out with people and clothed with plants.

Advice about the planting of the garden is given under the following heads:

Plants to liven up paths (page 24)
How to make lawns (page 28)
Plants and fish for a small pool (page 61)
Up the wall (page 96)
The front garden from a new angle (page 105)
Planting a one-colour garden (page 108)
Colour for autumn (page 129)
The scented garden (page 131)
Back to ferns (page 137)
A pick of the plants for ground cover (page 145)
Plants for tubs (page 160)

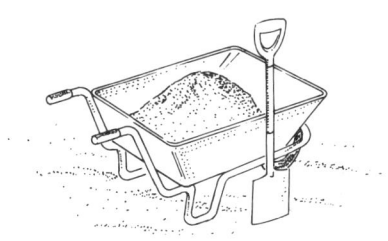

An important digression on fertility

With monotonous regularity we feed ourselves, our children, our pets and even our house plants – but we are far more lax about feeding our soil. Yet building up and maintaining a fertile soil is the number one priority of gardening. Plants, like us, need food to grow. They cannot live by sunlight, fresh air and rain alone – though all these play a vital part in their existence. They have a mass of roots so that they can draw up nutrients from the soil which, with the help of the sun and air, will provide them with the carbohydrates and proteins they need for growth. The nutrients they take out of the soil have to be replaced, and this should be a continuing process all your gardening life.

When I was a child loads of farmyard manure were delivered each spring, but those halcyon days are gone. Chemical fertilizers are not enough, for the soil must also be rich in humus if most plants are to flourish. Humus is the substance in the soil that is formed by the decay of organic matter. One obvious sign of humus-rich soil is its dark colour. It makes light soil spongy and water-holding, thus less liable to dry out, and heavy or clayey soils more friable and easy to work. But its main virtue is that its micro-organisms help to break down the minerals in the soil so that they can be absorbed by the roots of plants.

What the plants take out of the soil they can in part give back – with your help – in composting garden waste. A compost heap is not a pile of stinking rubbish left to look after itself. You have to provide the right conditions in which bacteria can convert dying organic matter into living humus; to do this bacteria need air, moisture, nitrogen and warmth. The warmth is in fact generated during the decomposition of the material, but if too much heat escapes the heap will cool before the conversion into humus has been completed. For a small garden the only reliable way to make compost is to do it in a container which will help to hold in the warmth. There are a number of compost bins on the market, and two of these would be suitable for a small garden. Better still you can build your own compost containers, either of stout wood, not creosoted, or of brick for longer life.

It takes from two to three months in summer and four to six months in winter for rubbish to decompose into compost, so build two containers side by side: when one is full the compost in it can be left to mature, while you fill up the other one.

What goes into a compost heap?

All leaves and soft stems from the garden. All vegetable waste from the kitchen. Keep this separate from tins and plastic containers and wrappings. Paper bags and wrappings will rot down.

Lawn mowings are all right in moderation, but a thick layer of young grass turns to revolting slime. Nonetheless it is a pity not to use it, and if you have a large lawn it is worth buying straw or wood shavings (not from conifers) to mix with the mowings. Alternatively there are proprietary activators available specially for rotting down grass cuttings.

What does not go into a compost heap

Anything which has recently been sprayed with weedkiller. Grass mowings must not be put on the compost heap if the lawn has been treated with hormone weed-killers unless you are certain that the compost will not be used on the garden for at least six months. Tough woody stems, except to use as the bottom layer of the heap for the sake of ventilation. The roots of perennial weeds. Diseased plants. Burn these instead, but do not let the potash-rich ash get wet. Store it for use in the garden, or sprinkle it on the compost heap.

How to make compost

Spread a layer of coarse garden rubbish over the base of the compost bin to a depth of about 8in (20cm) and put a 6in (15cm) layer of softer rubbish on top of that. Sprinkle a proprietary compost activator over the layer, following the maker's instructions: this provides the nitrogen necessary for decomposition. Add further rubbish in layers of 6–8in (15–20cm), watering if it is dry, and pressing it down if it is very loose. If it is too tightly packed there will not be enough air for the bacteria

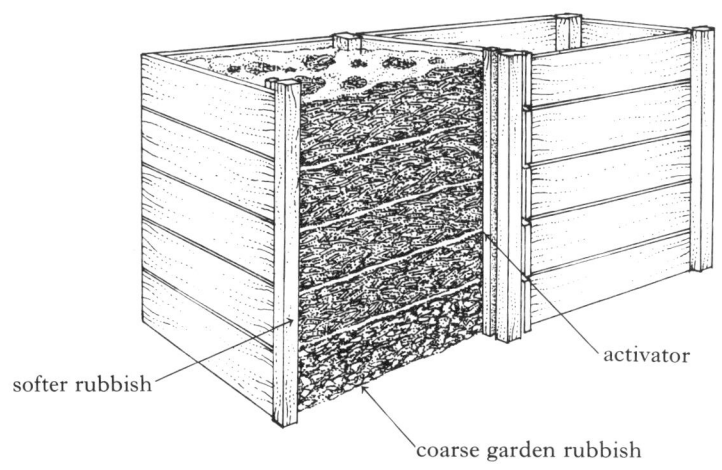

softer rubbish

activator

coarse garden rubbish

Wooden compost bins; cutaway shows layers of compost.

to work efficiently, but if it is too loose the heap will not stay moist, and the bacteria will again be inhibited. Water each layer, if necessary, and sprinkle with activator. If all goes well the heap will quickly heat up – most rapidly in summer – and it will also shrink. When the container will hold no more a shallow covering of soil can be put over the top layer, but this is not essential. It is vital, however, to cover it with black plastic sheeting to keep out rain.

How to use compost

Well-made compost is a complete plant food; it can be used in the first place to enrich the soil in the raised beds, and when planting shrubs, climbers and cordon fruit trees. After that it will maintain the fertility of the soil over the years.

Used as a mulch compost both improves the fertility of the soil and smothers annual weeds. Once a year spread not less than 2in (5cm) of compost on the surface of the soil. For suppressing weeds it is most effective if applied in the spring, but wait until the soil has warmed up after the winter. Spread the mulch when the soil is moist; it will help to keep the moisture in.

If you are able to make a considerable quantity of compost you will not only achieve a remarkably fertile garden but be free to give up digging and most hoeing and take to mulching instead. Before changing over to no-digging you will have to make a determined effort to get rid of deep-rooting perennial weeds, which mulching does not easily suppress. Start with a mulch of up to 4in (10cm) in spring and repeat it in early autumn. Constant mulching will encourage worms to breed and they will do the job of taking the humus down to the roots of the plants and aerating and draining the soil for you. This is what you imagine you are doing when you dig, whereas in fact the main result is to disturb all the good work which the worm population is doing more efficiently. Of course at first the worms have to be encouraged to breed by a fertile soil, but the compost provides that.

A mulch of well-made compost should suppress annual weeds and repeated mulches, undisturbed by digging, will make the surface soil so much more friable that perennial weeds will be more easily uprooted.

A fertile soil means healthier plants, and though no one can guarantee that disease will never strike a humus-rich soil it gives the plants a better chance to resist it. This is preferable to spending a fortune on the indiscriminate use of insecticides and fungicides, so many of which have undesirable side-effects. Of course there is a snag – the labour of making the compost. But that takes us back to our starting point: that fertility is the number one priority of gardening. Time and labour spent on that is time and labour that the gardener cannot use more profitably.

How to make paths and a patio

A garden path is meant for use: to walk on, push a barrow along or commandeer as a tricycle race track, for example. A paved garden is something different, and in a 'growing up' garden may sensibly be its ultimate stage, providing carefree permanent ground cover when we have only enough energy left to cultivate small areas.

When we start work on a virgin garden the only paving immediately needing to be done is for paths and a small paved area, call it a patio or yard or whatever you will. Extending the area of paving in order to cut down labour can begin in middle age, and before joints begin to creak if it is to be a do-it-yourself job. In this way the heavy expense of paving may be spread over a long period of years.

If you take over a garden with paths already laid any initial expense can be avoided or delayed if the existing paths fit in with the early stages of your lifetime gardening plans. Some, or all, of the paths can be changed or adapted later as the garden develops to meet 'the family's' needs. Do your best to anticipate what those needs will be and so avoid having to tear the garden apart because you didn't look ahead and get things right in the first place, especially with such costly features as paths.

Paving materials

The list of materials which could be used for paving is long, but most of them can be crossed off because they are too expensive, too hazardous for the young and old to walk on, plain ugly, or unsuitable for their surroundings. Newly quarried stone, slate and marble are out because of the cost; gravel and cobbles are murder for young and old to walk on; wood is slippery and crazy paving is likely to trip you up. Concrete laid in situ looks too stark. Asphalt or tarmac paths seem reminiscent of municipal gardens; concrete laid in situ is preferable to those for a drive or path which will get a lot of hard wear.

Having excluded so many materials, for whatever reasons, we are left basically with second-hand stone flags, second-hand and new bricks (hard, dense bricks, because soft bricks suffer damage through frost) and concrete slabs, which are cheaper than either bricks or stone flags, though more expensive than concrete laid in situ.

Concrete slabs are now made in many shapes, sizes, colours and textures – too many indeed, for an over-patterned path can be a disaster. However proud of it you may be at the start, because it is entirely different from the paths the neighbours have, you may soon come to hate it. This may happen even with the interlocking concrete blocks which are fast becoming a cliché. The simpler the pattern the less chance you will tire of it.

On the other hand there is no need to make it look like a street pavement; a restrained pattern can be achieved with plain concrete slabs using a contrast of sizes: 2ft x 2ft (60cm x 60cm), 2ft x 18in (60cm x 45cm), 1ft x 1ft (30cm x 30cm), and 1ft x 6in (30cm x 15cm) are stock sizes. (Warning: the two smaller sizes are only 1½in (4cm) thick whereas the larger are 2in (5cm) thick; mixing them all would therefore involve some tricky laying.)

Bricks, flags and concrete slabs may also be used for patios, but there are additional forms of paving suitable for them which might be too formal for paths. The best of these are brick paviors – brick-shaped but thinner than bricks and more hard-wearing – and quarry tiles, which are even harder-wearing. The main disadvantage of quarry tiles is that they are rather slippery when wet, but you are unlikely to be out on the patio then. They are also not easy laying for the amateur do-it-yourselfer. For more suggestions on paving, see pages 157–9.

Constructing a path or patio

A firm path depends on good foundations. To be on the safe side they should be 4in (10cm) deep, so dig out the soil to that depth, plus the depth of the bricks or slabs, plus the depth of the sand or mortar on which they are to be bedded. Start with a layer of rubble, ram it down hard, add a layer of smaller rubble and ram that down. On top of that spread a layer of sand, ashes or finely sifted soil, 1in (2.5cm) thick at one edge of the path but slightly thicker at the other edge; the slope will drain the water off. On top, lay the stone flags or concrete slabs. For better support put a dab of mortar at the point where the four corners of the slab will lie, and another dab in the middle. Use a mortar made of 1 part cement, 2 parts hydrated lime (soaked in water the previous day to make a paste) and 5 parts sand. Tap the slab gently into place.

The slabs may be laid hard against one another, or a gap of up to ½in (1.5cm) may be left between each one and pointed with mortar later. For this pointing use a tougher mortar without lime – 1 part cement to 4 parts sand.

Bricks are best laid on a bed of mortar 1in (2.5cm) thick, using a mix of 1 part cement and 4 parts sand. A ⅜in (1cm) mortar joint between the bricks would be suitable.

Patios can be constructed in the same way if you are using stone flags, concrete slabs or bricks. If the patio is laid right up against the house it is absolutely essential that it is 6in (15cm) below the level of the damp course of the wall; otherwise you will have built a source of rising damp. The paving should also slope away from the house; it need not be much – 1in (2.5cm) in every 10ft (3m) is sufficient.

Paviors and quarry tiles should be bedded in cement. This is probably best done by a professional, since learning by experience would be costly.

Making a concrete garden path

The path should be at least 3ft (90cm) wide so that two people can walk along it side by side. The concrete should be 3½in (9cm) thick, the mix being 1 part cement, 2 parts builder's sand and 4 parts coarse aggregate. You will need enough boards – old floorboards, for example – to line each side of the path to give a straight edge to the concrete and enough pegs – at least 1ft (30cm) long – to be placed 3ft (90cm) apart to hold the boards in position, plus a few wooden lathes, the width of the path, to lay between the boards at 5ft (1.5m) intervals.

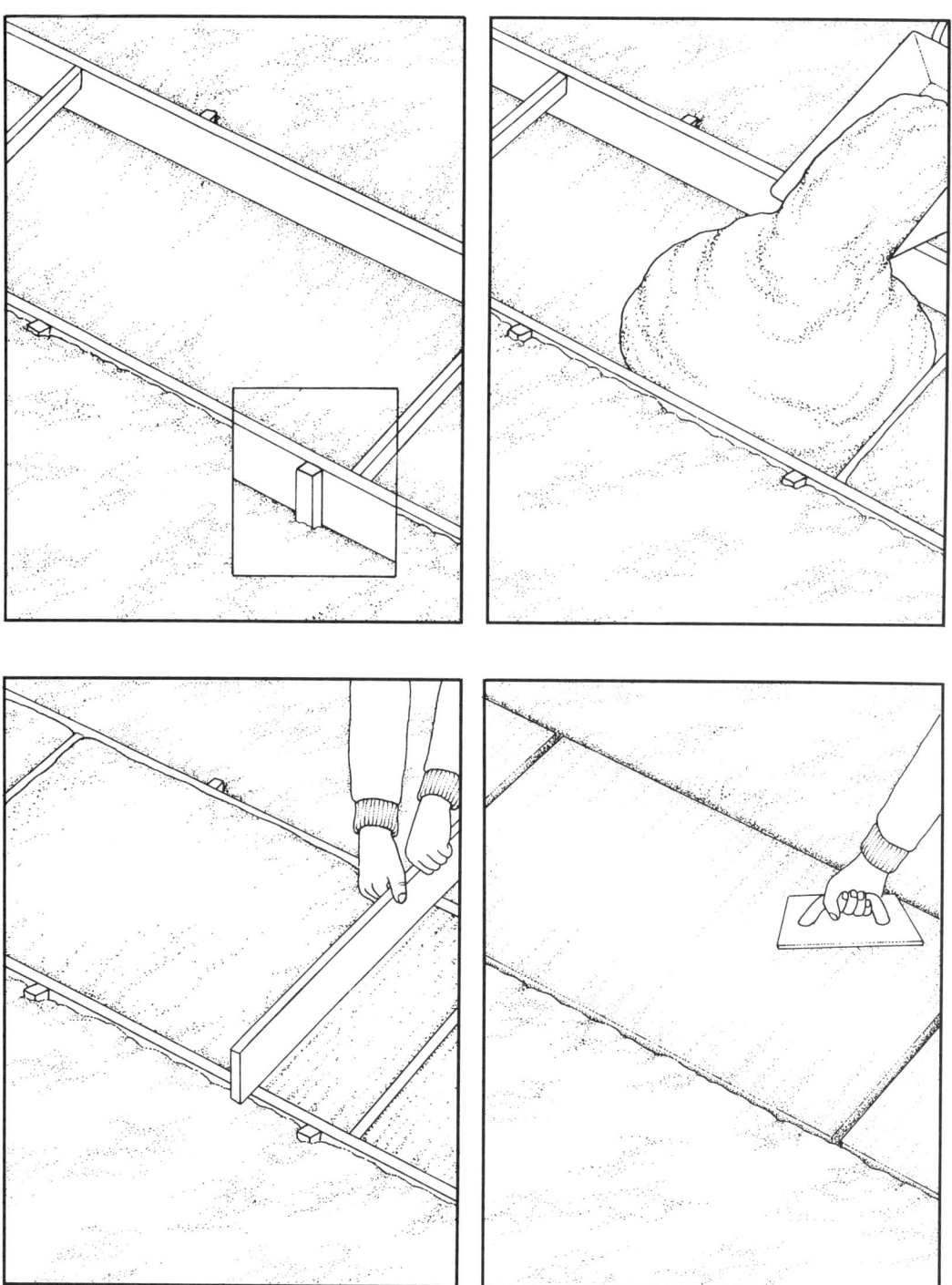

How to lay a concrete path. *Top left :* **framework of boards and lathes.** *Top right :* **pouring in the concrete.** *Bottom left :* **tamping the concrete.** *Bottom right :* **levelling with wooden float**

Mark out the course of the path and remove the soil to a depth of $3\frac{1}{2}$in (9cm) and to a width an inch or two wider than that of the finished path. If the ground is not firm at that depth remove more soil, enough to put down a 2in (5cm) layer of hardcore, well rammed down.

Drive the framework of boards, nailed to the pegs, into place so that the top of the board is at the height you want the path to be. To allow the water to drain off a path which is on level ground make one edge of a 3ft (90cm) path 1in (2.5cm) higher than the other side. Make sure the slope of the path is in the direction in which the water will drain away most readily and without causing damage – for example slope it away from any wall or fence, not towards it.

If no hardcore has been used spread $\frac{1}{2}$in (1.5cm) of sand over the soil – this is better than laying the concrete directly on the soil. This is not necessary if there is a base of hardcore.

To reduce the danger of cracks appearing in the concrete do not lay it in a long continuous strip. Provide a slight gap at 5ft (1.5m) intervals. This is done by wedging a 3in (7.5cm) batten on edge between the boards on either side of the path. Lightly grease or oil the battens before putting them in place so that they can be removed later. If you want plants growing out of the path, holes for pockets of soil can be made by standing greased plastic plant pots on the hardcore or sand base and laying the concrete round them. Remove when the concrete has set.

Have all this preliminary work entirely finished before mixing the concrete – and even more so if the concrete is being delivered; you will have little enough time just to lay the path in the couple of hours before the concrete starts setting. Tip the concrete between the boards as quickly as you can so that it is a little proud above the top of the boards. Then work a plank along the surface of the concrete a little at a time, lifting it up slightly and then letting it fall, to tamp the concrete. Use the plank also to work off any surplus concrete.

It is safer to have a rough surface to the path than a smooth one; it will also weather better. Tamping will achieve this roughness. But if the result is too rough for your liking, level off the surface with a wooden float (a flat piece of wood with a handle) as the concrete is setting and then roughen it up again as much as you wish by drawing a stiff bristled brush over the surface.

Cover the concrete with polythene sheeting so that it does not dry out quickly; the slower it dries the harder it will be. Leave the covering in place for at least ten days. After that the path can be used with care, but it will be at least a month before the concrete is thoroughly hardened.

Then remove the boards along the sides of the path. Ease out the battens across the path and fill the gaps with sand, so providing expansion and shrinkage joints which will prevent cracking. Or the gaps could be filled with soil in which small carpeting plants could be grown. The straight edges of the path can be softened by growing clumps of plants alongside and letting them encroach on to the concrete.

Making a concrete drive for a car

The drive should be at least 6ft (1.8m) wide, with the concrete laid 4in (10cm) deep on a bed of hardcore 4in (10cm) deep. 8in (20cm) of soil will therefore have to be excavated. An alternative method is to lay two strips of concrete 30in (75cm) wide to take the wheels of the car, with a gap between of about 20in (50cm). This could be filled with flags, bricks or gravel to relieve the boredom of unbroken concrete. It is no place to try to grow any plants, however, exposed as it will be to oil dripping from the car engine and fumes belching from the exhaust.

The actual construction of the drive is the same as for a path, but the gaps between the sections of the concrete could be filled with some bituminous mixture instead of sand.

Plants to liven up paths

Clumps of dwarf plants growing in gaps in paths or spilling over the edges can transform even a dull stretch of concrete. The more paving of any kind you have the more it will need enlivening in this way. Many rockery plants are suitable provided that the pockets of soil in which they are growing are well drained to allow the water from the path to soak away quickly.

Here are a few suggestions for suitable flowering plants for paved gardens, arranged in seasons of flowering. Most of them are evergreen.

Minuartia (Arenaria) verna caespitosa 'Aurea'
1–3in (2.5–7.5cm). Evergreen.
A cushion of narrow grey-green leaves with white star-like flowers in spring. Very hardy.

Aubretia deltoidea
4in (10cm). Evergreen.
One of the most popular carpeters, smothered in spring with flowers in all shades of pink, red and purple. Does best in limy, well-drained soil and sun. Suitable for the seaside. Can grow straggly if not trimmed back.

Phlox subulata (Moss phlox)
4in (10cm). Deciduous.
Large spreading mats of small narrow leaves and innumerable flowers in spring: 'Temiscaming' is magenta, 'G. F. Wilson' lavender-blue. Will grow in limy soil and by the sea. Trim back after flowering to prevent straggly growth.

Armeria caespitosa (Thrift)
3in (7.5cm). Evergreen.
Neat, dense cushions of grass-like leaves with pink flowers in early summer; 'Bevan's Variety' is one of the best. Should have well-drained position in sun; it flourishes near the sea.

Saxifraga paniculata (*S. aizoon*)
3–4in (7.5–10cm). Evergreen.
Mounds of silvery leaves with white, pink or yellow flowers in early summer.

Warning: a bent back can seriously damage your health

Right and wrong ways of lifting a heavy sack

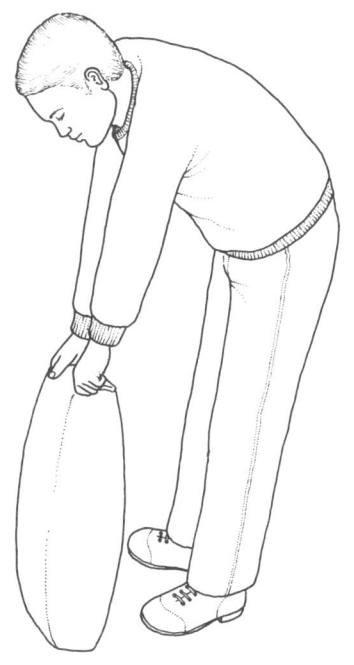

Laying paths, building walls, putting down lawns and other major construction work in the garden may be satisfying, but persons not accustomed to hard physical work will find it arduous. Do not charge at any such job like a bull, but use your head to work out how to make the most efficient use of your body. Your spine is the most vulnerable part of your body in many gardening operations; the first lesson to learn is to keep your back as straight as possible so that other parts of your body take the brunt of the work.

Faced with a delivery of cement do not bend over to lift the sack by the top; hoisting it up that way will put a great strain on your spine. Bend a knee, steady the top of the bag with one hand and put the other under the bottom of the bag. Straighten your knee, clutching the bag close to you as you get up.

Carry it in the same way, with one hand under the sack and the other holding it well up towards your shoulder and close to your body. Do not lean over to put down the sack; keeping your back straight, go down on one knee and lower the sack.

If in laying paths or lawns you have to sift soil or sand, again beware of injuring your spine. If you stand up straight, as you should for your back's sake, all the sifted soil will drop on your feet, but if you bend forward, as most people do, you will put enormous strain on your back. Instead raise the sieve off the ground on two boxes and shovel the soil through it.

Lithospermum diffusum
    8in (20cm). Evergreen.
    Forms a large mat of small hairy leaves with vividly blue flowers in late spring and early summer. Not for limy soils.

Veronica prostrata (V. rupestris)
    5in (12.5cm). Evergreen.
    A widely spreading mat of dark green leaves and a mass of bright blue flowers in early summer; 'Mrs Holt' is a rosy pink variation.

Dianthus gratianopolitanus (D. caesius)
    3in (7.5cm). Evergreen.
    A fairly open mat of grass-like leaves covered with a profusion of pink, heavily scented flowers in summer. Prefers well-drained, limy soil in sun. Will grow by the sea. An alternative is the popular *D. deltoides* (Maiden pink) which forms a loose mat, covered with pink or white flowers in summer.

Mentha requienii
    1in (2.5cm). Evergreen.
    A very ground-hugging carpeter. It grows more vigorously in the shade, but in summer bears more flowers – mauve and minute – if in the sun. Pungent when trodden on.

Cotula squalida
    2in (5cm). Evergreen.
    Rosettes of small, bronzy green, ferny leaves make a mat which will withstand a certain amount of treading on. Small, daisy-like, creamy flowers appear in summer. Thrives in limy soils and dry sunny positions.

Sedum acre (Stonecrop)
    2in (5cm). Evergreen.
    Forms a mat of rather succulent leaves (not to be trodden on) which may be smothered by bright yellow star-like flowers in summer. The leaves of *S. anglicum* are tinged with pink and its flowers are white. Plant in the sun.

Campanula portenschlagiana
    4in (10cm). Deciduous.
    Rapid grower to make a large mat of small dark green leaves with many lilac bell-like flowers in mid summer. Will grow in sun or part shade. Suitable for limy soils, and for town or seaside gardens. *C. cochlearifolia* (Fairies' thimbles) (3in (7.5cm)) has white or pale blue flowers – very pretty.

Thymus serpyllum
    2in (5cm). Evergreen.
    A creeping mat with small aromatic leaves and crimson, pink or white flowers in mid summer. Best when young, because bare patches develop as it ages. Needs warmth, sun and well-drained soil. It will tolerate the seaside.

Acantholimon glumaceum
    3in (7.5cm). Evergreen.
    A hummock of dark green sharp leaves with pink flowers in mid summer. It

needs a well-drained position in full sun. Suitable for the seaside.

Hypericum reptans (St John's wort)
   1in (2.5cm). Deciduous.
   A good spread of minute leaves with deep yellow flowers from summer to autumn. Prefers sun, but will tolerate shade and seaside conditions.

Hypericum reptans and *Lithospermum diffusum* can be propagated by cuttings. The rest are most simply increased by division.

How to make lawns

How right Margery Fish was when she wrote in *Carefree Gardening* (David and Charles): 'If there is no grass in the garden one's worries practically disappear.' Nonetheless most people still look on a lawn as an essential part of a garden. But there are lawns and lawns.

For a child a lawn is something to play on, not something which just lies there and looks pretty. A child's lawn must therefore be above all hard-wearing, while staying reasonably presentable. Those gardeners who still cling to the image of the English garden with immaculately manicured lawns dotted with beds of roses will aim at something more sophisticated. But be warned, the more beautiful you try to make your lawn the bigger sweat it will be looking after it. When you get older the attractions of a lawn will diminish as the effort needed to care for it becomes increasingly onerous and eventually impossible. Before that frustrating stage is reached it is better to have covered the ground with something other than grass.

Thus the six ages of man, from the mewling, puking infant to the lean and slippered pantaloon, can be served by three stages of lawn: the lawn utilitarian, the lawn beautiful and the lawn dispensed with. (At Shakespeare's seventh stage – 'sans teeth . . . sans everything' – the grass will be above us.)

The lawn dispensed with will be dealt with later (pages 144–59). At this stage of our garden we are concerned with:

1. What to do to improve neglected grass you inherit on moving into a house – or later when you want to change the lawn from the utilitarian to the post-children beautiful.

2. How, starting from scratch, to make a lawn – utilitarian or beautiful – from seed or turf.

3. How to keep the lawn in good shape.

Improving a lawn

If you move into anything except a brand new house you are likely to inherit some kind of lawn. Almost as likely it will be somewhat neglected. How neglected will depend on the care the previous owners gave it and how long the house has been empty and at what time of the year. If the house has been unoccupied during the winter and the grass untouched by human hands or feet you can start work on it in early spring where your predecessors left off. But a lawn that is left untouched for any length of time soon goes downhill; a mat of withered grass builds up, and the coarser grasses smother the finer grasses and seedlings, so leaving behind serious problems for the future.

Initial cutting

Let us start with grass which has been left uncut. First it has to be got down to a reasonable length. This will probably be more than a cylinder mower (see page 39) can tackle, especially if the grass is tangled. It is certainly not worth risking damaging a new machine just to find out what punishment it can take. Instead use the shears. This is tedious – and as soon as you start you will realize why the shears have to be sharp. There is, of course, no need to kill yourself doing it all at once. If the 'lawn' is obviously too big for your shears, or patience, hire a rotary mower (see pages 39–40) or ask a good friend and his rotary mower round for a drink.

At the first cutting do not shave the grass right down to its roots (indeed, never do that). Give it a few days' respite, so that the stems have a chance to raise their heads, to be taken off in a second cutting down to not below $1\frac{1}{2}$in (4cm).

Do not worry that the result looks a mess; it will look even worse before it begins to improve. Cutting the grass will have revealed how much rubbish there was lurking underneath, matted grass, the rotting leaves of weeds and probably moss.

Scratching

What it needs now is a good savage scratch to let in air and sun. Use the extraordinarily effective wire rake, with its tough springy tines; an ordinary garden rake is useless for this job. Even with a wire rake it is hard work, but it needs to be done thoroughly, though not necessarily in one mad burst of enthusiasm. Put the mounds of rubbish you remove on the compost heap, from which it will emerge as the humus your garden can never have too much of.

Some moss, clover and weeds will come away with this raking, but the main purpose is to get rid of the dead material; there are other less exhausting ways of getting rid of the unwanted growth later. ('Unwanted' only means that there is more than you are willing to tolerate; my own threshold of tolerance of 'weeds' in a lawn is pretty high.)

Spiking

If you start work on renovating the lawn in spring or summer the best thing you can do is to leave any further drastic treatment until the autumn. You will thus be able to use the 'lawn' during the summer and by regular mowing improve the quality of the grass.

If you start on the lawn in the autumn you can quickly follow the scratching by spiking the lawn, which is meant to let air down to the roots and improve the drainage. Grass, like other plants, can suffer from oxygen starvation in the ground. It is more likely to do so if you have a family walking, running, jumping and skipping over it, ramming the soil into a solid mass which air and water find hard to percolate.

Spiking, which should be done every year, can be carried out at any time between October and March, except (for the lawn's sake) when the grass has frost on it, or (for your sake) when it is sodden. If the area is not too great and the soil is fairly light an ordinary garden fork can be used. Press the fork into the ground, move back 8in (20cm) and press it in again, and so on until the whole lawn has been pricked. As you will realize this is a laborious operation, particularly on heavy soil. As spiking a lawn is a yearly operation you may think it worthwhile investing right at the start in a simple mechanical aerator, which looks like a lawn mower with spikes instead of blades.

Dressing

After scratching and spiking comes the 'dressing' of the lawn. This involves scattering all over it a mixture of equal parts of loam, sharp sand and peat (about 2lb (900g) to the square yard (or metre)). If you then go over the surface with the back of an ordinary garden rake much of it will be worked into the holes you have made during spiking.

By now the 'lawn' will be looking very sorry for itself, so leave it alone to recover until the spring, when the grass begins to grow again. Then you can tackle further rehabilitation – levelling out bumps and hollows, fertilizing, reseeding bare patches and getting to work on too impudent weeds and moss.

Levelling

In spring first sort out the minor bumps and hollows which fox the mower; it slices off the tops of the bumps right down to the soil and in the hollows cannot cut the grass close enough. Using a spade or a half moon lawn edger, mark the area of a rectangle of turf around the bump or hollow that will have to be removed for levelling. If it is small enough to be lifted in one piece that is fine, but with a larger area divide it into smaller rectangles to make more manageable turfs, each one not much bigger than the size of the spade you will lift them with. The reason is that turfs from neglected lawns tend to disintegrate easily when being handled.

To remove the turf first cut down about 2in (5cm) deep into the ground along the lines you have already marked. Then comes the tricky bit for the novice: slicing through the soil and grass roots beneath the surface so that each turf you remove is of uniform depth. The design of the spade and the angle at which you are having to use it conspire to force the blade deeper into the soil the further you push it along. However, if you start at rather more than $1\frac{1}{2}$in (4cm) deep and finish somewhat deeper the turfs can easily be trimmed when you have lifted them. Make a three-sided box with the sides $1\frac{1}{2}$in (4cm) deep. Place a turf upside down in the box and slice off the surplus soil to the height of the sides. It is essential to have turfs of uniform depth if you hope to get your lawn level; trying to contour the soil underneath to fit an uneven sod never works, whereas it is easy to produce a level base for a uniform turf.

Use soil, or a mixture of equal parts of loam, peat and sharp sand, to raise the level of the ground where a hollow was, firming down the new soil before re-placing the turf. Where there are bumps remove as much soil as necessary to give a level surface. Fill in the crevices between the replaced turfs with sieved soil, or loam, peat and sand.

If the edge of the lawn looks as though something has been chewing it, cut out and lift a square of turf and relay it so that the ragged bit faces into the lawn and you have a straight line at the edge again. Level up the damaged part with soil and leave it to heal itself – or you can encourage it with a sprinkling of grass seed when the weather is warm enough.

Feeding

The next step in the regeneration of the lawn is to feed it. The time to do this will depend on whether you live in the warm south, when it could be the beginning of March, or the cold north, when it might be into April. But the dates will also vary if spring arrives unusually early or unusually late. The correct time is when the grass is beginning to grow. The fine grasses are the first to start growing, and the idea is to encourage them to spurt ahead, giving them a better chance to hold their own against the coarse meadow grasses, which are late starters.

Misers and masochists can mix their own fertilizers, but the rest of us will probably settle for proprietary balanced lawn fertilizer containing nitrogen, phosphate and potash. Use it according to the instructions, which will probably recommend $1\frac{1}{2}$–2oz (40–50g) to the square yard (or metre). Do not imagine that giving more will do the grass more good; overfeeding is as bad for the lawn as it is for you. A heavy dosage of nitrogen will, admittedly, produce a luxuriant dark green growth within a few weeks, but the foliage will be soft and won't stand up to hard wear, and later the coarse, tough-stemmed grasses will become impossibly aggressive.

Overfeeding is not always deliberate; if you are scattering the fertilizer by hand it is hard to know how much you are distributing, or whether you are doing it evenly. Marking out the lawn, with a string, into strips of 2 or 3 square yards (1.7–2.5 sq.m) will help to ensure that you do not go diabolically wrong. There is something to be said for buying a simple spreader. Even then you have to master the art of pushing it in a straight line and controlling the rate at which the fertilizer falls out.

Choose a day when the ground is moist but the grass itself is dry (so that the fertilizer does not cling to the blades, scorching them). Then hope for a shower of rain to save you the trouble of having to water the fertilizer in.

Reseeding

Reseeding of the balding parts of a lawn is best done a little later in the spring, ideally when the weather is warm and showery and conducive to germination and certainly not when the soil is both stone cold and dry. For this kind of patching a general purpose grass seed mixture is adequate, for in no time the finest, most expensive strains will be swamped by the existing dominant grasses. Loosen just the hard surface of the bare soil, with a fork or rake, and spread over it some moist seed compost in which the grass seeds have already been mixed. Firm it gently with your feet.

Applying weedkiller

Finally there is the little matter of weeds in the lawn. Once upon a time gardeners spent far too much time plucking out the offending intruders, now they spend far too much money buying weedkillers to eradicate them. If you have a mind to spend the money you can achieve an almost totally weed-free lawn, but I doubt whether it is ever worth it, and certainly not for a lawn for children to play on. (What fun is a lawn for a child if it can't run to a daisy chain?)

Should you insist, you can easily discover from gardening catalogues and magazines what are the latest (constantly changing) weedkillers. Two warnings, however. Never spray liquid weedkillers on a windy day, for the drift will kill any plants on which it falls. And never use as a mulch any mowings from lawns which have been treated with hormone weedkillers during the previous six months. But these mowings can be put on the compost heap if you are absolutely sure that the compost will not be spread on the garden for at least six months.

The best time to use weedkillers is when the weeds and grass are growing well, probably some time during May. By this time the fertilizer applied earlier in the spring will be working, and as the weeds die the strongly growing grass will soon cover up for their absence.

Low-growing weeds such as dandelions and plantains duck the mower blades. They can be got rid of by sprinkling a little hormone weedkiller on top of the weed itself, instead of treating the whole lawn. A hormone weedkiller will not kill moss, but camomel dust (a mercury compound) will. Apply it in late summer to autumn.

The only lasting way to get rid of moss, however, is to discover the reasons for its presence, which include poor drainage, deep shade, lack of fertilizers or lime, and too close mowing. Start the attack on moss by thoroughly spiking the lawn and then fertilizing it. Only if that fails to discourage the moss apply ground limestone at 2oz (50g) to the square yard (or metre). In general acid soil is best for lawns.

Mowing

All the laborious operations so far described will be wasted unless you learn how to mow well.

Rule 1: the time to mow the lawn is when the grass needs cutting and not when you happen to feel like it. In spring and autumn it may need cutting once a week, in early summer perhaps twice a week, but it is the weather and not the calendar that will decide. In any case do not cut the grass when it is wet, and be in no hurry to cut it in scorchingly hot dry weather. Then it not only stops growing, but appears to shrink.

Rule 2: too close cutting is not only unnecessary but harmful. How close is too close? This depends on which grasses are the dominant grasses in the lawn. If you are surprisingly lucky enough to have a wealth of fescues and bents – the kind of grasses you find, for example, on the springy upland pastures grazed by sheep – they have the best chance of survival if you do not cut them less than $\frac{3}{4}$in (2cm) from the soil. Ryegrass and the coarser meadow grasses, which are more likely to make up your lawn, resent being cut shorter than 1in (2.5cm). So you can try to discourage those by cutting below 1in (2.5cm) but not below $\frac{3}{4}$in (2cm) for the sake of the superior grasses. Any resulting improvement is very gradual, and is perpetually threatened through recolonization by the seeds of meadow grasses from surrounding gardens.

If you are lucky enough to take possession of a reasonably well looked after lawn in early spring put off any major work until the late autumn, if only because there will be far more urgent jobs to be done both in the garden and in the house. But find some time to spread fertilizer as the grass starts to grow, and then you will be ready to have a go at the weeds in May, if your heart is set on that. Conscientious mowing during that first summer is the most useful thing you can do for the future of the lawn. Then in autumn embark on the raking and the levelling of humps and the filling of hollows.

Most neglected grass can be revived within a year to the kind of family lawn which will survive the ravages of children and pets without the parents having to impose too many nagging restrictions.

Making a new lawn

If you find that the lawn is too far gone when you take it over, or if the garden is little more than an expanse of builders' detritus, you will have to start from scratch to construct your own lawn. (That is, if you want one. If you can rid your mind of the conventional image of a garden you will find that a garden can be made beautiful without grass. How we will consider later in the book.)

There are two main ways of making a lawn: by sowing seed or laying turf. There is another way: planting creeping grass, the stolons of which will spread and root, putting up more tufts. This method is used in warm climates where seeding is likely to fail and it produces a coarse sward which cannot be cut close. I have tried it only once and the results did not encourage me to repeat the experiment.

Turf or seed?

There is little difference in the amount of work involved in preparing the ground for turf or seed. After that, turf is quite easy to lay and you are able to use the lawn far sooner than if you seed it. But turf is more expensive than seed, and good turf is both scarce and exorbitantly expensive.

The most readily available turf, and the cheapest, is cut from meadows. It is full of coarse grasses and weeds, like a neglected lawn, but it will improve with regular mowing, fertilizing, and annual scratching and spiking on the lines already described.

Turf cut from parkland, a mixture of coarse and finer grasses, is better and inevitably more expensive. The scarcest of all is Cumberland sea-washed turf. This you may be able to enjoy by taking up bowling at your municipal green, for even if you are able to raise the money to buy it for your own lawn there are far better ways of spending it.

The lawns of the future may be made from rolls of turf laid as though it were carpeting. The grass seed is sown in a growing medium which is bonded by Netlon mesh. The thin strips of turf so produced are 11ft (3.3m) long and 30in (75cm) wide. The rolls are light to handle and do not easily break because of the bonding; if they have to be cut this can be done with scissors. The cost is higher than for most ordinary turf, but a fraction of what you have to pay to carpet a room (and that for carpeting which wears out instead of keeping on growing).

Seeding a lawn is much cheaper than turfing it, and you can choose exactly the seeds to sow for the kind of lawn you want (but don't imagine it will long stay unsullied, for the wind is full of the seeds of unwanted grasses and of weeds looking for a home). There are two major drawbacks to growing a lawn from seed, firstly the danger of a dry spell just after the seed has germinated, and secondly the long time you have to wait before the lawn can stand any hard wear. Hence the wisdom of getting a sown lawn well established, if possible, before the children need it for rough games.

Preparing the ground

Time spent in getting the site of the lawn into first-rate condition is time saved for years ahead. The first job is to get rid of the jungle of undergrowth and/or the desert of builders' rubbish. A weedkiller based on paraquat will soon kill the green top growth of all plants (except moss). Paraquat is immediately broken down in the soil and succeeding growth is not affected; that unfortunately means that weeds will spring up again. There are more vicious weedkillers, but they are best left alone since you may then have to leave the soil alone for a year or more.

When you have removed the dead vegetation you will at least be able to see what you are doing. If the builders have been there all the bricks and milk bottles they have left behind will now be exposed. Remove them all. Bottles are particularly dangerous if you intend to use a machine to do the cultivation.

You can now get down to the serious business of preparing the soil for seed or turf. Autumn is the best time for both turfing and seeding a lawn; late August and early September for seed, while the soil is still warm and the dews heavy, and September and October for turf, giving it a chance to settle ready for use the next spring. The second best time for sowing is April, and for turfing is March to April.

The longer the time you give to preparing the site before seeding or turfing the better, even up to a year. The longest timetable would be:

Autumn: dig or rotovate the ground, removing as many docks, thistles, nettles and other persistent perennial weeds as you can lay your hands on. Get the area roughly level at this stage, but then leave the soil to be weathered by rain and frost during the winter.

Spring: when the soil is reasonably dry finish off the autumn's levelling in order to get an even surface. Some people can achieve it by eye alone, but most of us are easily deceived and have to resort to a straight edge (any piece of wood with a straight edge, at least 6ft (2m) long), a spirit level and a supply of flat-topped wooden pegs about 1ft (30cm) long. Having fixed the level needed at one corner of the lawn, hammer in a peg until 6in (15cm) of it are left sticking out of the soil. A couple of yards (2m) or so away knock in another peg, using the straight edge and a spirit level to get the top of it level with the top of the first peg. Repeat this, spacing the pegs all over the lawn. The back of a rake is a good weapon with which to push the soil around until it is a level 6in (30cm) below the top of each peg all over the area. Work peat evenly into the surface of the soil (about a bucketful to the square yard (or metre). If the soil is heavy clay a dressing of sharp sand helps to improve drainage.

Summer : hoe the area as often as you have the energy to do so in order to kill off weeds as they germinate. Root out any perennial weeds you missed the first time round. Even out any humps and hollows which develop as the soil settles. Once again, time spent now is more time saved later.

Autumn : the passage of time and the cultivations of the summer will have produced a firm base and a fine loose surface tilth ready for sowing late in August or turfing a month or two months later. (Seed needs a finer tilth than turf.)

A few days before you intend to sow the seed rake off any stones which have surfaced, spread a general fertilizer at the rate of 3oz (75g) to the square yard (or metre), and gently rake it in.

You can get a usable lawn in a hurry by using turf and telescoping the time-table. Dig the site in early autumn, working in peat and fertilizer. A few weeks later break down the lumps of soil with the back of a rake. Choose a day when the soil is fairly dry and friable, i.e. when it does not form clods on your shoes when you walk over it. After getting rid of the lumps, firm the soil by shuffling all over it with your feet close together. If you can borrow a small roller use that, but don't overdo it. Once lengthwise and once across should be enough. Then rake well, with luck finishing up with a surface without bumps and hollows, free of largish stones and rubbish, and with a crumby soil ready for laying turf.

Alternatively, on lightish soil and weather permitting, it is possible to dig the site in early spring and get the soil in a fit state for turfing in April. You then hope that there will not be a dry spell until the grass has become established.

The snag about speeding up the process is that the soil is likely to settle further after the turf has been laid. After a few months you will probably have to remove any bumps and hollows which have developed, but at least you will have had a usable lawn sooner than you would otherwise have done.

You cannot hope to get a lawn from seed in a hurry: even if you skimp the preparing of the ground you will have to wait nine to twelve months after sowing the seed before the lawn is usable.

How to lay turf

The vital equipment for laying a lawn is three planks. If you haven't got them they can usually be hired, but make sure you have them before the turfs are delivered. The turfs may be 1ft (30cm) square, or 18in × 12in (45cm × 30cm) or 3ft × 1ft (90cm × 30cm); these will be rolled up with the grass side inwards. Try to lay them as soon as possible after delivery, but only if the soil is reasonably dry. If they are not of an even thickness shave off the bumps, using the three-sided box as described on page 30.

Mark one edge of the lawn with a line of string and lay a row of turfs lengthwise up against it, but overlapping each end a few inches to allow for later trimming; it is hard to get a perfectly straight edge at the start. Each turf must be laid very snugly against its neighbour. When the first row is in position place two planks

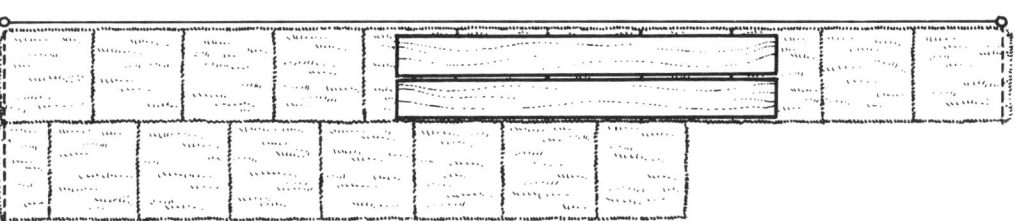

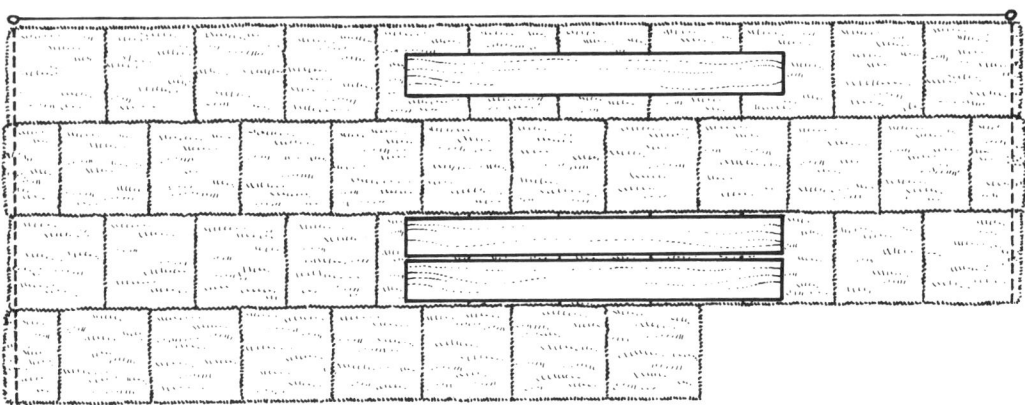

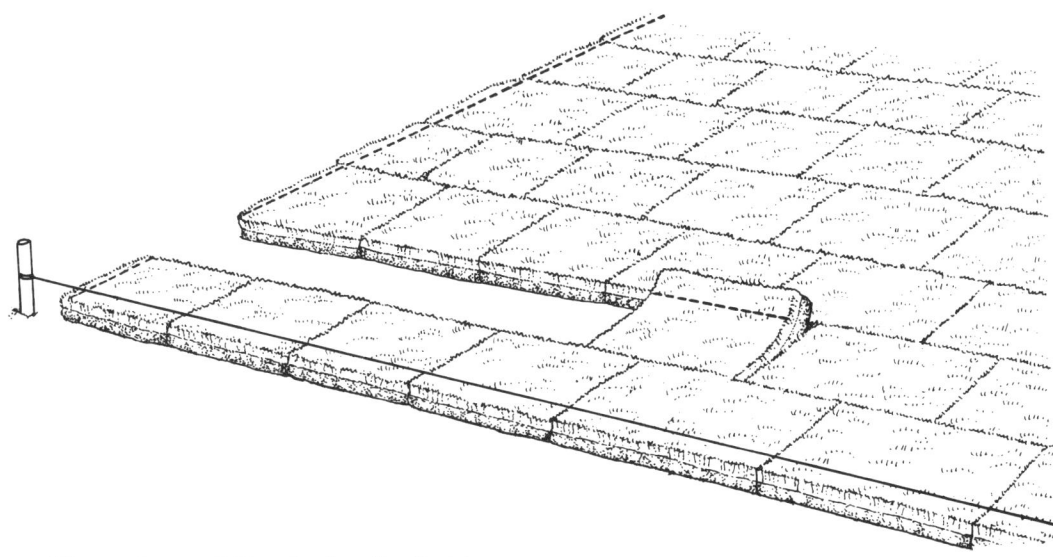

How to lay turf. *Top :* **laying the first two rows.**
Centre : **using the three planks as you move forward.** *Bottom :* **laying the last two rows**

over it and kneel on them to lay the second row. The purpose of this is to work forwards over the lawn as you lay it, thus not treading on the soil and leaving footmarks on the surface which you have so carefully levelled. Kneeling on planks ensures that you do not damage the turfs already laid, while at the same time pressing them firmly against the soil beneath.

When laying the second row cut one turf in half and start the row with that; use full-sized turfs along the rest of the row, but finish with the other half of the turf you cut. The third row is made up of full-sized turfs, and the fourth row starts and finishes with a half turf. This produces a pattern like bricks in a wall, and the purpose of it is to make the lawn knit together more readily.

When kneeling on the planks take care not to dig your toes into the grass you have just laid. As you move the two planks forward place the third plank so that your feet press on that instead. In this way work your way forward covering the whole length of the lawn. When you have almost reached the other end mark with the line of string where the edge of the lawn has to be, and lay a row of full-sized turfs against it. Then trim turfs to fit the gap behind.

Now spread a dressing of equal parts of fine soil, sand and peat over the whole lawn. Allow about 5lb ($2\frac{1}{4}$kg) to the square yard (or metre). Use the planks to carry out this operation to avoid walking on the turfs. As you move across the lawn brush the compost into the grass, particularly into the joints between the turfs. Then keep off the lawn for three or four weeks to give the roots time to spread from the turfs to the soil below. Wait until the turfs are firmly rooted before trimming the edges of the lawn.

Although September and October are the best times for laying a lawn it can also be done in early spring. An early spring dressing of fertilizer will give a fillip to an autumn-laid lawn, followed in May by a selective weedkiller.

How to sow grass seed

Choose a day to sow when the ground you have prepared is dry enough to walk over without picking up soil on your boots. A usual rate for sowing (at least for the less expensive grasses) is 2oz (50g) to the square yard (or metre), and to scatter such small amounts evenly over a whole lawn is not exactly easy. To make it less difficult mix the seed with three times as much sand, so that you will be scattering at 8oz (225g) to the square yard (or metre). To increase further the chance of getting an even spread divide the seed into two equal parts. Use half of it to cover the whole area of the lawn from end to end. Then sow the other half, working from side to side of the lawn – that is at right angles to your first sowing. Also, or alternatively, you can mark the lawn with string into smaller sections of a few square yards and ration the amount of seed to each accordingly.

After sowing gently rake the grass seed into the soil. The seed may well have been dressed with a bird repellent which will keep it safe from some birds. But they wreak as much havoc by taking dust baths in the soil, so it is wise to cover the lawn with Netlon, held above the surface of the soil by small twigs.

In favourable warm, dampish weather the grass will germinate in about fourteen days – and so will the weeds. If you wish you can kill these with a selective weed-killer but it absolutely must be a mild one specially devised for newly sown lawns.

The ordinary weedkillers should not be used until the grass has been growing for at least six months.

Tedious though it may be, the first cutting of the lawn, when the grass is rather more than 2in (5cm) tall, should be done with shears, since a mower is more likely to tear the seedlings out of the soil than slice off their tops. For the first season it is better not to cut the lawn closer than 1in (2.5cm), especially if the seed mixture consisted largely of the coarser grasses.

The cheapest way of buying seed is to take the blends offered by nurserymen, preferably those who specify exactly what is in them. Many merely give them fancy names, advertising only that they are either with or without ryegrass. Ryegrass got a bad reputation because of its long wiry stems, which cock their snook at most mowers, but the newer strains have shorter, more cuttable stems. They are not to be despised for the workaday lawn since they grow well and wear well. If you start asking for special mixtures you may have to pay three or four times as much as for a pre-packed mixture.

Mixture for a family working lawn

Most of the grasses for such a lawn have broad, tough leaves. A typical mixture might consist of:

36 per cent of Perennial ryegrass (*Lolium perenne*), using the new short-seeded strains. Not over-fussy about soil as long as it is well-drained and fertile (and you won't get a good lawn with any grass without that).

15 per cent of Rough-stalked meadow grass (*Poa trivialis*) or Smooth-stalked meadow grass (*Poa pratensis*), which make a good turf quickly. The Rough-stalked does best on heavy soil and the Smooth-stalked on lighter soils.

10 per cent Crested dog's tail (*Cynosurus cristatus*), a grass which can stand up to the children tramping over it and to prolonged dry weather.

These coarser grasses may be combined with finer but pretty resilient fescues:

20 per cent Chewing's fescue (*Festuca rubra fallax*), which helps to give a good colour to the lawn.

20 per cent Creeping red fescue (*Festuca rubra genuina*). Its habit of spreading by underground stems eventually puts springiness into the turf.

The snag about these fescues is that they are only thoroughly at home on lighter soils. If you are unfortunate enough to garden on cold clay forget the fescues and sow Timothy (*Phleum pratense*) instead. A possible mixture would be 35 per cent Timothy, 25 per cent Rough-stalked meadow grass (the heavy-soil meadow grass) and 40 per cent short-seeded Perennial ryegrass.

These percentages are only rough guides, however; it is far more sensible to buy a slightly different off-the-peg mixture than to have a far more expensive bespoke mixture specially made for you.

Seed mixtures for a posh lawn

Only fine grasses make fine lawns, so you sow fescues and varieties of fescues and bents. The wind, however, will be less discriminating and will carry to your lawn the seeds of other grasses, as well as weeds. How well you look after the lawn (especially mowing) will decide whether you or the guerilla wind wins the war.

A mixture for a fine lawn might consist of 60 per cent Chewing's fescue, 20 per cent Creeping red fescue, and 20 per cent Brown top bent (*Agrostis tenuis*). This has fine but tough leaves and does not wilt readily in a dry summer. It is the bent usually found in British lawns, but there are others. Creeping bent (*Agrostis stolonifera*) has stolons that spread along the surface of the soil and then root. This is popular in the United States but not widely used in Britain. If you aspire to putting green or bowling green standards, and wish to become a slave to your lawn, the simple mixture to sow is 80 per cent Chewing's fescue and 20 per cent Brown top bent.

Looking after the lawn

Having spent time and money on creating a good lawn it would be absurd to skimp either time or money on keeping it that way. Fertilizers will be a recurrent cost and scratching, spiking and mowing recurrent chores. But after the original outlay on a mower the running costs are not excessive (fuel, if it is a motor mower, and sharpening and overhauls each winter). A poor mower is useless so economize as little as you have to and buy a good machine. There are three widely used types of mower – the cylinder mower, the rotary mower and the hover mower, which is a rotary mower that floats over the grass on a cushion of air. I should admit that my bias is towards the cylinder mower.

A typical *cylinder mower* has a revolving cylinder carrying the cutting blades, a box to catch the grass as it is cut and a light roller. How closely the mower cuts the grass is controlled by adjusting the height of the cylinder, but how efficiently it cuts depends on how many blades there are on the cylinder. There may be up to a dozen and you are wasting money, not saving it, if you buy a machine with fewer than eight.

A motor mower takes a lot of the hard sweat out of mowing, but not all, and the larger it is the harder it is to manouevre in turning. And you still have to empty the grass box, which is the real curse of mowing. Even so, do not make a regular habit of leaving off the grass box and letting the mowings rot on the lawn. The only time when that is wise is in a dry spell when the cut grass protects the soil a little from a scorching sun. Only a cylinder mower will give that light and dark striped effect to the lawn which is achieved by moving backwards and forwards the length of the lawn. To be able to do this perfectly is to me the main satisfaction of mowing. Occasionally mow across rather than along the lawn because if you cut always in one direction ridges may be formed.

Rotary mowers have two or four blades fixed to a circular metal plate which revolves at high speed (hence all rotary mowers are motorized). The plate is raised or lowered to adjust the height at which the grass is cut. These mowers can cope with far longer grass than cylinder mowers – which may be a temptation not to mow your lawn often enough. They do not produce such a pretty effect as cylinder mowers, but they are excellent for rough work. Some, but by no means all, collect the grass.

Hover mowers are rotary mowers which, like a hovercraft, float along on a cushion of air. They are therefore very light to handle and very manoeuvrable, and are often recommended for cutting grass on steep banks. An easier solution to this problem is not to grow grass on banks, for there are plenty of other forms of ground cover which do not need cutting. Everyone who writes about a hover mower adds the warning that you should wear very stout boots when using one, presumably for the sake of anyone careless enough to get their toes in the way.

Hand mower or motor mower?

Mowing the lawn is one of the sounds of summer. Heard some way off it can be almost soothing, but less so when you are walking behind a power mower belching out petrol fumes. (For several hundred pounds more you could, of course, sit on an even noisier, smellier machine.) For a small lawn a motor mower is more trouble than it is worth; a really good modern cylinder mower is not particularly hard work for a young person to push and much healthier. And in the wisdom of age one can be expected to have dispensed with the burden of cutting grass by finding something else to cover the soil with.

Electric-powered mowers are somewhat quieter than petrol-driven mowers, and not malodorous. They may be run off the mains, but unless you are a very methodical mower there is always a risk that the cable may become involved with the revolving blades. Certainly children should never be allowed to use them. There are also battery models, which are safer; the snag is remembering to re-charge them. Whichever type of mower you choose, buy the best you can afford. With a cheap mower you will end up with a bad lawn and an even worse temper.

Warning: mowing can seriously damage your health

Right and wrong ways of mowing the lawn

Many people push a mower along by leaning over so much as to be at risk of falling flat on their face. They tend to do this especially when the grass has been allowed to grow long. Lowering the angle of the handle of the mower will help to break this bad habit. Stand up as straight as possible when mowing, whether with a manual or motor mower, to avoid strain on the spine.

You can not only damage your health by incorrect mowing; you could kill yourself with a mains electric mower if you carelessly cut through the cable.

How to build a raised bed

When you build a raised bed you are building for a lifetime so there should be nothing shoddy or ramshackle about it. Beds made of old tyres or railway sleepers, as sometimes suggested, are an eyesore at the start and worsen as they age. Stone walls are expensive and their width is out of proportion to the size of the beds. Stone or concrete flags set on end on concrete foundations are cheaper and can look attractive when weathered. Concrete walls built in situ between shuttering look severe but when covered with white cement paint (and regularly repainted to maintain its freshness) can be effective if they blend with the style of the house.

Bricks in subtle colours, not harsh red, would be my own choice. If possible they should already be mellowed by age, but if not they can be relied on to weather gracefully. I like bricklaying and I am sure that, given patience, most people would find it a perfectly feasible and enjoyable do-it-yourself operation.

Building a brick raised bed

You may prefer to employ a professional, but if you set about building a brick raised bed yourself you will need:

Bricks: You can buy new bricks, or second-hand bricks from buildings which are being demolished. Many old bricks are very attractive, having developed a patina through long weathering. Probably cheaper than new bricks, they have the drawback that you may have to chip old mortar off them. Also, because they are likely to be more uneven than new mass-produced bricks, they are a little harder to lay. Unlike modern standard bricks they will have no frogs, the name for the hollow in the laying surface of a brick.

There is a wide range of modern bricks to choose from, varying in colour, texture and, of course, price. Avoid those known as common bricks, since they will deteriorate through the effects of soil inside the bed and frost on the outside. For use in the garden choose facing bricks, which stand up to the weather better. L.B.C. bricks, made by the London Brick Company in vast quantities, are obtainable in various colours and textures, and are a reasonably economical buy.

Bricks have undergone metrication; the standard size is now 215mm × 102.5mm × 65mm. But when working out how many bricks you need the mortar between the joints has to be taken into account, and that brings you pretty near the old Imperial reckoning for brick plus joint, which is 9in × 4½in × 3in. From that you can work out that you need forty-eight bricks to the square yard (0.8 sq.m) for a single brick width wall, but when ordering add a few more in case any are broken or too damaged to use.

Concrete : The amount of concrete needed for the foundations of even a fair-sized raised bed does not justify the delivery of the usual load of ready-mixed concrete (and don't imagine you will be able to fit in other concreting jobs as well, for the cement will be setting within two hours). However, in some areas there are firms which specialize in delivering small amounts. Dry cement, sand and gravel can be bought ready mixed and bagged at many do-it-yourself shops, but while this is convenient for small jobs it is uneconomic if you need a fair amount of concrete. You have to pay for the cost of mixing and bagging, and you are still left with the labour of mixing it all over again when you add the water. The cheapest way is to buy cement, sand and gravel separately (you will also need cement and sand for the mortar for the walls). You will probably find that the major cost of sand and gravel is in the delivery, so look ahead: if you are going to build several raised beds, a summerhouse, a pool, a patio, a sandpit, or whatever, it would be economical to order the sand and gravel at one go. But not cement, which should be bought fresh as you need it.

A usual mix for foundations is 1 part cement, $2\frac{1}{2}$ parts fine washed sand and 4 parts gravel, all measured by volume.

Mortar : a suitable mortar for brick-laying consists of 1 part cement, 1 part hydrated lime and 5 parts sand. Dry mixes in these proportions are obtainable from do-it-yourself shops or builders' merchants, or you can mix your own.

Tools : you will need a large trowel for spreading the mortar (called a laying trowel); a small trowel for pointing the mortar in the joints; a builder's level at least 2ft (60cm) long (this combines a spirit level and a plumb rule to check whether you are building the walls both level and absolutely upright); a builder's square to ensure that corners indeed run at right angles (it is a right-angled triangle, and you can make one yourself out of three wooden battens – 18in (45cm), 24in (60cm) and 30in (75cm)); a long length of string and pegs to mark out the foundations; string and two 6in (15cm) nails to help you to get the courses level when building the wall.

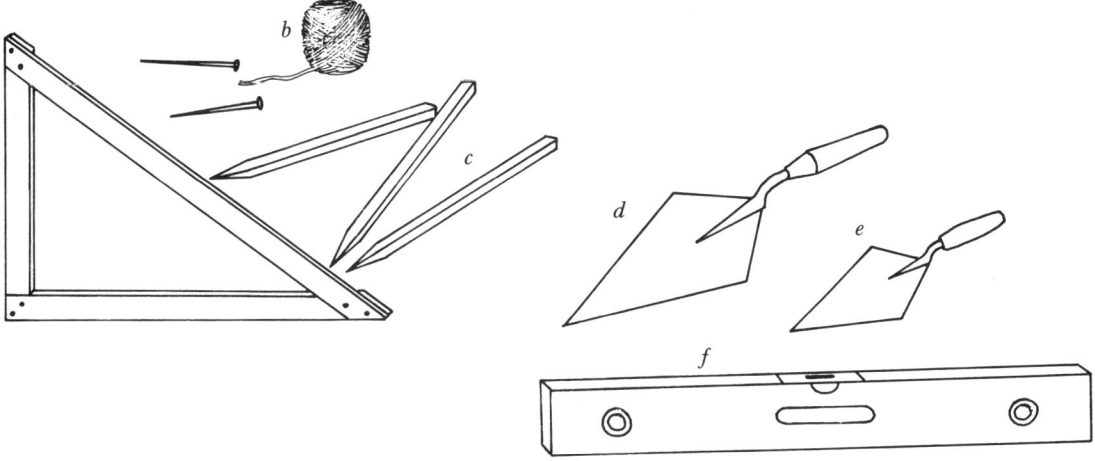

Tools needed for brick-laying. a. builder's square. b. nails and string. c. wooden pegs. d. laying trowel. c. pointing trowel. f. builder's level

Preliminary decisions

The recommended height for raised beds is about 2ft (60cm), so the walls need be only a single brick in width, $4\frac{1}{2}$in (11.5cm). The one practical way in which a single brick wall can be built is in what is known as the stretcher bond, which gives the familiar pattern of most of the brick walls we see. All the bricks are laid lengthwise (hence the name of stretchers), but with the joint between two bricks in one course arranged to fall in the middle of a brick in the course below.

It is not the most inspiring pattern for a wall, but the more interesting patterns can be achieved only by building a double wall, with bricks laid not only along the wall, but also across the width of the wall (headers). This both doubles the cost of the wall and reduces the inside measurement of the bed by 9in (23cm) all round. That would mean losing a lot of growing space as well as making a small bed look absurdly out of scale. So that is one decision already made for you: the raised bed will be a single brick width in stretcher bond.

The recommended width for a raised bed which can be approached from only one side (for example if the garden wall is made to serve as one side) is 2ft (60cm). If the bed can be approached from both sides the recommended maximum width is 4ft (1.2m). But if you stick meticulously to these figures you will find yourself involved in cutting many bricks down to get them to fit, an infuriating and time-wasting chore for an amateur. Instead fix the size of the bed to avoid any cutting at all.

A standard brick laid lengthways takes up 9in (23cm), allowing for a little mortar at the joints as well, but less than the amateur is likely to use. So a 4ft (1.2m) bed could be made 47in (118cm) wide; that would take five bricks, leaving 2in (5cm) overall for the mortar in the four gaps between the bricks. That is, in fact, rather more mortar than is necessary for that course but you have to allow for the fact that the course above, and other alternate courses, will have five mortar joints and not four, and you must leave enough room for adequate mortar between them.

If you are planning a nominal 2ft (60cm) wide bed you can add 4in (10cm) to the width without putting the back of it out of your reach. The 28in (70cm) would then conveniently take three bricks and 1in (2.5cm) of mortar. Other labour-saving lengths for beds of standard bricks can be similarly worked out, and the sums adjusted for bricks of other sizes. You must, of course, work out the exact size of the bed before you begin to dig out a trench for the foundations.

There is one major decision to be made: how are you going to provide water for your raised beds? The soil in them dries out more quickly than soil in beds at ground level and you will soon tire of carrying water to them. Using a hose saves some of the labour but still takes up time. Eventually you will probably want to install labour-free watering throughout the garden, but that can be done in stages. However, the first stage should be carried out while you are building the raised beds and laying the paths alongside them. Run a length of pipe under the foundations from inside each bed to a convenient point outside the bed where it can later be connected to the mains. The cost of this small length of pipe will not be great, whereas it would be expensive and awkward if beds and paths had to be disturbed later. The sprinkle or trickle or whatever automatic watering device you finally choose can easily be fitted later.

Laying the foundations

With all decisions taken, all materials delivered, and your tools ready you can start the actual work.

The first thing is to make the trench in which to lay the concrete base on which the walls will be built. Start by marking out the outline of the bed. Push a wooden peg firmly into the soil at each corner of one end of the bed, and stretch the string between them. Then take the string at right angles along one side of the bed to whatever length it is to be, and secure it round another peg. Use the builder's square you made to make sure you have a right angle. Mark the other end of the bed in the same way, double-checking that it is exactly the same width as the opposite end. Finally, continue the string along the remaining side, checking for that right angle again, and secure it to the first peg. You now have a rectangle of string marking the outside measurements of the walls you are going to build. Check that you have a perfect rectangle by measuring the two diagonals, which must be the same.

The trench itself can now be marked out to take a concrete foundation extending 3in (7.5cm) on either side of the wall. To get the outer line for the trench, mark with pegs, and string a rectangle 3in (7.5cm) wider all round than the rectangle you have already marked out. The inner line of the trench is established by marking out a rectangle within the original one, $7\frac{1}{2}$in (19cm) smaller all round; this allows for the width of the brick wall and the extra width on that side for the foundation. The trench you have marked out will then be $10\frac{1}{2}$in (26.5cm) wide.

Remove the middle piece of string and trenching can begin. The trench should be 10in (25cm) deep. This gives room for 6in (15cm) of concrete plus the first

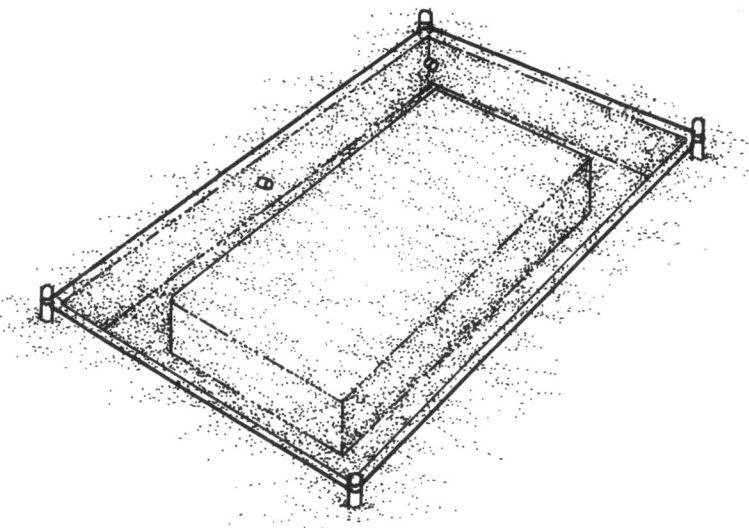

Digging a trench in order to lay foundations for a brick raised bed

course of bricks, which is laid below the level of the surrounding path or lawn. If you make a clean cut down the sides of the trench along the lines of the string, the trench itself will act as a 'form' for the concrete, so you won't need to mess about making a wooden one.

The soil you remove from the trench will be needed to help fill the raised bed. But do not pile it up in the area between the trenches; if you do, as will emerge within a few lines, you will have to move it again. So stack it well out of your way.

The bottom of the trench must be level; to check use a spirit level laid on a longish straight piece of wood. If there are any dips do not fill them up with loose soil, but wait to level them out when laying the concrete.

To get the correct depth of concrete, hammer pegs into the soil at each corner (and if the bed is long at intervals down the sides), so that the tops of all of them are a level 6in (15cm) out of the ground.

Reminder: the mix for the concrete is 1 part cement, $2\frac{1}{2}$ parts sand and 4 parts gravel.

If you are mixing the material yourself start by mixing the sand and cement and then mix in the gravel. (If you are using a dry mix give it a few turns.) Make a well in the middle of the pile (like a small volcano) in which to pour the water, not too much at a time. Shovel dry material from the outside of the pile into the middle, add a little more water and so on, until the whole pile is moist. Turn it over well, and, if necessary, add more water to bind it together, but don't get it sloppy; too much water weakens the concrete.

When you start emptying the concrete into the trench the tops of the wooden pegs will indicate the depth needed. Use a piece of wood to tamp the concrete down as you go along. Check thoroughly to get the levels absolutely right; if you don't get them right at this stage the walls will probably finish up cockeyed.

Rest from your exertions for a few days while the concrete sets. Then remove the soil, to the depth of a spade or so, from within the area bounded by the foundations. Be careful not to dig too near them, in case you disturb them. At some stage this soil has to be removed and replaced by rubble to ensure adequate drainage in the bed. It is obviously easier to take the soil out now rather than later when you would be cramped within the walls.

Building the walls

Don't go bullheaded at the brick-laying, but tackle it in stages so that you get it right; it should last at least your lifetime.

A mortar containing lime is much easier to handle and less likely to fall off the trowel of its own volition. If you are using hydrated lime put three-quarters of a bucketful of it to soak in water the day before.

The bricks have to be dampened a few hours before you start operations; a dry brick will draw the moisture out of the mortar before you can say Jack Robinson, giving you no chance to do a bit of fiddling about if you don't get it just right in the first place. After watering the bricks, arrange them in small stacks handy for the stretch of wall you are working on.

Reminder: the usual mix for bricklayer's mortar is 1 part cement, 1 part hydrated lime and 5 parts sand. If you are using a dry mix turn it well before adding water. Beware of making it too wet or the weight of the bricks will squeeze it out of the joints like melting ice cream. If you are mixing your own start with the hydrated lime which has been soaking. Pour away any water which has not been absorbed, leaving only the lime, which will now have the gooey consistency of synthetic cream. Mix this thoroughly with five times as much sand.

Do not add cement to all the lime-sand mixture at once, or you may find that you have a lot of mortar which has set hard before you have managed to use it up. Though the sand and lime mixture will go hard when it dries it will not set when wet until the cement is added, so mix only a little mortar at a time. Use only enough water to produce a stiff mortar. It is fatal to make it too sloppy. As you become more proficient you will be able to estimate your hourly bricklaying potential and mix more mortar accordingly.

Before mixing the first little batch of mortar the novice would do well to have a dry dummy run. Lay a line of bricks lengthways along the centre of the concrete base, choosing an end rather than a side – being shorter, there is less to go wrong. Start 3in (7.5cm) in from one end of the base and allow 3in (7.5cm) on each side of the bricks. Space them out so that there is ½in (1.25cm) between them. Five bricks make a double bed; three bricks a single.

If it works out make a mark which there can be no mistaking across the whole width of the concrete base to show where the first and last bricks in the row have to be laid. Move the bricks out of your way and begin.

Lay the two corner bricks first with ½in (1.25cm) of mortar under them. Place a batten from one to the other and with a spirit level check that the two bricks are level with each other. With the spirit level check that each one is level lengthwise and also level across its width. Either a little more mortar added, or a little taken away, or sometimes just a little tap with the handle of the trowel, will get the levels right. Make absolutely sure they are, because the corner bricks of the wall are vital.

When you are satisfied complete the first course. A string secured round the two end bricks will give you a straight line to work to. Don't forget to check levels with the spirit level.

In building a brick wall the corners are kept a few courses ahead of the rest of the wall. To be able to do this, at the start you will have to lay two or three first-course bricks along the sides of the bed. Use the builder's square to make sure that these are at right angles to the end wall.

The way in which the bricks are laid at the corners and how the building of the walls then proceeds is simply shown in the illustration on page 48.

When one end of the bed is well under way start on the other end and then on the sides; do this when it becomes obviously convenient to do so for ease of working.

Keep the spirit level in constant use – horizontally to make sure all courses are level and vertically to see that the wall is plumb and diagonally to confirm that the wall is plumb and to discover if any bricks are out of line. A sharp tap will often put this right while the mortar is still wet.

The mortar in the joints will look pretty rough as you build and needs pointing to give a good smooth finish. This not only looks better but makes the wall more weather-resistant. Pointing should be done as you go along while the mortar is

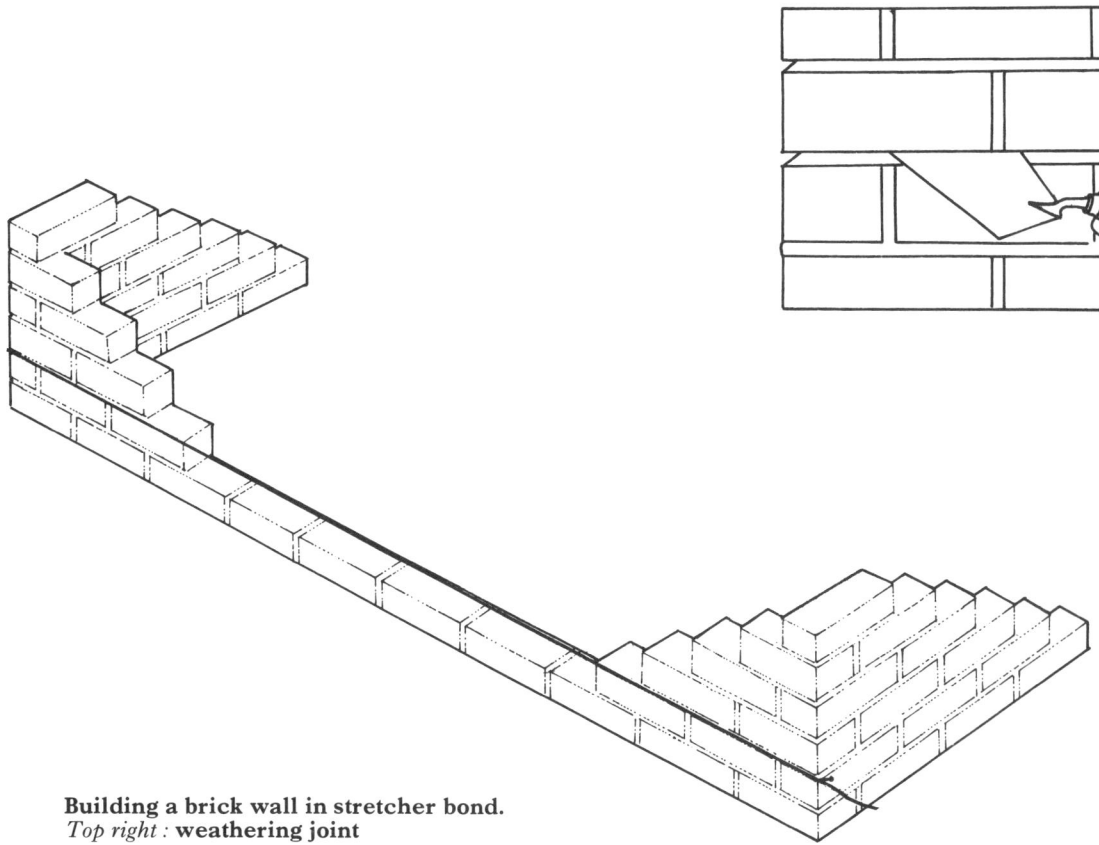

Building a brick wall in stretcher bond.
Top right : **weathering joint**

still wet, the vertical joints first and then the horizontal. Several patterns are possible but the 'weathering joint' is one of the most common and useful. This is done with the pointing trowel.

The mortar should not be allowed to dry out rapidly. For a week or so after building the walls cover with polythene sheeting or spray each day with a fine spray. Then let them dry out for two or three weeks before you start filling the bed.

Filling the bed

At the bottom goes 1ft (30cm) or so of rubble, stones and broken bricks, followed by layers of turfs upside down if you can lay your hands on them. Failing that put in a layer of smaller stones a few inches deep; the purpose is to stop the soil from being washed down among the rubble and cutting down on drainage. On top of that goes the soil which you have saved from various excavations, to which you can add peat, and compost; you can also work in a slow-acting organic fertilizer such as bonemeal (2oz (50g) to the square yard (or metre)).

Fill to within about 3in (7.5cm) of the top of the walls; you may have to add a little more soil as it settles, so do not plant until it has done so.

A sensible refinement is to lay a small strip of flags across one end of each raised bed to serve as a seat, and, more importantly, as somewhere to put tools,

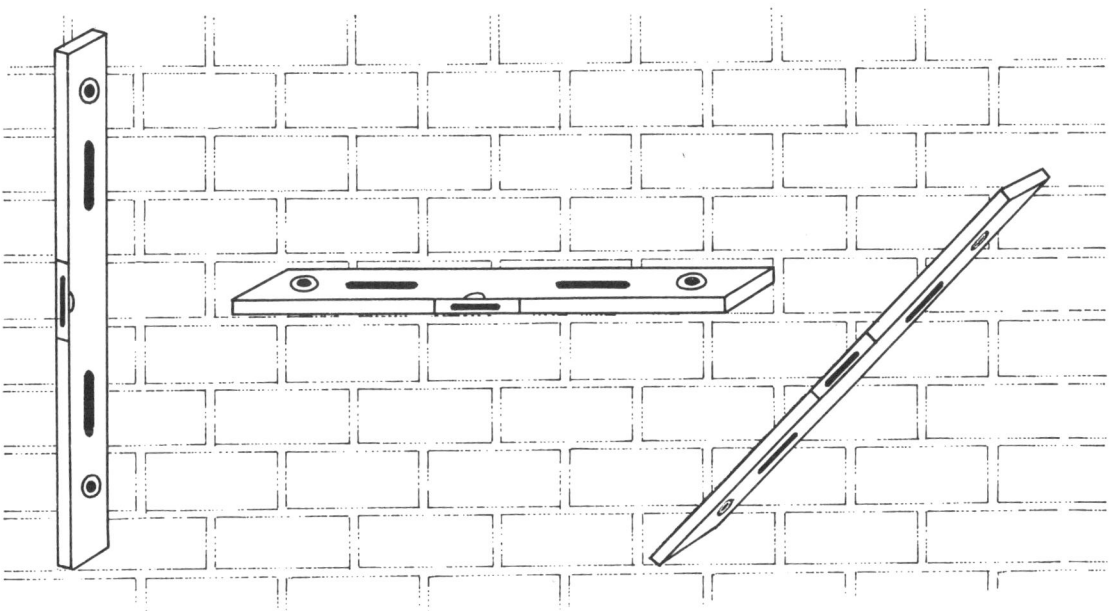

Three uses of a builder's level: vertically, horizontally and diagonally

seeds, plants and fertilizers while you are at work at the bed. Flags a foot (30cm) square are suitable. Their edges rest on the brick walls but they will need other support. On the soil directly under them put a layer of rubble, topped with sand, up to the level of the walls. If there are young children about fix the flags so that they do not overhang the outside of the bed, to avoid the danger of banged heads. Also set the flags in mortar on top of the brick walls so that the children do not dislodge them; both they and the cat will enjoy using the flags as a seat. You can, of course, add the workbench/seat later when stiffening joints remind you of the folly of unnecessary bending. But why wait?

Making a raised bed out of concrete flags

This is simpler than making a raised bed of bricks, but it does involve first laying the paths around the bed. The concrete flags to use are the stock size of 3ft × 2ft × 2in (90cm × 60cm × 5cm). Two of them at each end will form a bed 4ft (1.2m) wide, the optimum width of a raised bed, and the length will be what you wish in multiples of 2ft (60cm) plus 4in (10cm), the width of the end flags.

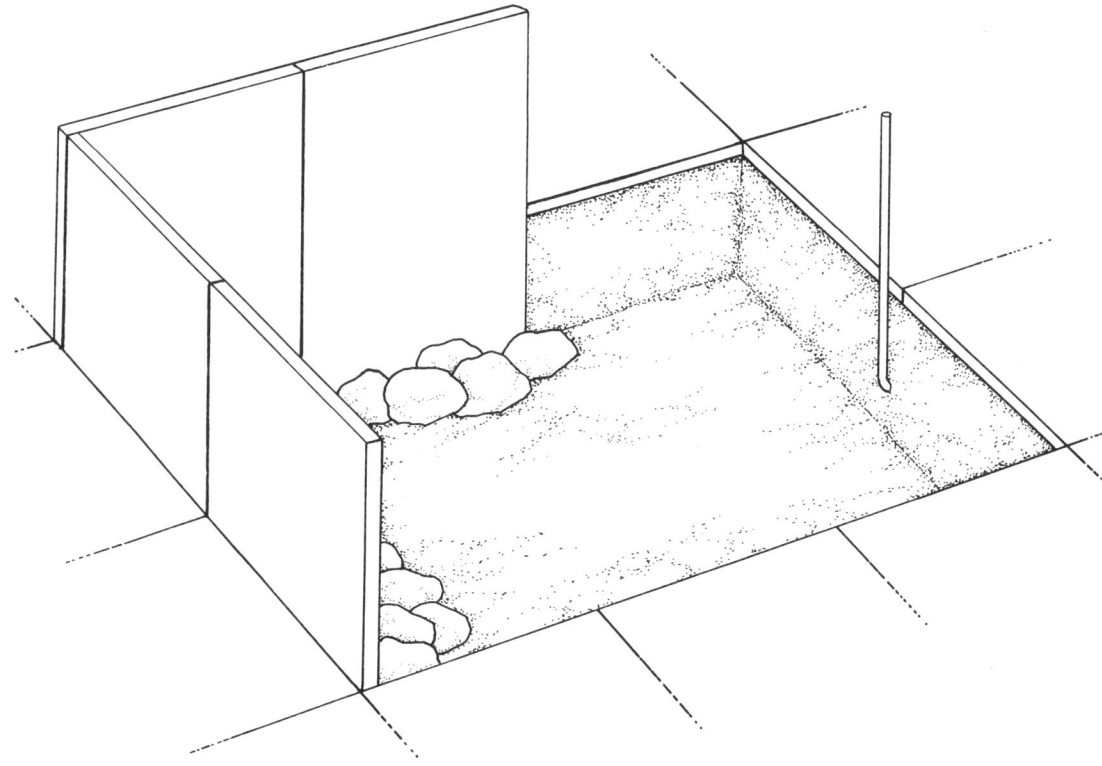

How to make a raised bed using concrete flags

Mark out the size of the bed and construct a path round it, with paving or concrete, as already described. Lay the path so that it will slope away from the bed. That completed, remove the turf (if any) from the area of the bed and put the turfs on one side. Remove the soil to a depth of 1ft (30cm): you will need this to help to fill the bed. Test meticulously that the ground is level or you will finish up with a raised bed of drunken tombstones.

Start with one end of the bed, upending one flag into the hole, long side (3ft (90cm))right against the edge of the path. Prop it up with stones while you test that it is both level and vertical. Put another flag alongside it to complete the end, also packing stones against that to keep it upright. Continue right round the bed, with each flag right up against the next one, checking that all the flags are level and vertical. To prevent water from seeping between the flags fill the joints from inside with a sealant.

Fill the bottom of the bed with rubble to the depth of 1ft (30cm). This should keep the flags securely in place, but if you have any doubts lay a strip of concrete against the base of the flags before putting in the rubble. On top of the rubble place a layer of the turfs you saved, grass side down, or some smaller stones. Fill the bed with good soil to within 3in (7.5cm) of the top, adding a little more as it settles.

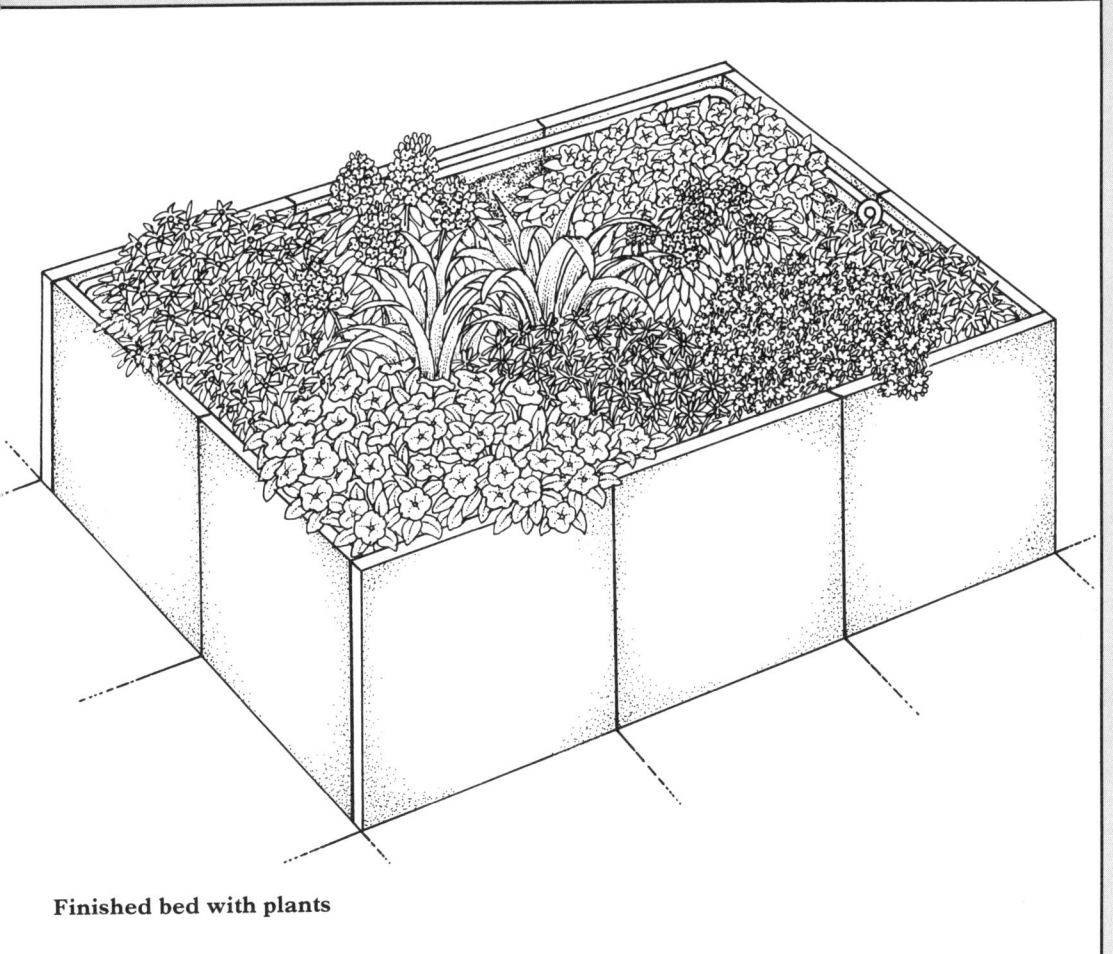

Finished bed with plants

How to build a raised pool

It is less easy to build a raised pool than the usual sunken pool. It is also harder to build a raised pool than a raised bed. But the enjoyment to be got from a raised pool throughout your lifetime far outweighs the labour and cost involved.

The advantage of a raised pool over one at ground level is that it provides somewhere to sit with water not far below eye level so that you can see properly what is going on in the pool. If you grow scented plants in the water you will actually be able to smell them without having to kneel down. A raised pool also has the important practical advantages that children and old people are less likely to stumble into it and it is less effort to look after since you do not have to bend.

How big you decide to make the pool is partly a question of taste, the space available, and cost. You are unlikely to want the pool to overwhelm the garden; on the other hand a pool should not look puny. Also, it is difficult to keep a pool reasonably free of algae if the surface is less than 40 square feet (3.7 sq.m). If the pool is smaller there will not be enough room for the number of water plants needed to keep the water clear, and the algae will have to be controlled with chemicals. Anything wider than 5ft (1.5m) becomes inconvenient to look after.

The minimum depth of a pool is 15in (38cm), and 18in (45cm) is far better. This gives adequate depth of water for a large number of aquatic plants; they vary in their needs from an inch or so to nearly 6ft (2m) at the other extreme.

The wall surrounding the pool should be no higher than 2ft (60cm); around that height allows your legs to dangle a little when sitting on it. If you like your feet on the ground make the wall lower, but not too low or it will be awkward to get up from when you grow older.

To ensure that the pool survives as troublefree as possible throughout your lifetime it has to be built well with first-rate materials. The life expectancy of various materials differs widely. A concrete pool is not as long-lasting as one might imagine: poor concrete might last only two years, while a well-constructed concrete pool could last two decades. One expects a life of five years for semi-rigid moulded plastic pools and double that for the more expensive glass fibre pools. Heavy duty butyl liners may last half a century, and are the obvious choice to line an excavated pool where the earth itself provides the 'mould'.

For an excavated pool all you would have to do would be to dig out the earth to the shape and depth you need for the pool and then line it with butyl. With a raised pool you first of all have, as it were, to build a hole above ground. This feat can be achieved in a number of ways. The simplest are:

1. For a formal pool build brick walls, face them inside with cement mortar and then line with butyl.

2. For informal pools build stone walls around a prefabricated shell of glass fibre or plastic.

Formal (top) and informal raised pools

Whichever you prefer you have first to decide, within the overall garden plan, where to put the pool. Avoid at all costs siting it under a tree. A tree in full leaf in spring and summer will cast too much shade over the pool, which should be in sunlight for at least half the day, preferably more. And a tree overhead in autumn is an even greater curse, for the falling leaves have tediously to be fished out if the water is not to turn foul.

Having chosen a suitable site decide whether you want still or moving water, provided by either a fountain or a mini waterfall. Reflections of clouds in still water are absorbing to watch, but the pleasure may be marred if the mirror image is mainly the back of the house next door. Moving water obliterates reflections, but the movement itself is fascinating. On the practical side a fountain or fall does help to aerate the water in summer. However the movement must not be violent; indeed some plants flourish only in still water.

In the scale of a garden pool do not try to emulate either Versailles or Niagara. A gentle jet of a fountain, worked by a submersible pump, is all that is needed to bring movement to the pool. Providing a supply of electricity to run the pump would be part of the early planning of the garden. Electricity will also be needed for the summerhouse and, eventually maybe, a greenhouse.

A waterfall can be created by having a second smaller pool at a higher level with water pouring down from it over a projecting lip, the water being circulated by the pump. However, this makes the pool far harder to build and the result can easily look pretentious on the inevitably small scale.

Whether to have a formal or an informal pool depends largely on your taste, but there are some practical considerations. A formal pool looks fine with walls of bricks matching the style and materials of the raised beds. On the other hand, an informal pool would look odd, to say the least, with curvaceous brick walls. If you plump for an informal pool, therefore, you are in fact committing yourself to building stone walls, probably using what is known as random rubble, which is not easy for a beginner. Brick walls will be far easier to build, especially if you have already gained experience with the raised beds.

To make a brick-walled formal pool lined with butyl

Start by marking out the area of the pool. How to do this, how to lay foundations and how to lay bricks are all explained in detail in the chapter on building raised beds (pages 45–8). The difference in building a raised pool is that a double 9in (23cm) wall is needed. Therefore dig the trench 15in (38cm) wide – so that the concrete foundation will extend 3in (7.5cm) beyond each side of the wall. The trench should be 10in (25cm) deep. In it lay 6in (15cm) of concrete, the mix being 1 part cement, $2\frac{1}{2}$ parts sand and 4 parts gravel. Let the concrete set for a few days.

Remove the turf, if any, and soil to a total depth of 5in (12.5cm) over the whole area within the foundations in order to get a firm base. (Stack the turf to let it rot down; there are many uses for it in the garden – filling the baskets in which the aquatic plants will grow is one.) If the soil is loose ram it down as hard as possible. You can then start laying the bricks.

When building a single brick wall only the stretcher bond can be used (where all the bricks are laid lengthways), but for a double wall there is a choice of patterns which will give greater strength. A suitable one for a pool is the English garden wall bond. For this you start with three courses of stretchers and then follow with a course of headers: headers are bricks laid across the width of the wall instead of along it, and they bind the two sides of the wall together.

A course of headers raises one slight problem. Two headers laid next to each other at the corner of the wall would make the joint at the edge of the second header fall directly in line with the joint of a stretcher below. This pattern would then be repeated the whole length of the wall, making it both weak and ugly. You avoid this by using as the second brick from the end what is known as a closer – a brick which has been cut down in width to $2\frac{1}{8}$in (5.3cm). Fortunately closers can be bought ready-made to this size, so when ordering bricks have some of this size included.

English Garden Wall Bond

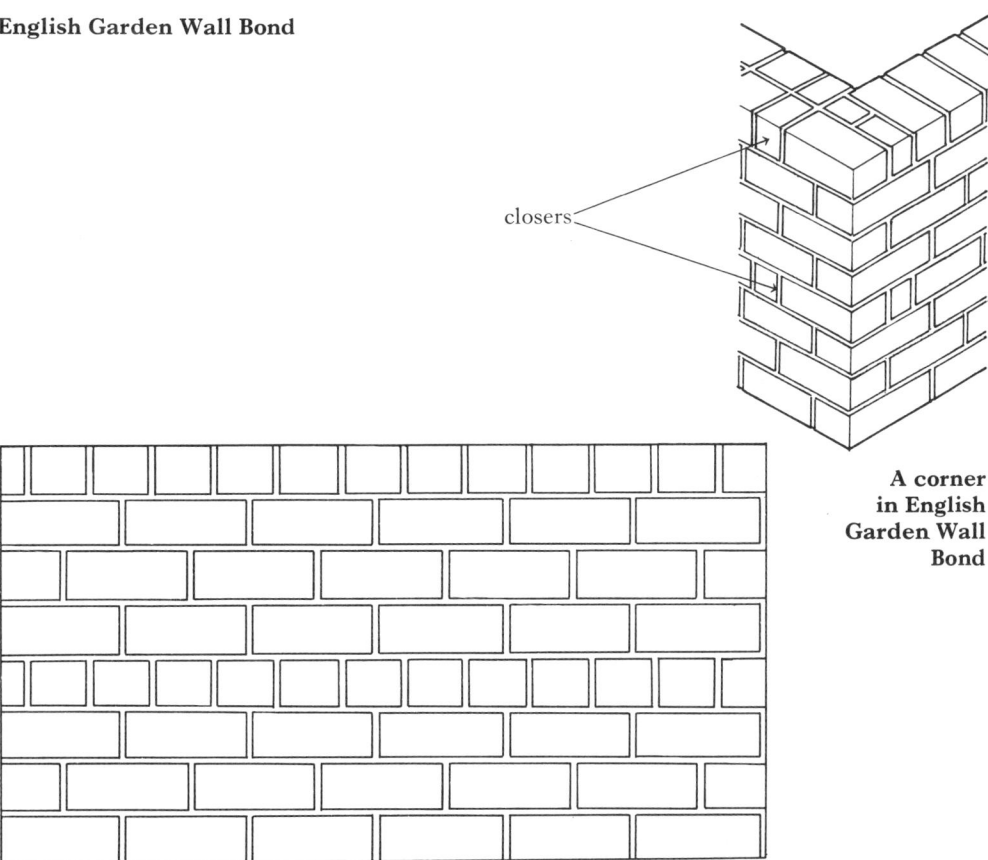

closers

A corner
in English
Garden Wall
Bond

After the row of headers there are three more courses of stretchers and then another course of headers – eight courses of bricks in all. The wall will be finished off with topping flags 1ft (30cm) square and 2in (5cm) thick. The result is a wall 22in (55cm) high above ground level, if you have laid the concrete foundation correctly and have not been too lavish with mortar between courses.

It helps greatly to mark on a stick the height each course should be, allowing 3in (7.5cm) to a course – that is, the height of the brick plus a layer of mortar. If you check each course against the marks on the stick as you go along you are unlikely to go astray.

Do not lay the topping flags immediately after the eight brick courses; that comes later. Make a start now with the inside of the pool.

At the bottom put a layer of stones and broken bricks 3in (7.5cm) deep. Ram them down. On top of that lay 4in (10cm) of concrete; this will give a pool to hold 18in (45cm) of water. If you wish to grow plants which must have only a few inches of water above them you will have to construct a shelf inside the pool 9in (23cm) below the top edge of the pool. A shelf along only one side would be enough unless the pool is large. It can be made by constructing a platform of broken bricks and stones bound together with cement mortar (1 part cement, 5

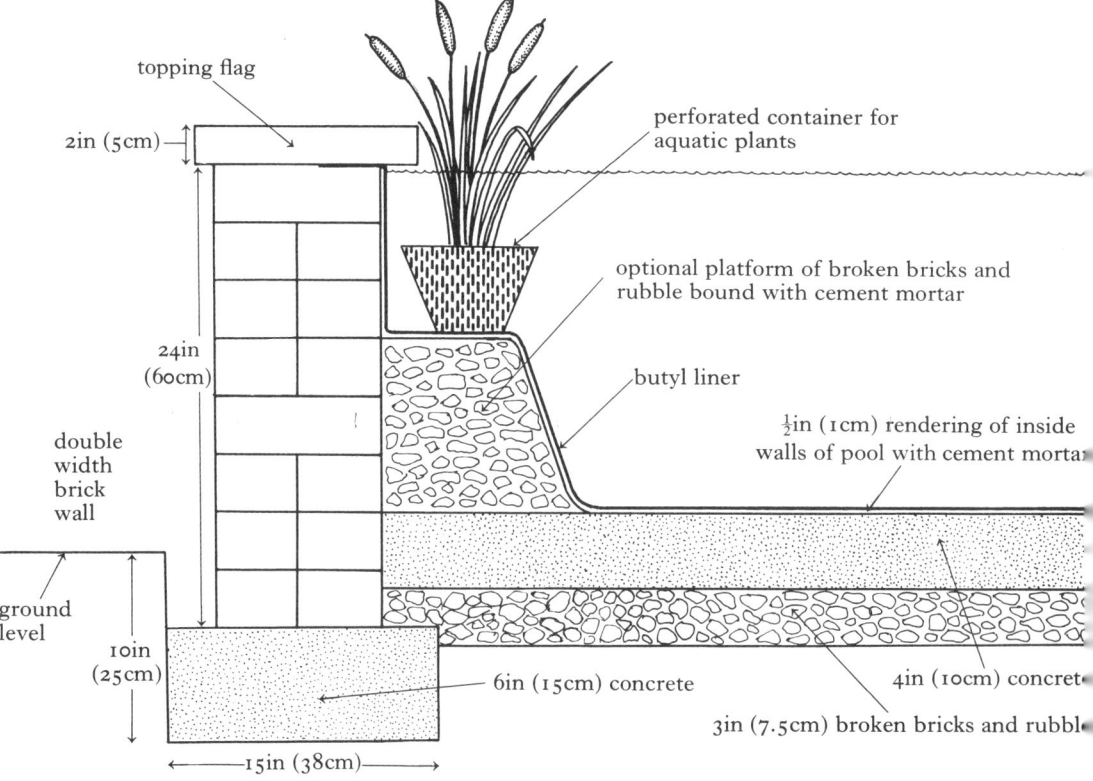

Cross-section of formal pool, showing construction

parts builder's sand). The platform should be 1ft (30cm) wide at the bottom of the pool, sloping inwards a little so that when it is 9in (23cm) high it is 9in (23cm) wide. If you intend to plant only water lilies (in addition to the essential oxygenating plants) there is no point in going to the trouble of building this platform.

With or without a platform the inside of the pool needs rendering with a coat of cement mortar about $\frac{1}{2}$in (1.5cm) thick (1 part cement, 5 parts builder's washed sand). This gives a smooth surface on which the butyl lining will not be damaged, as it might be on a rough surface.

The next stage is to fit the liner. To work out the size of liner to buy is simple. Its length must be the length of the pool plus twice the maximum depth of the pool, plus 1ft (30cm) for overlap at the edge of the pool. Its width must be the width of the pool plus twice the maximum depth, plus 1ft (30cm) for overlap.

Before putting the liner into the pool make sure that there are no sharp bits of concrete on the top of the wall which might damage the butyl. Spread the liner evenly over the pool and ease it a little into the pool. Hold it in place by weighting it with bricks along the top of the wall. Start filling it slowly with water from a hosepipe. As the pool fills up lift the bricks briefly from time to time to let the liner settle to the shape of the pool. Adjust the liner as it does so, folding it neatly into the corners, and along the shelf, if there is one. When the pool is full and the liner has been tucked in everywhere to your satisfaction the overlap can be trimmed so that 4–5in (10–12cm) overlaps on to the wall. Use the bricks to hold the overlap in place, removing them only as you lay the topping stones.

These are laid on a bed of mortar spread partly on the bricks and partly on the butyl (1 part cement, 3 parts sand). Flags 1ft (30cm) square can be laid to overlap the pool by 2in (5cm), leaving an overlap of 1in (2.5cm) at the other edge. Point carefully between the flags, leaving one joint unpointed if you want a submersible pump so that the cable can be led into the pool without showing. Take great care at this stage that no cement drops into the water, since it is dangerous to plants and fish. If any does fall in empty the pool, clean it out and fill it all over again. You can syphon the water out with a hose.

Pools can be planted any time between May and September – that is, when the plants are growing. It is advisable to wait two or three days after filling the pool before planting, but with a butyl-lined pool there is no need to wait any longer. After planting let a few weeks pass before putting fish into the pool so that the oxygenating plants have had a chance to get to work aerating the water.

If the pool is surrounded by grass there is a risk that pool watchers, especially children, will wear bare patches. A formal path all the way round a formal pool is overdoing formality to the point of boredom. Instead lay a few paving stones at intervals round the pool, to cope with the traffic. At other suitable points round the pool grow a few shrubs or herbaceous plants to break up the starkly straight lines of the pool. To be effective these plants must grow higher than the pool walls. Poolside planting is particularly valuable as an alternative to growing marginal plants inside the pond. It avoids the performance of building a platform shelf inside the pool and you can then devote the pool itself to floating water-lilies (plus the essential oxygenating plants which grow from the bottom of the pool).

To make an informal pool, using a prefabricated glass fibre shell within stone walls

This is a trickier operation than constructing the formal brick pool just described; it will be more expensive, and, as already pointed out, glass fibre has not as long a life as butyl. (However, when the glass fibre pool approaches the end of its natural life, it can be lined with butyl to add perhaps fifty years more. If you can afford it, you could use the glass fibre pool as a mould and line it with butyl in the first place.) On the other hand, stone is a very beautiful material and an informal pool may fit in better with the kind of garden you are aiming at.

Fully dressed stone is too formal looking, as well as frighteningly expensive. With roughly dressed stones of the same thickness you can build a wall with regular courses – as in the style of a brick wall. The cheaper random rubble is used for an uncoursed wall. If there is suitable local stone it is sensible to use that to save on transport. You may be lucky enough to find second-hand stone available from demolition work. Avoid mixing stone; if, for example, the house or garden walls are built of stone you should use similar stone. Some reconstituted stone blocks are convincing, but not if you put them near real stone.

As well as assorted sizes of stones for the wall, large flat stones or flags of equal thickness will be needed for topping off the walls to provide a surface even enough to sit on. A stone wall, being wider, will be more comfortable to sit on than a brick wall.

Glass fibre shells are made in various sizes, shapes and depths. The simpler the shape the easier it will be to build the wall and the better it will look.

The larger the pool you can find room for the less it will look dominated by the thick stone walls.

Choose a shell that is 18in (45cm) deep, with a plain flange (not pretending to be crazy paving or rocks) and moulded with a shelf for growing marginal plants.

First lay the prefabricated shell on the ground on the site chosen for it, flange upwards. Mark out on the ground, with pegs, the outline of the top of the pool. (Then move it out of harm's way.) Mark a similar outline 18in (45cm) away. Between those two lines dig a trench 8in (20cm) deep. Lay concrete in the trench to a depth of 6in (15cm) and the full 18in (45cm) width of the trench. This provides a foundation extending 3in (7.5cm) on each side of a 1ft (30cm) wall. Carefully test the level of the foundation.

Let the foundation set and then remove 3in (7.5cm) of soil from all over the area within it, ramming the soil down hard. Then make a start on building the wall, in the first place up to a height of only some 9in (23cm). Spread a strip of mortar about 1ft (30cm) wide and 1in (2.5cm) deep along the centre of the concrete foundation, doing about 2–3ft (60–90cm) at a time. For the first layer choose substantial stones of roughly the same thickness and put plenty of mortar between

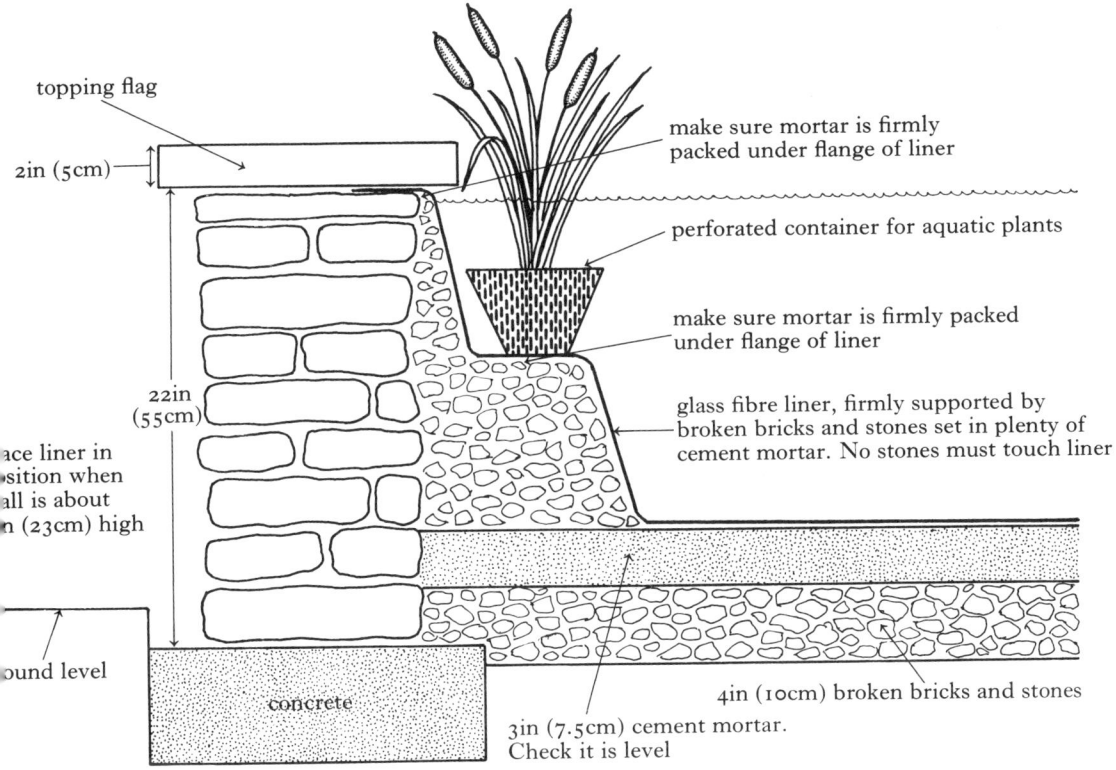

topping flag

2in (5cm)

22in (55cm)

ace liner in
osition when
all is about
n (23cm) high

ound level

concrete

make sure mortar is firmly
packed under flange of liner

perforated container for aquatic plants

make sure mortar is firmly packed
under flange of liner

glass fibre liner, firmly supported by
broken bricks and stones set in plenty of
cement mortar. No stones must touch liner

4in (10cm) broken bricks and stones

3in (7.5cm) cement mortar.
Check it is level

Cross-section of informal pool, showing construction

each stone. Continue the whole way round the pool. You are in fact building only
a retaining wall, one side of which will not be seen, so you can concentrate on
making the public side presentable.

There are two important points in building a stone wall. Avoid laying the stones
so that there are continuous vertical joints. Secondly, lay the stone so that the
grain runs as near horizontal as possible. Stone has a natural grain, more evident
in some types of stone than others. If a stone is laid with the grain running at a
considerable angle it is liable to split with the weight of the stones above. Also it
looks cockeyed, whereas even an irregularly shaped stone gives the impression of
having been laid level if the grain is horizontal.

When the wall is about 9in (23cm) high it is time to place the prefabricated shell
in position. Put a 4in (10cm) layer of bricks and stones over the area within the
wall and on top of this a 3in (7.5cm) layer of cement mortar (1 part cement, 6 parts
builder's sand). Test that it is level. On top of the mortar place the glass fibre pool,
checking that the pool is level from side to side and from end to end, using a spirit
level and a long piece of wood. If you don't get this right the water will show you
and everyone else that you haven't when the pool is filled.

Continue building the wall, filling the gap between the wall and the shell as you
go. This is a vital part of the operation, even though it will not be seen. Water is

heavy and when the pool is full – perhaps with 200 gallons (900 litres) of water or more – there will be great pressure on the glass fibre shell. It must therefore be supported thoroughly both underneath and all round the sides. It is particularly important to provide full support under the shelves of the pool. The best infill, especially with a large pool, is small pieces of broken brick and stone mixed with plenty of cement mortar (1 part cement, 6 parts sand). Make sure that no stones are touching the glass fibre.

When the wall is 4in (10cm) or so below the rim of the pool start packing the cement mortar under the flange of the pool. This must be strongly and evenly supported. When you are satisfied, complete the building of the wall exactly to the level of the rim of the prefabricated shell. Complete the filling in.

The final stage is to lay flags along the top of the pool wall all round the pool, bedding them on $\frac{1}{2}$in (1.5cm) of cement mortar, on the wall and the flange. If you want a fountain, leave a gap between two flags where a cable for a submersible pump can be concealed.

The pool can be filled straight away, and also planted, if between May and September. Fish can be introduced a few weeks after the oxygenating plants have been planted.

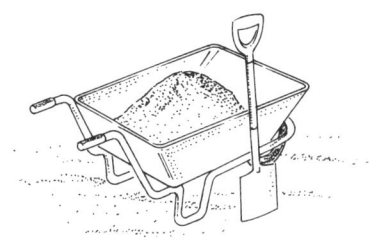

Plants and fish for a small pool

Having gone to the trouble of building a raised pool one might as well make it as interesting as possible. A bare stretch of water, even if it includes a fountain or waterfall, is less fascinating to watch than a pool in which plants are growing and fish swimming about.

Plants

Apart from the attractiveness of plants they are important in keeping the water clear. Without them a pool is almost certain to be invaded by algae, turning the water to green pea soup, or covered by green blanket weed. Small pools are the most difficult to keep clear, but given a surface area of not less than 40 square feet (3.7 sq.m) it should be possible to starve out algae or blanket weed for most of the year by a judicious use of plants. As a last resort it is possible to treat the water with chemical preparations which, if used properly, are harmless to fish and plants. In a newly built pool you are bound to get algae after a few weeks, but once the plants are established this should disappear – though it may appear each spring until the plants are growing vigorously again.

The most efficient pond cleaners are the oxygenating plants which grow from the bottom of the pool. The simplest way of 'planting' them is to attach them to a small stone with a rubber band and sink them into the water. Plant generously, allowing a dozen plants for every 20 square feet (1.8 sq.m) of surface area of the pool. Some grow too vigorously, but of the dozen or so generally available a good choice is:

Lagarosyphon major, probably the best of the oxygenators for the small pond. It is not unlike the rampageous *Elodea canadensis* (Canadian pondweed), which is widely sold, but it is far easier to keep under control.

Ceratophyllum demersum (Water hornwort), with branching stems of attractive, feathery, bright green foliage, which are easily kept under control.

Fontinalis antipyretica (Water moss). Grows in graceful shining green strands on the sides of the pool. It will tolerate both moving water and a fair amount of shade.

Hottonia palustris. Though called the Water violet, this is not a violet but a member of the primula family. Feathery emerald foliage grows below the surface of the water, but in May and June pale lilac flower spikes poke out above it.

Ranunculus aquatilis (Water crowfoot). This produces a mass of stems, leaves and white flowers on the surface of the pool. It will grow in moving or still water, once you have induced it to grow.

While you need plenty of oxygenators go easy on the number of other plants you put in the pool. Many plants which grow in water are far more rampant than those growing on land and can quickly swamp a pool. To avoid constant hacking away so that you can get a glimpse of the water (after all, that is the attraction of a pool), restrict yourself to a few and choose those which are in proportion to the size of the pool. Floaters such as water lilies (*nymphaea*) seem to take over the moment your back is turned. But there are more than fifty species and countless cultivars of water lilies to choose from, and from these it is possible to find one suitable for the smallest – and shallowest – pool. One water lily would be enough for 20 square feet (1.8 sq.m) of water.

The following list is mainly confined to miniature and small water lilies, which are less numerous than those on sale for larger, deeper pools. The area of the pool which they are estimated to cover is, of course, only approximate. The depth of water given is the depth *above* the plant. The time of flowering is much the same for all of them – mid June onwards.

The following miniature varieties form a circle of leaves about 18in (45cm) in diameter, for up to 9in (23cm) of water:

Nymphaea pygmaea alba. White with a golden centre and very delicate looking. This is probably the smallest water lily, and can be grown even in tubs.

N. candida. Small white flowers with a yellow centre; very free-flowering.

N. laydekeri 'Purpurata'. Wine-red flowers with white shading; scented.

N. pygmaea 'Helvola'. Leaves with brown mottling and flowers of sulphur yellow.

These small varieties form a circle of leaves about 2ft (60cm) in diameter, for 6–18in (15–45cm) of water:

N. caroliniana nivea. Large white flowers; strongly scented.

N. odorata turiensis. Soft rose flowers with elongated petals. Scented.

N. 'Froebelii'. Crimson; free-flowering. A popular old favourite.

N. 'Paul Hariot'. When the flowers open they are pale yellow, but they age to copper red.

N. 'Sioux'. Buff-yellow flowers become peach as they age.

N. 'Graziella'. Deep apricot; free-flowering.

Finally, these slightly larger varieties form a circle of leaves about 3ft in diameter, for $1\frac{1}{2}$–2ft (45–60cm) of water:

N. 'James Brydon'. A very widely grown water lily with dark leaves and large rose-pink flowers. In large, deep pools it will grow quite vigorously, but in shallow water it shows more restraint. It has the great advantage that it will tolerate more shade than most water lilies.

N. 'Rose Arey'. Rich pink flowers with dainty incurved petals. Delightful scent.

Water lilies do best if they get plenty of sun – at least for half the day. Plant them in boxes or planting crates, lined with hessian and filled with heavy loam or rotted turf. At the start support the crate on a platform of bricks in the pool so that the lilies are covered with between 3 and 4in (7.5–10cm) of water. As they grow lower them gradually, removing the bricks as needed, if they are varieties which need deeper water. Ordinary fertilizers encourage algae so use only the special fertilizers made for aquatic plants.

Water lilies, however, are by no means the only attractive water plants. Here are some others which are among the best for smaller pools, though a few of them may have to be kept under control:

Aponogeton distachyus (Water hawthorn)
    Floating leaves. Depth of water: 6–18in (15–45cm).
    The oval leaves grow from small tubers. The flowers, which smell of hawthorn blossom, are white with black stamens, and appear from spring through summer to autumn and later. The plants need full sun and still water. They may seed themselves, needing to be thinned out.

Nymphoides peltata 'Bennettii', syn. *Villarsia bennettii* (Water fringe)
    Height above water: 3in (7.5cm). Depth of water: 4–18in (10–45cm).
    Like a miniaturized water lily, with round crinkly-edged leaves and golden yellow fringed flowers only 1in (2.5cm) in diameter. They appear in July on short stems above the water. Small though it is, it has to be kept under strict control.

Pontederia cordata (Pickerel weed)
    Height: 18in (45cm). Depth of water: 3–5in (7.5–12.5cm).
    The leaves are heart-shaped and glossy and there are spikes of soft blue flowers in late summer. It is deservedly popular, not only because blue flowers are not common among aquatic plants but also because – in spite of its name – it is not invasive. Plant in April and May; this is also the time to propagate by division.

Orontium aquaticum (Golden club)
    Height: 10in (25cm). Depth of water: 3–12in (7.5–30cm).
    The waxy, silvery leaves stand above the water if planted in shallow water, but float in deeper water. The flowers are spadices without spathes, looking like pokers with a yellow tip, and they appear in profusion in April and May. Plant in at least 6in (15cm) of rich loam.

Sagittaria sagittifolia (Common arrowhead)
    Height: 1ft (30cm). Depth of water: 3–5in (7.5–12.5cm).
    The plants get their name from the shape of the leaves. The British native has white flowers with purple centres which appear in July. It can soon get out of hand, so in a small pool it would be better to plant *S. japonica flore pleno*, with large double white flowers, even though it does take time to establish itself. It needs to be covered with only an inch or so of water. Propagate by division in spring.

Acorus calamus 'Variegatus' (Sweet flag)
Height: 30in (75cm). Depth of water: 3–5in (7.5–12.5cm).
The iris-like leaves are striped with green and cream and the poker-like spadix is brown. The smaller *A. gramineus* 'Variegatus' (6–8in (15–20cm); depth of water: 2–6in (5–15cm)) has narrow grassy leaves, which, unlike those of *A. calamus,* are evergreen.

Iris laevigata
Height: 18in (45cm). Depth of water: 2–4in (5–10cm).
This is the most popular of the hardy water irises. The brilliant blue flowers appear in June and July and often again in September. Propagate by division.

Calla palustris (Bog arum)
Height: 6in (15cm). Depth of water: 2–4in (5–10cm).
The leaves are heart-shaped and glossy; the white, strongly scented, arum-like flowers appear from June. The plant has a running rootstock and can be propagated in spring by cutting up pieces of the roots with shoots attached and planting them.

There are two very lively-looking plants for growing at the edge of the pool if a ledge can be arranged for them so that they are hardly standing in the water. They are:

Caltha palustris (Marsh marigold, Kingcup)
Height: 1ft (30cm). Depth of water: up to 3in (7.5cm), but it flourishes equally in mud.
This is one of the best plants for the water's edge, with its smooth heart-shaped leaves and vivid golden yellow flowers in April. *C.p. plena*, which grows to around 6in (15cm), carries masses of double, quite long-lasting flowers in April. *C.p. alba*, about 6in (15cm), is a white single version of *C. palustris*.

Mimulus luteus (Yellow monkey musk)
Height: 1ft (30cm). Depth of water: 0–2in (0–5cm).
Small yellow flowers with chocolate spots appear from July onwards. There are other species (but avoid *Mimulus guttatus* like the plague it is) and many hybrids and cultivars, such as 'Whitecroft Scarlet', the crimson 'Red Emperor' and the yellow 'Canary Bird'.

Rushes and grasses can also look effective when planted in shallow water near the edges of the pool. Here are three possibles:

Scirpus albescens
Height: 3ft (90cm). Depth of water: 2–4in (5–10cm).
The attraction of this rush is in the variegated leaves, with vertical stripes of green and white. The Japanese rush, *S. tabernaemontanus* 'Zebrinus' (plant in 3–5in (7.5–12.5cm) of water) has horizontal stripes of green and white. To

maintain the variegation cut away all plain leaves which appear. Plant in spring, also the time to propagate by division.

Butomus umbellatus (Flowering rush)
   Height: about 18in (45cm). Depth of water: 3–5in (7.5–12.5cm).
   This rush has smooth glossy leaves. Flower stems, about 30in (75cm) tall, bear rose-pink flowers in July and onwards. Plant in loam in April or May and in autumn cut down the leaves and stems to about 6in (15cm). It is best to split up the roots and replant them each spring.

Glyceria spectabilis variegatus (Manna grass)
   Height: 2ft (60cm). Depth of water: 2–5in (5–12.5cm).
   Showy striped grass of many colours, but it does tend to get out of hand.

Fish

The best fish for the size of pool we have been considering are goldfish and golden orfe. In milder parts of the country the multicoloured shubunkin could be added to those two. They would all get on together.
   Goldfish (*Carassius aurata*) are not furiously active and therefore do not demand a lot of space to swim in. They are usually red, but yellow and silver fish are available. Few of the more bizarre forms of goldfish are hardy enough for outdoor pools, but it would be worth trying the Comet longtails, rapid swimmers with flowing tails. Fantails, though attractive, are not particularly hardy.
   The salmon-orange coloured golden orfe (*Idus idus*) is more active than the goldfish so you are likely to see more of it, especially as it swims near the surface.
   Shubunkins have transparent scales displaying a mottled pattern of yellow, brown, red and blue. They also turn up in a Comet form with flowing tails and fins.
   The most dramatic, and expensive, of the hardy cold water fish are the Japanese Koi carp, the colours of which range through yellow, blue, red, silver and gold. But they are rapid growers and can reach 3ft (90cm), so they are unsuitable for the small garden pool.
   Snails are not necessary.
   Fish can be put into the pool between May and September. Do not overstock. The rule of thumb is to allow a square foot (0.1 sq.m) of water for every 2in (5cm) of fish, assuming that the pool is adequately stocked with oxygenating plants. Allow several weeks for these plants to become established before introducing any fish. Shortly before the fish are put in add a water conditioner to the pool. This helps the fish to adjust gradually to the change of water from that to which they were accustomed. They are very touchy about that.
   Fish are usually transported in a sealed plastic bag containing water and air. Do not empty them out at once. Place the bag on the surface of the pool for half an hour or so to ensure that the temperature of the water in the bag and the pool are the same. Then release the fish.

If the pool is new and the vegetation in it is not fully established the fish will have to be fed for the first season, either daily or twice daily, according to how hungry they appear to be. They should be eager to eat, but their appetites will vary according to the weather. Do not overfeed; the fish should gobble up everything within five minutes. Remove uneaten food; this will be easier to do if you use floating pellets which can be scooped up in a net. Food left in the water will foul it up.

From October through the winter feed only when the weather is warm and the fish eat readily. Even in later years when there is enough natural food in an established pool it helps to give the fish a supplementary daily feed in spring and autumn.

If you have bought a pool heater remember to turn it on on frosty nights. It is not meant to coddle the fish by warming all the water in the pool but it will keep a little area free from ice. This allows the gases given off by any rotting leaves in the pond to escape. If trapped in they are liable to kill the fish. Hammering away at the ice to make a hole risks harming the fish.

The summerhouse

The summerhouse in our first garden was quite a simple affair. It consisted of a room about 8ft (2.4m) square, with windows facing west and south, but windowless on the north and east. The door was also on the south side. One important feature was the verandah, about 30in (75cm) wide, which was built on the south and west sides. You could therefore sit out of the sun or rain and still be in the open air. It was at first, above all, a sheltered place for the pram.

It was not quite perfect. It was built on a wooden platform, which created an unnecessary step up on to the verandah. A concrete base, level with the path, would have been better. One other improvement would have been to extend one end of the summerhouse to provide a separate store for a mower and other gardening tools. Garden sheds are bought by the million but they are invariably eyesores. A summerhouse and garden shed combined need not be if well designed and constructed, an important proviso. I would not attempt to build one myself but it is certainly not beyond a really competent handyman.

You may need planning permission and you will have to comply with local building regulations. (When my summerhouse was built there were no such problems.)

To get the fullest value out of a summerhouse it is essential that it should have electricity laid on, and this should be done when it is built and not later. Without electricity the summerhouse will be used spasmodically in summer, and will be unusable when it is dark and cold – that is, for most of the year.

A garden for a young family to grow up in

Garage

Summer house

Back of the house

Children's Garden

Raised Pool

Raised bed

Raised bed

Raised bed

Compost bins

Hide hole

Play mound

Rough grass

Sandpit

Barrier shrubs

Children come first

This section of the book concentrates on the planning and creation of a family garden until the time when the emphasis ceases to be on its use by the children and when the parents can come into their own again.

There are four basic stages in a conventional family life. The first runs from marriage until the first child is born. The second stretches (endlessly, it seems at times of exasperation) from the birth of the first child until the last one leaves home. In the third stage the husband and wife are on their own again, nowadays probably still young with an active middle age ahead of them. Finally, together they grow old. The transition from being husband and wife, to father, mother and puling infant is abrupt, but later stages merge more gradually with each other.

All kinds of events may occur to wreck this conventional pattern, but thinking about them is probably not at the forefront of anyone's mind when moving into a first home (and garden).

For a young couple the move into their first home is almost as intoxicating as was falling in love, and as dangerous, for emotion takes over from rational thinking. There is a resurgence of the white wedding syndrome, which can lead to an orgy of misdirected spending to achieve a *House and Garden* home, and garden to match. In the average house, for a couple who plan to have children, this is folly. Right from the start infants and their impedimenta turn exquisite surroundings into an untidy shambles. Children growing up in such a house will predictably wreck it – not maliciously or even intentionally but just in the process of growing up.

A sensible couple will therefore start by furnishing as economically as possible with the minimum of furniture, and that of a kind to withstand the presence of children. You are unlikely to want to spend all your life with that kind of stuff, and in any case after perhaps fifteen years of use and abuse it will either be looking disgusting or falling apart. Then is the time to replace it with the kind of furniture you wanted in the first place, or a different kind if your taste has changed.

Children's outdoor activities are even more potentially destructive than those indoors, and plants are even more fragile than furniture.

Saki wrote a story about a prince who told his gardener that he wanted to keep pigs in his garden. The gardener pointed out that the prince could not have pigs and flowers. The prince chose pigs. Similarly, if you have children, or hope to, you should shelve for a time any ambitious dream garden fantasies. Accept that while the children are young the garden should above all cater for their needs. If you try to combine your picture book garden with their mini-playground you will be infuriated by the destruction they wreak while they will resent your unreasonableness and nagging.

Never forget that your children are young only once, and will be able to enjoy the pleasure of a garden to play in for only a few years, whereas you have all the rest of your lives for gardening. While you are waiting for your turn, concentrate on enjoying your children and their enjoyment. It is a fleeting time and will never recur.

Take as a starting point a young couple moving into their first home. They may be taking over a well-kept garden, a neglected garden or a bit of virgin land, if that can be used to describe a site ravaged by builders. The methods of tackling each of these will be different, but the aim is the same: to turn it as quickly as possible into a garden to fit the uses you want to put it to.

If there is a child, or if a child is on the way, the most urgent task is to prepare the garden for it. If children are hoped for, but the first is not actually in prospect, plan the garden with children in view but do not necessarily carry out the plans. For instance, there is no point in building a sandpit until a child is born; there will then be plenty of time to get it done before the child is ready to use it. But it would be wrong to waste that first burst of new garden enthusiasm by doing no major work in the garden. Channel it into preparing for times much further ahead than only the next few years. Make a start, as set out in Part One, on building paths, a paved area and raised beds, perhaps a raised pool, and a summerhouse if possible, for a summerhouse is valuable above all when there is a growing family.

Giving priority to your children need not mean giving up gardening altogether (unless you want an excuse). In the average garden there are two generally under-used areas: the front garden (see pages 105–7) and the walls of the house and other walls and fences (see pages 96–105). These can largely compensate for the space given over to the children in the main part of the garden.

Safety warning

A front garden is not a safe place for young children to play in, however little traffic there may be about and however secure the gate. The gate will be left open by the milkman, the postman, the dustman and all those people who stuff bargain offers through the letter boxes. To a small child an open gate is an open invitation to satisfy a natural and very praiseworthy curiosity. Even when children grow older there will be times when they forget the dangers of traffic and dart out after a lost ball, or just for the hell of it.

If children have the run of the garden behind the house – as they should – and are excluded for safety's sake from the front garden, some kind of effective barrier must be erected between the two areas. Just saying 'No' is not enough. An unscalable fence or wall will give you greater peace of mind than reliance on a child's unfailing obedience. Better still a hedge or ornamental screen which can be peered through but not escaped through; it seems less prison-like. Obviously there will have to be some way through the barricade, but equally obviously a gate is pointless if it can be opened by young children. It must be kept locked, however infuriating that may be at times for adults who must remember yet another key.

(For suitable shrubs for barriers, see pages 80–81.)

The garden as a playground

Having decided to shelve your dream garden for a few years for the sake of a growing family it would be absurd not to make sure they get the most out of it. It is hard to recall what we liked most of all about the garden of our childhood. Highlights stand out, but there are long stretches where memory is blank. The early days are oblivion, and when we try to remember the later days of childhood we go wildly astray about the ages at which we enjoyed doing what.

Even if our recall were perfect there is no guarantee that our children's interests will be the same as ours were. I hated games, but had a precocious interest in my father's garden. My children, like many people, had no interest at all in gardening until they married. There are also fashions in play, as in everything else, but fortunately many of the activities that can be provided for in a garden are unchanging: for example, water and sand play, and hiding.

A little espionage in your neighbours' gardens, local nursery schools or adventure playgrounds will help to show you what is most popular with children of various ages. But not only do children have different interests; there is considerable variation in the ages at which those interests may be aroused. Beware of trying to live your childhood over again; accept that your children may prefer reading to training for the First Division or the Olympic Games gymnastics. Strange as it may seem to some parents, some children may not even like climbing trees.

With all these provisos it is possible to give a rough guide to some stages of a child's development and the way in which a garden can be planned and used to meet them.

The first year

Being outdoors adds a whole new world of experiences even to a child in a pram, even before he or she can focus properly. There is more movement – light and shade, and currents of air – and a different repertory of sounds. A child born in the summer can be put out in the garden in a pram right from the start. On fine days find somewhere where the child's face is not directly in the sun, and go out to check from time to time because the sun whips round in the sky faster than you think. But do not put the pram directly under a tree, for you never know what will fall out of the branches. On wet days use the verandah of the summerhouse to protect the child from rain and wind. Fix a fine mesh in front of the pram hood, to keep out insects, to deter curious cats and to discourage doting humans.

Take the playpen on to the lawn by all means, but do not use it as a cage for the child for long; the garden should give greater freedom than the house ever can (for thoroughly practical reasons). When the child begins to crawl and shuffle never leave him alone in the garden. And always check that the gates you have fixed for your children's safety are shut and the catches secure.

A sandpit can be a problem at this age. Many children, before they start to crawl, enjoy just sitting in sand. But they also like trying to eat handfuls of it and, more dangerously, they may rub it into their eyes. So be prepared to watch them with undistracted hawklike eyes if you introduce them to the sandpit at this stage. Also, without fail, fix the cat barricades whenever the pit is not in use or you will have more unpleasant problems than sand.

The second year

The more mobile your child becomes the more you will find yourself shouting 'Don't'. Some of these occasions can be avoided with a little foresight: by seeing that gates are shut, garden tools are not left lying about, and garden fertilizers, pesticides and insecticides are locked away. And though you may have to tell him not to climb into the garden pool, make sure (for your own peace of mind) that even if he does he will not drown because the safety net is always securely in place. (A wooden frame with wire netting attached is all you need.)

After making safe as many Don't places as possible provide him with something he *can* do. Water play and sand play are the great standbys, and they will probably stay so for several years, taking new forms as the child's skills develop.

Water play will have begun in the bath at a very early age, but it is far more exciting outside. The raised pool you may have built is useless for water play, however fascinating it may be to watch, but you can easily provide better alternatives – water to splash in and water to pour – the two basic pleasures of playing with water.

First the splashing. There is no point in providing a permanent paddling pool; it will be expensive to build and not easy to keep clean. A portable plastic pool is a far better buy; a shallow circular model with inflatable sides will be adequate at this stage and can be replaced later with a larger, deeper pool. The small pool needs only 3 or 4in (7.5–10cm) of water. Even that is enough to drown a small child, so you will have to be present all the time to prevent any danger of that. Empty the water out after using the pool and leave it upside down to keep out dirt, cats, birds and the like.

It is a chore if you have to refill the pool with buckets of water – hence the sense in having a small pool. If you use a hose to fill it add some hot water before the child gets in so that the water is not stone cold; the bodies of small children lose heat quickly. For that reason splashing sessions should not be protracted.

Secondly the pouring. This ritual is basically a standing up pastime. The equipment needed is not elaborate: a good-sized plastic washing up bowl half filled with water, a stool or box to stand it on at a comfortable height for the child (or you can buy a specially designed water trough on a metal stand; an unused baby bath and stand is also ideal), yoghourt and ice cream plastic tubs in many sizes and an enveloping tough plastic apron. Expect a lot of spilled water. In hot, dry weather the water play can be done on the lawn without turning it into a mud bath, but in general it is better to choose a hard surface – the patio, for instance. Put the tackle away when not in use – another role for the summerhouse.

Sand play has an even longer lasting attraction than water play because it becomes incorporated in other more complicated forms of play. But at the start

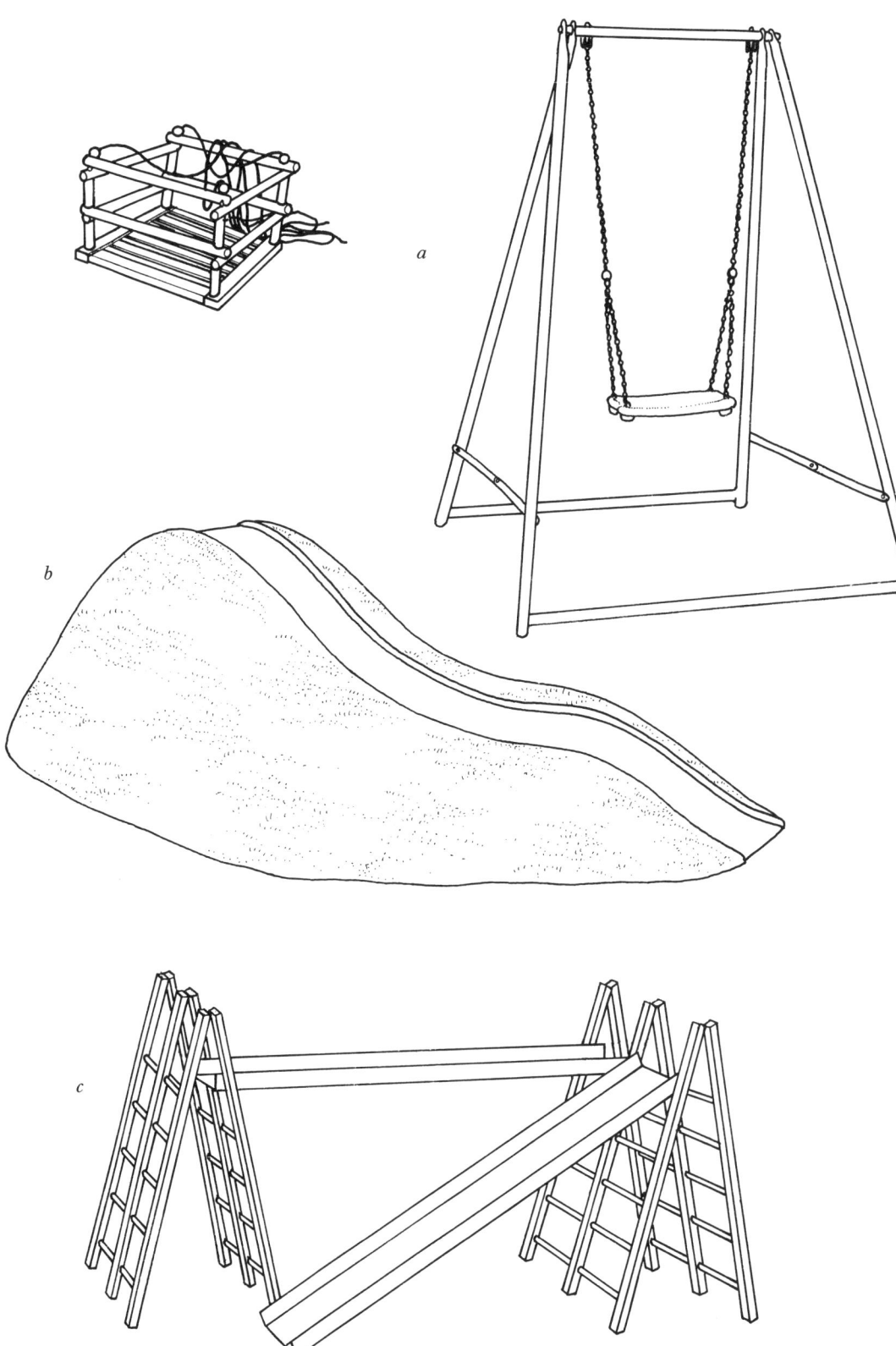

Play equipment. a. swing, with alternative seat for very small child. b. slide on contoured mound. c. slide on climbing trestles. d. climbing frame. e. barrel to crawl through. f. wooden log, for stepping stones. g. plank for balancing. h. seesaw

the play is very simple: patting the sand, filling anything fillable with it and then emptying it, and, infuriatingly, carrying it out of the sandpit.

At this early stage the equipment needed is a small plastic spade (not a metal one yet), a bucket, and more yoghurt and ice cream tubs or any other plastic containers (but never, never anything made of glass; broken glass turns a sandpit into a disaster area).

When the pit is not in use keep the cat-proof cover in place. Fork the sand over regularly to keep it loose and let the air in. Shovel back any sand that strays out of the pit. Top up occasionally from your secret store.

Playing with sand may lessen the nuisance of a child playing in similar ways with soil but will certainly not prevent it. You will have to be reasonable about this, possibly tolerating it where no great harm is done, but discouraging it elsewhere.

The third year

The garden becomes more and more the domain of the increasingly active child, who has now discovered the pleasure to be got from things on wheels – a tricycle (small at this stage), a truck or a miniature pram. He/she may also enjoy climbing, swinging and sliding, but equipment for these activities must be within the capabilities of the child at that age even though you will have to replace it with something more challenging in a year or two. Hiding, with the excitement of being found, is a game you will be expected to join in at this stage; the raised beds are marvellous places for hiding behind. (Hiding with the intention of not being found comes later.)

The fourth and fifth years

The activities are the same as in the third year, but more so in this period up to school age. Nursery school, if the child is lucky enough to go to one, can provide some of the opportunities and equipment for play. Failing that it must be encouraged at home. Instead of buying gimmicky toys which are abandoned within a few days or weeks any money is better spent on simple permanent equipment, which will also be an invaluable investment for any younger children as they grow up.

How to make a sandpit

This is the way to make a good sandpit:

Sink it in the ground.

Surround it on three sides with a wall broad enough to sit on or to make sand pies on.

Do not enclose the fourth side. In place of a wall have a gentle slope into the pit which allows a very young child to walk instead of climbing (and falling), while helping to prevent the sand from creeping out.

Have a paved area, not grass, at the entrance to the pit so that any straying sand can be brushed back in.

Pave the floor of the sandpit as well, or the children will soon be digging down into the soil. Concrete flags make a good base if 1in (2.5cm) gaps are left between them to provide the absolutely essential drainage.

The size of the sandpit depends on how much of the garden you think you can spare and how large you imagine your family is going to be. In childhood terms a sandpit has a long life, for even when a child has outgrown the sand pie stage a decent-sized sandpit will provide the setting for quite sophisticated games with all kinds of toys. If there are several children in the family make it as large as you reasonably can. Even if there is only one child, there will be a multitude of best friends eager to share it.

Circular sandpits may look pretty, but they need skill to make and the shape is hard to put to other uses when its life as a sandpit is over. A rectangular pit is more easily adapted for other purposes.

While a single brick width will do for a raised bed a sandpit should have a double brick thickness, both to provide a seat wide enough to sit on and because it will get a lot of hard usage. The foundations therefore need to be wider and thicker and laid deeper to make allowances for the slope towards the back of the pit.

When working out how big to make the pit – rectangle or square – bear in mind that because of the thickness of the walls the pit will be 18in (45cm) narrower than the outside, which makes quite a difference to how much sand and how many children the pit can hold. Mark out the site. (How to mark out the site, dig the trench for the foundations, and lay the concrete base is explained in detail in the section on building a brick raised bed (pages 45–6).) A trench needs to be dug on only three sides of the square or rectangle; if it is to be a rectangular pit it is better to have a shorter end as the open end; that way less sand is likely to escape.

The trench must be 15in (38cm) wide and 15in (38cm) deep. In the trench lay concrete to the depth of 6in (15cm).

After laying the concrete leave the foundations to set for a few days. You can then begin to remove the soil from inside the pit to make a sloping floor. At the entrance to the sandpit take out soil to the depth of 3in (7.5cm). This allows for laying concrete slabs 2in (5cm) thick on a bed of sand about 1in (2.5cm) thick.

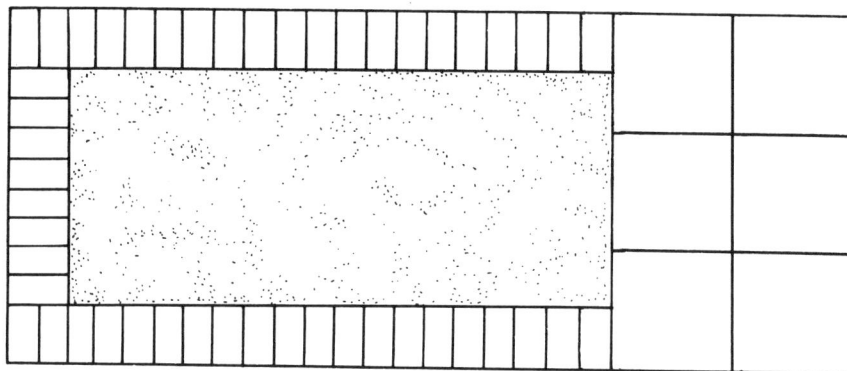

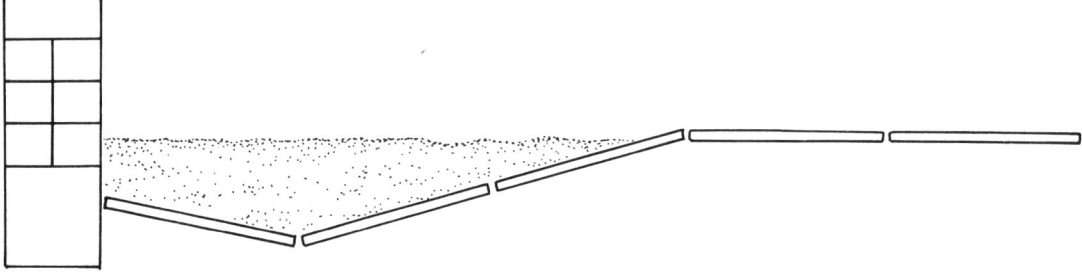

How to build a sandpit: view from above and cross-section

From there grade a slope evenly so that at a point 2ft (60cm) away from the end wall you have dug out 9in (23cm) of soil, making the surface level with the top of the concrete base. From that point to the end of the pit the slope should turn upwards, rising by about 3in (7.5cm). This will prevent rain water from the pit draining straight under the foundations of the wall.

The soil from the sandpit may be used to fill any raised beds you may be building or to make a grassy mound for children's play. Removing the soil at this stage makes the building of the wall easier and your treading about on it while brick-laying will firm the surface ready for flagging.

The next step is the wall. As we have seen there is a choice of bonds for a double wall. A suitable bond for the sandpit is the English garden wall bond, as described on pages 55–6. Lay three courses of stretchers followed by one of headers, including closers. Then lay three more rows of stretchers and finish with a row of headers, which on the final course can be laid with their narrow face (3in (7.5cm)) upwards if you wish. (If you are using bricks with frogs make sure that at the corners you leave the flat face of the brick exposed.)

Finish the pit off by laying concrete slabs on the floor. Two standard sizes are 2ft × 2ft (60cm × 60cm) and 2ft × 18in (60cm × 45cm); both are 2in (5cm) thick. Bed them down in 1in (2.5cm) of builder's sand, leaving a gap of 1in (2.5cm) between each one for drainage so that the pit does not become waterlogged.

Remember that the final row of flags must slope away from and not towards the end wall to drain the water away from it.

Concrete flags may also be used for an apron of paving at the entrance to the sandpit. This will be needed only if the pit abuts on the lawn and not a path.

The pit is now ready for the sand. While young children enjoy pouring dry silver sand, it is impractical to provide for this in an outdoor pit. Damp sand is much more versatile; a fine, washed builder's sand fits the bill (and the other bill will be less than it would be for silver sand). Sand is sold by the cubic yard or metre, and how much is needed can be worked out from the size of the pit. Do not skimp; a mysterious property of sand is to diminish for no apparent reason.

Sand is very heavy, so the charges for delivery make up a large proportion of the total cost. If you have in mind any building jobs that need sand look ahead and buy enough for the whole lot. Till you get round to doing them the sand can always be parked in the pit.

Cats regard sandpits as a public convenience built especially for them, and dogs bury bones in them. To defeat them build a simple frame of wood and netting to cover the top and front. Train the children to put it in place when the pit is not in use, or to remind you to do it if they are too young to handle the frame. Do not use any cover that excludes air – for example polythene sheeting. Air, sunlight and rain are needed to keep the sand sweet. Turning it over occasionally also helps. Clear out leaves that sneak in during autumn; they play havoc with sand pie making.

Somewhere to hide

Children need somewhere to hide. They need hiding places when playing games and they need secret places to escape to. Adults often forget the need they had as children for some privacy from the gaze of adults, and tend to assume that when their own children are out of sight and quiet they are up to no good – especially if the neighbours' children are with them.

The bottom of the garden – or anywhere far enough away from the house – is a good place to provide a hideaway. Allow as much space for it as possible, depending on the size of the back garden, but even a small area is better than none. Shrubs can form a screen from prying eyes, and it is very important that they be tough enough not to be trampled down by children taking short cuts.

Many years ago the British Embassy garden in Moscow was overrun by Russian demonstrators who played havoc with the rose beds. I then drew up a list of plants suitable for gardens liable to be overrun by demonstrators. The following recommendations for shrubs which may prove a barrier to children is a somewhat less punitive version. There are many others: they need not necessarily be prickly (though that helps), but they should form dense growth.

Berberis darwinii
10ft (3m). Evergreen.

Small, shiny, prickly leaves; clusters of orange-yellow flowers in spring; bluish berries in summer. It would be a foolhardy child to challenge the dense, prickly growth of *B. wilsoniae,* even though it is only about 3ft (90cm) tall, and slow to reach that. It is deciduous.

Chaenomeles japonica
3ft (90cm). Deciduous.

This ornamental quince makes a good barrier shrub as well as a wall plant. The dark red flowers in early spring are followed by yellow fruits. Hardy and not fussy about soil. The hybrid 'Crimson and Gold' is taller; it has darker leaves, orange flowers and suckers furiously.

Clethra alnifolia
6ft (1.8m). Deciduous.

White racemes of sweet-smelling flowers in late summer; in autumn the leaves turn yellow. Suckers are produced freely. Unfortunately the shrub is not particularly hardy.

Cornus alba (Dogwood)
4ft (1.2m). Deciduous.

This is the red-stemmed dogwood, and because the densely growing stems are so striking in winter it is no great matter that the leaves do fall. *C. alba* 'Sibirica', the 'Westonbirt' dogwood, is the brightest.

Cotoneaster conspicuus
Around 6ft (1.8m). Evergreen.

Small leaves and scarlet berries, which may last until spring. It is a great spreader, and eventually can reach 20ft (6m) tall. *C.c.* 'Decorus' also spreads but is not so tall. Likes a limy soil, but tolerates others, and also sun or shade.

Forsythia suspensa sieboldii
6 ft (1.8m) or more. Deciduous.

Dense-growing with arching branches. Striking in spring when covered with yellow flowers but boring for the rest of the year. See page 102 for cultivation.

Gaultheria shallon
   4–5ft (1.2–1.5m). Evergreen.
A thoroughly rampageous plant, but an effective barrier if kept under control. Sprigs of pinkish bell flowers in early summer, followed by purple grape-like fruits. Needs a rich, lime-free soil in the shade.

Genista hispanica (Spanish gorse)
   2ft (60cm). Deciduous, but numerous spines make them look almost evergreen.
It would be a brave (or foolish) child who chose to do battle with such a prickly bush. When young it has a shapely roundness, but it can become straggly with age and needs cutting back hard to make it bushy again. Covered with aggressively yellow flowers in spring. Needs warmth and full sun. Will grow in limy soil and thrives near the sea.

Juniperus x *media*
   5ft (1.5m). Evergreen.
If you like conifers, and are afflicted with a cold, shady, windswept garden, *Juniperus* x *media* (*J. chinensis*) 'Pfitzeriana' is as dense-growing a plant as you can get. The branches develop a great spread, from a moderate 6–7ft (2m) to a possible 20ft (6m). This is the variety to choose; some are narrow at the base and broad at the top and therefore more penetrable.

Mahonia japonica
   6ft (1.8m). Evergreen.
The leaves are just a little prickly, but the plants are far less fearsome than the berberis because the stems have no spines. It makes a dense, wide-spreading bush. *M. japonica* is one of the most attractive; hardy, tolerant of shade, and unfussy about soil, it carries deliciously scented long racemes of yellow flowers. Unfortunately they bloom in late winter and early spring, so if you plant mahonias at the bottom of the garden you will catch little of their Lily-of-the-valley smell. *M. aquifolium* (the Oregon grape, because of its blue berries) grows to a rather more manageable 4ft (1.2m).

Pernettya mucronata (Prickly heath)
   2–3ft (60–90cm). Evergreen.
Smooth, small, dark green leaves ending in a sharp point – hence its name of Prickly heath. Clusters of small white bells in late spring and early summer. According to variety the berries, which appear in autumn, may be white, pink, red or purple. 'Bell's Seedling' and Davis's hybrids are self-fertile, but otherwise you will need a male plant among the females to ensure berrying; plenty of sun also helps. Given a rich, lime-free soil the plant should make a dense shrub, but if it shows signs of growing lanky cut back the long shoots in spring.

Rosa rugosa, R. x *paulii, R.* x 'Macrantha'
   5ft (1.5m). Deciduous.
There are some pretty savage roses which make excellent barriers. Among the rugosas are the double white 'Blanc Double de Coubert', the pale pink 'Fru Dagmar Hastrup' and the winy red 'Roseraie de l'Hay'. *R.* x *paulii* (white and fragrant) and *R.* x 'Macrantha' (pink and fragrant) are sprawlers.

The summerhouse as refuge

There are countless uses for a summerhouse in a family garden. Here are some, from infancy to adolescence:

A parking place for the pram, with or without the infant. He or she is the first justification for the L-shaped verandah; the pram can be put where it is out of the rain, wind or sun and still be in fresh air.

A playroom from an early age. After a few days indoors, staring through rain-obscured windows, a child becomes bored to tantrums, not so much with doing the same things as with having to do them in the same place. Fix a large piece of hardboard to one wall, paint it with blackboard paint and let the children scribble or draw on it without your fidgeting about spreading chalk dust. A 3in (7.5cm) shelf along the bottom of the blackboard will catch some of the dust and provide a place for the chalks and blackboard duster.

Inside the summerhouse when the children are small

An activity room, to give it a grand name. Furnish it with a small trestle table, easel and chairs, with shelves or cupboard for any equipment. The children can then paint and model to their hearts' content without having to clear away when they are half-way through what they are doing.

Clearing away may well be necessary in the house, but to a child it seems an infuriating adult obsession. Avoiding parent–child frictions such as this is another argument in favour of a summerhouse: it will permit a modicum of that mess which children believe to be their birthright.

Fix a board to pin things on, using that part of the windowless wall not taken up with the blackboard. Use the type of board into which drawing pins can be pushed easily; hardboard is useless.

A refuge in which to engage in such unsocial activities as practising the recorder, the violin or the like.

A quiet haven for homework, with no distractions but one's own thoughts.

Simply a place to get away from the rest of the family, perhaps to read a book or just to sulk things out.

A hobby room. Whereas stamp collecting can be carried out on a bedroom floor, or even in bed, woodwork cannot. Put a bench under the window to get a good light. A cupboard will be needed for tools, and it must be locked so that younger children do not amputate their limbs.

A room to be secretive in, with friends, out of the earshot of parents.

A place to play the record player too loudly.

A place to snog in.

Which pets to choose

Children in the garden are one problem. Animals in the garden are another. Children and animals together are yet another. It needs considerable devotion to both species to make the combination a pleasure rather than a pain in the neck.

If you have animals before you have children you will presumably have already accepted the inevitable compromise between your concept of a garden and that of the animals. So you should be able to adjust to a new relationship involving you, child, pet and garden. A dog may find it harder to accept the situation through being ousted from the centre of attention.

Children who are accustomed to animals from birth usually do not become so obsessed by them as those who develop a passion for them which for years they are not allowed to satisfy. There are exceptions: some children are terrified of both dogs and cats even when their parents like them. Children cannot be bullied into liking animals and in such cases the parents will have to forego pets for some years, in the same way that they accept a less than dream garden for the sake of their children.

On the other hand there are many adults who, for some reason or another, do not like pets. The reasons may seem utterly stupid to their children, but are none the less real to their parents. This is a tricky situation. It will certainly not make for family harmony if the children are allowed to have an animal which is resented or openly hated by the adults, and it is certainly grossly unfair to the animal. If children are refused pets they may become involved with a friend's pet, or the school hamster, and these attachments should be respected and not ridiculed. They can be very intense. When my own daughter was about eight years of age she used to blush with adoration every time she saw a horse.

Why children are so attracted by a certain animal is mysterious. When I was very young the only thing I longed for was a red squirrel in a revolving cage; the very idea now fills me with horror. Fortunately I was never given one, and that desire was overtaken by an obsession for fluffy day-old yellow chicks. This longing was also never realized – just as well, for I would have been heartbroken when they ceased to be fluffy and yellow and started to grow white feathers.

Young children, say between five and seven, tend to prefer small animals, probably furry. The obvious choices are rabbits and guinea pigs, which can be housed out of doors, and golden hamsters and gerbils which are indoor pets, but could go out of doors in summer. Hamsters and gerbils were not around in my youth, but for centuries before that rabbits and guinea pigs had been popular (either as pets or as food). Here is a brief guide to the pros and cons of these four animals.

I have no great affection for *rabbits*, remembering vividly from my youth the misery of cutting up frozen swedes for my elder brother's rabbits, but they have many advantages as pets. They are hardy and are far better kept out of doors than in. A hutch, to which a wire netting run can be attached for moving round the lawn in spring, summer and autumn, will give the rabbit exercise and help keep the grass under control. The hutch itself needs to be well insulated against excessive heat in summer and cold in winter.

Rabbits are fairly placid creatures if treated considerately; they should be fussed over at times and at others left alone to get on with their nibbling and contemplation. They are comparatively easy to look after, and will eat almost any greenstuff; this should be supplemented with hay for roughage, and, for extra nourishment, if need be, with rabbit pellets from pet shops. They are clean animals and tend to use only one corner of the hutch for their droppings. This part should be cleaned out every day, however, and the bedding there (straw or sawdust) renewed; the whole hutch should be cleaned once a week.

Expect young children to get bored from time to time with the endless routine. It is counterproductive to say, 'It's your pet, you've got to look after it.' If you don't step in when the child *does* shirk the routine, it is the animal which will suffer; and the child will come to think that after all it isn't vital to feed or clean it regularly. However infuriating it may be you should fill in any occasional lapses to show that routine must be observed since these are living things, not toys. Of course, if the child becomes totally, rather than intermittently, bored, get rid of the creature – but preferably not by eating it. Young children not hardened off on farms are sensitive about eating a friend, even an erstwhile one.

One of the joys of keeping rabbits is the appearance of the young: this is also the greatest disadvantage. Once you introduce a buck to your doe you will soon have an awful lot of rabbits. (But keep the buck away from the young rabbits, otherwise he will eat them.)

Guinea pigs (cavies) need much the same food as rabbits, but more of it. They are less hardy than rabbits and will need far more warmth in winter. On the other hand they have certain advantages over rabbits. They are less prolific, and unlike rabbits the male and females can usually be left in each other's company. The young, born after a gestation of just over two months (twice the time rabbits take), arrive equipped with teeth, fur and open eyes and are running about within a few hours. Avoid the long-haired Peruvians, as their coats need too much attention.

The popularity of the *golden hamster* I find puzzling, in spite of its appealing looks. It has an uncertain temper, a potentially nasty bite and a habit of gnawing its way out of wooden cages. Moreover it tends to be lethargic during the day, foraging in the early morning and towards twilight. It is even more prolific than the rabbit if given the chance; one female could produce up to forty young a year. Like rabbits, the male and female should be kept apart, except for mating, to prevent his being murdered; otherwise the natural span of life in captivity is up to two years. They could be transferred to the summerhouse during the summer months, probably on the verandah if it is well protected from wind and rain.

The *Mongolian gerbil* is altogether a better bet than a hamster – more placid, less given to biting when being handled, healthy, less prolific; above all, it is a daylight animal. Like hamsters they gnaw and so must be housed in metal, not wooden, cages. Mating them can sometimes be a problem, since they are fussy about the choice of partners. But if a pair get on together they make excellent parents and stick together till death. The death of one of the pair can create difficulties, however, with the survivor often refusing to take another partner. Take care not to disturb the young gerbils for almost a month or the doting mother may kill them. They are, of course, indoor animals, but they could spend the summer months in the summerhouse or on the all-purpose verandah.

Whatever responsibilities these small mammals create for parents they hardly upset the running of the garden, and their droppings will be a valuable addition to the compost heap. The apex type of rabbit hutch can circulate round the lawn for much of the year, and perhaps find a temporary home on the patio in winter. Here it will be handier for feeding and the ground less soggy underfoot. Tiered hutches are best placed against a wall, in as sheltered a place as possible so that the rabbits do not freeze in winter or fry in summer.

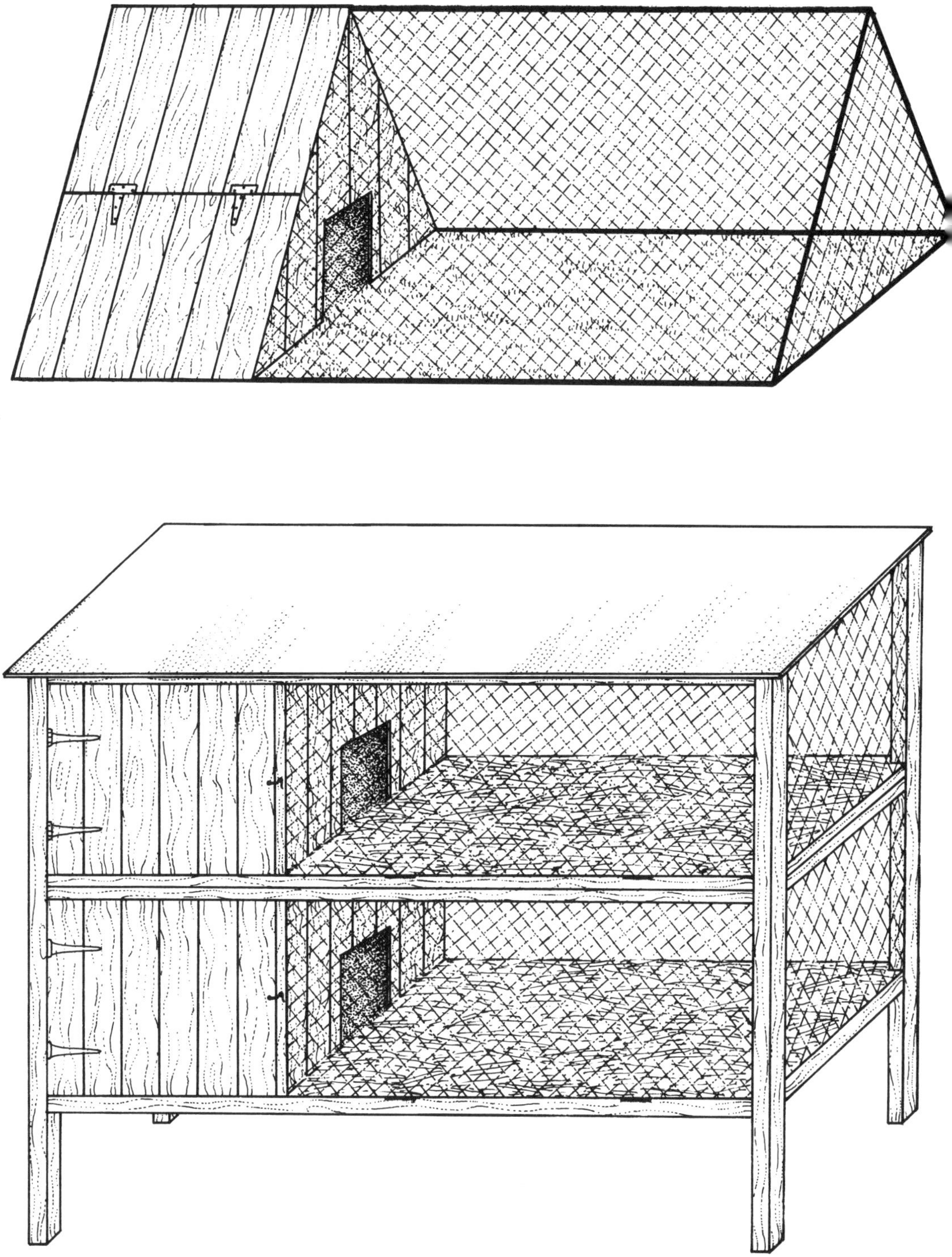

Rabbit hutch with run (top) and tiered rabbit hutch

These four pets are probably the most suitable for the very young. Later there are innumerable other small pets which your children may dote on. Not all will be outdoor pets or for outdoors all the year round. They could include mice and rats (whose musky smell I loathe), tortoises and terrapins (but these have surely suffered enough already at the hands of man), cage birds (setting me, as well as heaven, in a rage, though free-flying pigeons are a different matter), bantams, toads and snakes. Most children also go through a fish phase. Goldfish bowls and aquariums are indoor pursuits but outdoors a raised pool is all the more interesting, and not only for children, if it has a few fish in it (see pages 65–6).

Some of those which I have mentioned, and many others which I have not, are pets which many parents would prefer not to have either around the house or in the garden. To avoid pressure building up for one of these it is better, in good time and with a good grace, to welcome into the bosom of the family a more acceptable species.

That leaves *cats and dogs*, which might seem the most straightforward choice as pets. This is not necessarily so, for the relationship of a child with an animal can be entirely different from that of an adult. A child won't usually start agitating for a dog or cat until around the age of seven or so. With some children it may only be a passing urge, perhaps because a friend has been given one. This is no adequate reason for owning any animal, let alone a dog or cat. No harm is done in resisting such fleeting fancies.

Other children will go on nagging and nagging for a dog because they have a genuine need of one. If possible this should be satisfied. At this stage in the process of growing up a child may feel lonely or exposed and require the support of an unquestioningly loving, uncomplaining and uncritical friend such as a dog can be. An already existing family dog is not a complete answer, for it has other prior loyalties; it must be 'my dog'. (Loneliness in old age gives rise to the same need, but that of children will probably not last more than a couple of years or so, whereas the dependence of the old becomes permanent. Cats can fill this supportive role with the old, but they are too independent to be of much use to children.)

If you are getting a *dog* (for the first time) various questions arise. What breed? And what about the garden?

It is impossible to be objective about dogs. If you are not a dog-lover you are likely actively to dislike them. If you like them you will probably be blind to the faults of the breeds you like and ignore the virtues of the breeds you don't. My prejudices are straightforward: I adore large beautiful dogs, I dislike small ones – but here what is important to consider is which dogs are suitable for children in the comparatively limited space of modern gardens.

It is unfortunate that many of the dogs with a reputation for being fond of children are big dogs which take up a lot of room, eat a lot of food and need a great deal of exercise. But if you can cope with all that this group includes some devastatingly attractive dogs. Outstanding among them are several sheepdogs, in particular the Border collie and the shaggy Old English sheepdog, though their coats require a lot of attention. So does that of the striking white Samoyed, which is particularly affectionate with children. For sheer beauty the setters possibly take the prize (the black and white English and the red Irish setter are favourites of mine). They are also loving, but at times they can be both neurotic and headstrong.

There are some fearsome-looking dogs among the large smooth-haired breeds, but though suspicious of strangers they are affectionate within the family. Both the Boxer and the Bulldog like children, and blessedly the Bulldog does not bark or fight. The rather smaller Bull terrier, though also fond of children, tends to be aggressive with other dogs and must have a firm degree of handling which is beyond most children. The much smaller Pug is another affectionate dog, but runs to fat if not given regular exercise.

In purely physical terms small dogs may take up less room, but there are many small dogs which are so restless that they seem to take up far more. Terriers in particular can be extremely wearing and children are easily infected by their excitability. The Fox terrier is certainly one to avoid – aggressive, noisy and hard to control. The Airedale, Welsh, Scottish, West Highland White and Cairn terriers are all affectionate types with varying degrees of cockiness, need of exercise and firm control. Sealyhams have the advantage of being less demanding of exercise.

Of the spaniels the loving Cocker and the pretty King Charles are probably the best bet, though the Cocker especially will need plenty of exercise to prevent its becoming fat. For a sedate and gentle dog the choice could be a Bassett hound, but it still needs exercise.

Some dogs are to be avoided. The beautiful Afghan hound is too aloof for children. The Chow hates being teased. The Alsatian should never be trusted with children. Miniature toy dogs are at home only on the laps of old ladies and in the bosoms of film stars.

Whatever dog you introduce to your garden you have brought in trouble. In cahoots with your children it will treat the garden as its rightful romping ground. It will also treat it as its lavatory, and without the discretion that cats show. The solution is not to let the dog regard the whole world as a public convenience. In a large garden they can be trained to use the unfrequented parts, but everywhere the priority should be to discourage them from fouling the lawn. Besides the potential danger to the children's health there is the certain menace of showering the nauseous mess around when mowing the lawn. (Incidentally, it is unreasonable to expect the dog to respect your grass if you encourage it to use the grass in a public park.) Scooping up is an inevitable burden you should reckon with when adopting a dog, and the child owner should not escape some of the responsibility. The compost heap is an appropriate depository, allowing the dog to make some small return for your hospitality.

The urine of bitches can ruin a lawn, creating nasty yellow patches, especially in dry weather. Shrubs and tree trunks will be targets for dogs, and a dog's obsession for a particular shrub can kill it. Unfortunately the corners of raised beds may also prove irresistible.

Even if you choose not to have a *cat* of your own, you will have no control over the visitations of your neighbours' cats. There is not much you can do about it because in law cats are regarded as wild animals. Your neighbours, therefore, are not responsible for any damage their cats may do in your garden, and conversely you are not responsible for what your cat gets up to next door. And while gardens can be made reasonably dog-proof – as long as some fool doesn't leave the gate open – it is impossible to make it cat-proof. If you have a dog it is not wise to encourage it to chase cats away; the joy of the chase will cause far more damage than any straying cat.

I think a cat is a wonderful animal, but its alternating moods of affection, aloofness and disdain do not make it the ideal only pet for a young child. Far better to have a dog and a cat, the dependability and dependence of one complementing the unpredictability and self-reliance of the other – teaching the child quite a lot about human characteristics.

It is best to start with a kitten, as long as it can be protected from the excessive attentions of an adoring child. There will be no difficulty in getting one; far more non-pedigree kittens are waiting for homes than there are homes for them. There is no need to have a pedigree if all you need is a pet, but if you want one of the more exotic breeds you will probably have to have a pedigree cat, and, of course, pay for it. Each cat has its own character, but by and large long-haired cats are lazier and hence more amenable than short-haired cats.

Never take a kitten until it is at least two months old. Friday evening is a good time to collect it, so that it has a whole weekend with you around so that it can settle down and get to know the house and you. Its first wish will be to explore, not chase a piece of string. When it has wandered round as many rooms as it wants – with you at a discreet distance – it may feel disposed for a little wash. Let it: that is a good sign. Then offer it a saucer of slightly warm milk. After that it may let you stroke it or sit on your lap, but do not force it to accept your attentions. Do not let the children maul it.

For the next few days the best thing you can do is to talk to it softly, and be ready to play with it if it wants to. But a kitten tires of play more quickly than children will, and when it does tire it must be allowed to drop straight off to sleep. Children often take an evil pleasure in waking a sleeping animal, but they must somehow be made to understand that a kitten needs an awful lot of sleep, however boring that may be. On the considerate early treatment of a kitten the whole future relationship between the cat and the child may well depend – determining whether you have a jumpy or a relaxed cat.

A tom or a female? A tom sprays its urine all over the place, indoors and outdoors, and no amount of training will make it desist. Neutering is a simple operation, and is best done between four and six months; after that an anaesthetic is required. The side effects of neutering are that the cat will be less likely to wander, more likely to get fat and more cuddly – and unfortunately it doesn't always stop the spraying.

The neutering of a female cat (spaying) involves removing the ovaries; this is a major operation which is best done when the cat is young, between four and five months old. This means that the children, as well as the cat, will never enjoy the birth and rearing of kittens. On the other hand, the almost inevitable killing of an interminable stream of unwanted kittens is distressing for young children.

Cats are by nature clean animals, but their habit of burying their excreta can play havoc in the garden. You are lucky if they choose a bit of the garden hidden by shrubs, or if they prefer to go next door (though it would, obviously, be antisocial to encourage it, and it would not preclude other cats coming to you). An alternative to a scratched-up bit of garden is to encourage the use of a cat tray, tedious chore though that may be for you.

Cats like to roll on their backs. This is all right on grass, but isn't good for the plants. A simple solution is to plant a small area of catmint – most adult cats will prefer rolling in that to anything else. There is obviously some kind of sexual connotation, but no one appears to know what is the magic ingredient that induces such ecstasy.

A cat and dog need not be enemies if you go about introducing them to one another in the right way.

Kittens and puppies : when brought into the house as 'babies', they will reach some arrangement without undue mediation, but be ready to intervene if things get rough.

Adult animals : to introduce a newcomer to an existing cat or dog, for three or four days take turn and turn about, keeping one shut in a room while the other has the run of the house. Though they don't meet they get accustomed to the smell of each other. Then have them together in a room with you for, say, a couple of hours, talking to both of them from time to time. Then let both of them follow you round. After a few days the established resident will forgive your perfidy and accept the interloper.

When buying a pet do buy a book which explains how to look after it. You may have to read the book yourself and regurgitate the information for your youngsters, but it is only fair to the animal that someone in the family should have some clue about how to treat it.

A child's own garden

There is no such thing as a born gardener; people have to learn how to garden, often through their failures. Probably what is meant is that some people are curiously interested in gardening, whereas many people look on it as boring. Boys and girls, in general, do the latter.

There are many reasons for this. The conventional garden is very much a 'Don't do that' place for children. The small child's reaction when faced with a pretty flower is to pick it – and usually only the head! Parents often expect children to know by instinct that they must not walk on newly dug beds or newly sown grass.

When older, they are soundly berated when they fail to resist the overpowering temptation to swipe the heads off tall plants. Attempts to help daddy and mummy to weed or cut the hedge are usually brought to an abrupt end.

When a child beats his parents into submission and persuades them to give him a little plot of his own they assume, probably with justification, that this interest will be exceedingly transient and while it lasts will lead to an appalling mess. As a result he is given a miserably small patch of ground which never gets any sun, thus ensuring that he will lose interest rapidly (I use 'he' for convenience).

If, however, he is lucky enough to be given a more promising bit of the garden his enthusiastic gardening parents will be forever interfering to impose an adult gardening approach. On the other hand, if he is allowed to go his own sweet way the rate of failure will be so great that he gives up in despair. Furthermore, gardening involves thinking in the long term: this is beyond many adults – let alone children, for whom next week can seem aeons away.

Nonetheless, even though they may not be born gardeners, some children are sufficiently interested in gardening to overcome its drawbacks. In order to give such a child every possible encouragement, the parents should offer advice but not take over. An only child has a better chance of making a go of his bit of ground than one in a family of several children, especially if the others look on the garden solely as a playground. A child with a garden is an easy target for the petty jealousies of brothers and sisters, who can turn to all kinds of sabotage. Even a favourite pet can become an enemy.

For very young children messing about with soil is an interesting change from the sandpit. If it is called pretend gardening it is acceptable to parents, who would disapprove of making mud pies. For this activity it is enough to provide a trowel and a hand fork with blunt prongs. Buy sturdy ones; it is very frustrating for a child to have to cope with cheap tin tools which bend.

The serious young gardener will need trowel and hand fork, spade, fork, hoe and rake. Providing him with a set of his own will show that you are taking him and his gardening seriously, making it slightly more likely that he also will. Moreover, it avoids squabbling, for it is an odd fact that when two people are working together in the same garden they always seem to need the same tools at the same time. Looking ahead it is sensible to buy tools – spade, fork, hoe and rake – which are smaller than yours. When the child has no further use for them put them away, oiled and wrapped, for your old age when you will find lighter tools easier to handle. Other less often used tools you should be able to share without too much acrimony, apart from bullying him to keep them clean and put them away.

As well as a decent bit of ground and some decent tools a child needs something worth growing. It is pointless to fob him off with a few cheap packets of seeds. There *is* satisfaction in growing plants from seed but in a child's timescale it is in general too slow a process; some seeds do germinate quickly, but there is a limit to the excitement to be got out of growing mustard and cress.

Since adults have become addicted to instant gardening, thanks to the growth of garden centres, it is unreasonable to expect children not to be attracted by it. Take your child to the garden centre, equipped with whatever money he is free to spend, and let him choose what he wants to grow – *not* what you want him to. Merely warn him off things which are certain not to grow: a tropical houseplant, for instance. Supervising the planting of them when you get home requires tact; try to appreciate how strongly he feels that it is his garden, not yours.

When he has some plants showing quick results he can then be encouraged to grow a few seeds. If possible buy pelleted seeds; they are more expensive, but they are easier to handle and space out economically (and not only for a child).

Children, like adults, are usually most eager to garden in spring when, as Stella Gibbons has described it, 'the sap is rising in the sukebind'. But it makes sense to encourage a child to plant spring bulbs in the autumn and provide them for him – snowdrops, crocuses, scillas, muscari and daffodils. As he will be out in the garden less during the winter he will not be as impatient about their non-appearance. In spring, when they do appear, he will not have long to wait; in that sense bulbs are among the most satisfying plants to grow. When they have flowered they can be replanted in other parts of the garden.

Some children – though not all – have the patience to grow things to eat – and I do not mean just radishes, of which a family can become heartily sick. Strawberry plants are one idea, but likely to lead to looting and squabbling if there are several children in the family. Dwarf peas and tomatoes are a good choice; picked and eaten off the plant they are far better than any snitched in the kitchen.

Exit children

The garden will no longer be the centre of your children's outdoor life from around the age of ten. They will want to go somewhere where there is more space and less parental presence. Growing up demands some breaking away from the family; children have to learn how to enter into groups of their peers, whether for vaguely organized games, kicking a ball around, loafing or just being with 'best friends'.

At the start this exodus from the garden will be erratic, and serious gardening – if that is what you long for – should not be rushed into straightaway. Nonetheless, the time is approaching when you will be able to reclaim the garden from the children.

It is quite likely that they will find more use for the summerhouse than for the garden at this stage. It will provide a gang meeting ground, somewhere to giggle away from parents' disapproval, a place for games that do not have to be cleared away before going to bed, an arts and crafts workshop, a place for music-making or record-playing – all depending on the children's interests. It will also be a haven for the solitary child, who does not want to join groups and is often harried by adults to go out and get some fresh air.

Even before the garden ceases entirely to be a playground, a start can be made on clearing up after the children – removing the no longer used play equipment, the empty rabbit hutches, the hillock of earth you built on the lawn, and so on.

How to garden in spite of the children

Tall shrubs

New
Magnolia tree

Drive

Up the wall

Lateral thinking is a way of trying to solve problems by unorthodox methods; in the garden this could involve thinking vertically. We are so conditioned to gardening on the flat that we neglect all those vertical surfaces – the walls of the house, or the boundary fences and walls – which are crying out to be used as part of the garden.

These walls and fences are especially useful when our children have first claim on so much of the garden. They drive *us* up the wall; and in a garden full of boisterous children plants are probably as safe there as anywhere.

There are a number of ways in which you can bring the walls into service:

1. Plant *perennial climbers* against them. These may be self-clinging (though many people have an exaggerated fear of the supposed damage they do to house walls), or climbers which need support, by trellis or wires, for example.

2. Grow *shrubs* against them.

3. Train *cordon fruit trees* against them – profitable as well as attractive.

4. Grow *annual climbers* against them, or fix *containers* on them, and fill them with trailing greenery or striking flowers.

What to grow and where depends not only on the needs of the plants – sun and shade, for example – but on considerations for their safety when exposed to children.

One bit of the garden which the children are most likely to avoid is the narrow strip of ground adjoining the boundary walls or fences down the sides of the garden. Except when they want to peep into the garden next door they will not generally go too near them. Nor are the plants growing there, in the average rectangular garden, so exposed to ball games: children tend to play down the length of the garden rather than across its width.

However, if you choose to grow cordon fruit trees against these side walls some protection will have to be given against the depredations of both children and birds – more of this later.

The walls of the house itself may be comparatively well-protected places, because, for the sake of the windows, ball games are often prohibited near them. On the other hand, plants growing up the boundary wall at the bottom of the garden are vulnerable, either because that wall has to serve as goal or just because it is less easy for parents to keep an eye on that end of the garden.

Perennial climbers to grow up walls

A list of the climbing plants which could be chosen would itself cover a wall; we must be satisfied with a more modest selection.

Some climbers grow to an enormous height when conditions are just right for them, taller than most houses. The estimates of their heights given here indicate what the plants are capable of rather than what they will necessarily reach. They can, of course, be kept under some kind of control with shears, secateurs or a saw.

The following pages list climbers in a range of heights appropriate for the walls of the house. These are divided into plants which will need, or will do best, on walls facing south or west, and those which will be either happy or not too dis-satisfied with north- or east-facing walls (there are more such climbers than one might imagine). Each of these groups is itself subdivided into climbers which will cling to walls on their own and those which need some support. The plants in each group are listed according to height.

Those climbers which depend on tendrils or which twine can be helped on their upward journey in a number of ways. One is to fix battens to the wall, and fasten to these plastic trellis with a 2in (5cm) square mesh. The battens must be made thoroughly secure, for a well-grown climber is a heavy weight to bear.

For a large area of wall an alternative is to use vine eyes with lines of wire tightly stretched between them. Drive 4in (10cm) vine eyes into the mortar, about 6ft (1.8m) apart from each other, in a horizontal or vertical line. Allow 18in (45cm) between each line of wire. Pull the wire as taut as possible.

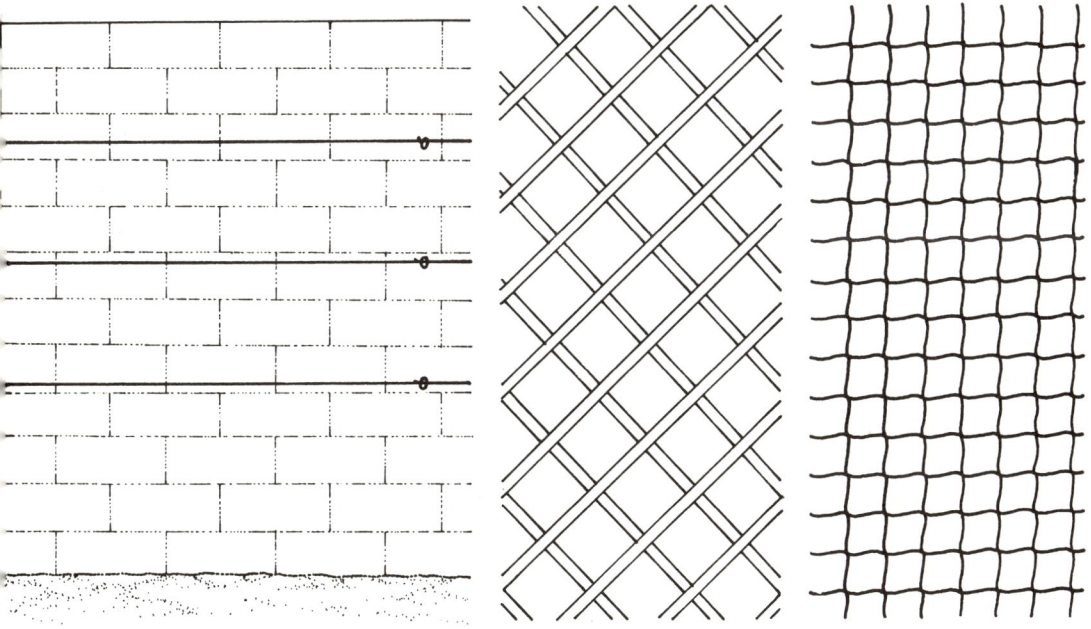

How to support climbing plants. *Left :* **using vine eyes and wires.** *Right :* **different sorts of trellis**

Self-clinging climbers for south- or west-facing walls

Parthenocissus (Virginia creeper)
    To 70ft (21m) or more. Deciduous.
    Virginia creepers will grow on all walls, whichever point of the compass they face. However, they look most dramatic where they catch the sun to show up the brilliance of their autumnal colours.
    Most popular is the Boston ivy, *P. tricuspidata* 'Veitchii', the summer coarseness of its large dark green leaves fully compensated for by the splendours of its range of reds and yellows in autumn.
    The true Virginia creeper is *P. quinquefolia*, the bright green leaves of summer turning in autumn to scarlet and orange. A wall covered with Virginia creeper involves a lot of sweeping up in the autumn, and there is a brief period, when the leaves have fallen off but the leaf stems are still sticking out from the branches, when the plant looks not so much naked as half-dressed. Propagate by hardwood cutting at the end of autumn.

Campsis radicans (Trumpet vine)
    40ft (12m). Deciduous.
    Strictly for warm, sheltered, sunny walls. The leaves are light green and the trumpet-shaped flowers, in late summer, a coppery red. Propagate by root cuttings or layering.

Polygonum aubertii (Russian vine)
    Reaching 40ft (12m) in five years. Deciduous.
    Just the thing for camouflaging an ugly garage, with mid green leaves and masses of white flowers tinged with pink from July to late September. There are far more attractive and less aggressive climbers for the house itself, however. Propagate by cuttings.

Climbers needing support, for south- or west-facing walls

Wisteria sinensis
    100ft (30m). Deciduous.
    Few houses are so attractive that they would not look better in spring and early summer smothered in wisteria. But short of buying a house where the wisteria has reached that stage already you may have to wait until the plant is twenty years old before it even begins to flower, and then only with proper pruning. It would be in time for your silver wedding and then continue even more magnificently into your old age. *W. sinensis* has racemes of mauve flowers; those of the variety 'Alba' are white. Worth waiting for.
    Wisteria floribunda, of Japanese origin, may grow to only 30ft (9m) but the racemes are longer; those of the white *W. floribunda* 'Alba' may reach 2ft (60cm) and those of the lilac-purple *W. floribunda* 'Macrobotrys' up to 3ft (90cm).

Clematis

10ft (3m) to more than 30ft (9m). Most deciduous, a few evergreen.

There are far too many species, varieties and hybrids to go into detail but if you covered the whole house with a selection of them you could have them in flower from late winter to late autumn. You can have them red, white and blue, violet, mauve and purple, pink, yellow and orange. The flowers of some are barely 1in (2.5cm) across while those of the large-flowered hybrids may be 6in (15cm). They climb by twining their leaf stalks round whatever they can get hold of.

For a succession of clematis possible choices are: *C. armandii* (evergreen) 'Apple Blossom', pink, and 'Snowdrift', white – for early spring. *C. macropetala* (deciduous) 'Markham's Pink' and 'White Moth' would follow a little later, while *C. montana grandiflora* (deciduous), white, and *C.m. rubens,* pink, appear in late spring. These are followed by the large-flowered garden hybrids. For late summer there are the deciduous *C. orientalis*, which is yellow, and *C. flammula*, with tiny white flowers.

Jasminum officinale

30ft (9m). Deciduous, but semi-evergreen in mild winters.

This is a climber to grow near a window so that on fine evenings and nights from early summer to early autumn the fragrance of the white flowers can be enjoyed indoors as well as outdoors. The plant climbs by twining. Propagate by cuttings.

Passiflora caerulea (Passion flower)

30ft (9m). Evergreen.

The interest of this plant is in the curious construction of the flowers – the numbers of petals, sepals, stamens and so on supposedly representing Christ's Passion. The colours are very subdued, and while the plant is seldom without a few flowers during the summer each bloom lasts only a few days. Although evergreen the leaves look a mess at the end of winter, and the plant is easily killed by frost. It climbs by tendrils, which must have something to hang on to.

Aristolochia macrophylla (Dutchman's pipe)

20ft (6m). Deciduous.

The large leaves are mid green and heart-shaped; the tubular flowers are yellow, green and brown. Propagate by cuttings.

Campsis grandiflora (C. chinensis)

20ft (6m). Deciduous.

Like *C. radicans* – and perhaps more so – this needs a warm, sunny, sheltered wall, but this differs from *C. radicans* in that it is a twining climber and not self-clinging. Clusters of orange-scarlet trumpets are produced at the end of summer and the beginning of autumn.

Solanum jasminoides album

20ft (6m). Evergreen.

This should be planted against a warm, sunny south wall; there it will produce sprays of white flowers from early summer until late autumn.

Solanum crispum 'Glasnevin', 15ft (4.5cm), semi-evergreen, is hardier than *S. jasminoides*. It grows less vigorously but flowers more profusely, with dark purple flowers through summer to late autumn. An untidy grower.

Lonicera (*Honeysuckle*)

From 6ft (1.8m) to 20ft (6m). Some evergreen, some deciduous.

Most people associate honeysuckles with their scent, but not all are scented – though they may still be worth growing for the good colouring of their flowers. The most beautifully scented honeysuckles are varieties of the English woodbine.

Lonicera periclymenum 'Belgica', or Early Dutch honeysuckle, has creamy white and crimson blossom in May and June, while the Late Dutch honeysuckle, *L.p.* 'Serotina', with darker markings, flowers from July through to October. Both are deciduous. The semi-evergreen *Lonicera japonica*, also heavily scented, has carmine-tinted creamy flowers from mid-summer to November. The hybrid *L. americana* (deciduous) is a vigorous grower with lots of yellow-pink flowers in summer.

Two attractive scentless deciduous honeysuckles are *L. brownii* 'Fuchsioides', with scarlet flowers in summer, and *L. tragophylla*, with large deep yellow flowers in early summer.

Most honeysuckles prefer some shade and many are suitable for north-facing walls (see page 101); however the two scentless honeysuckles listed here are somewhat tender. Propagate by cuttings.

Actinidia kolomikta (Kolomikta vine)

12ft (4m). Deciduous.

The leaves, rather than the modestly fragrant small white flowers (early summer), are the attraction of this plant. When they appear in the spring they are a metallic green, but if exposed to full sun they become splashed with pink and white during the summer.

Self-clinging plants for north- or east-facing walls

Hydrangea petiolaris

60ft (18m). Deciduous.

The leaves are dark green on the top surface and pale green on the undersides. It is covered with large lace-cap type white flowers in June, but they do not last long. A longer-flowering alternative is *Schizophragma integrifolia*, 40ft (12m), deciduous. The large white flower heads with creamy white bracts appear from mid summer to early autumn.

Pileostegia viburnoides (20ft (6m)), another self-supporting climber in the hydrangea family, is evergreen. It carries dense clusters of small white flowers in September.

Hedera (Ivy)

50ft (15m). Evergreen.

For the coldest and shadiest situations there are varieties of the common or English ivy, *H. helix,* to choose between: 'Sagittifolia', with its beautifully shaped all-green leaves, 'Goldheart', with its lively foliage (green with a central splash of yellow), 'Buttercup' (golden leaves) or 'Glacier' (silvery). Large leaves may look more effective on a large wall, and the ivy to choose for that is the green-leaved Persian ivy *H. colchica* 'Dentata'. A large-leaved variegated ivy is the Canary Island ivy *H. canariensis* 'Gloire de Marengo', but unhappily it is less hardy than the others, and can be seriously damaged in a bad winter. Propagate by cuttings.

Parthenocissus henryana
50ft (15m). Deciduous.

The best Virginia creeper for a north wall is *P. henryana*. In summer the leaves are a rich green with silvery and pink veins, turning a flaming red in autumn.

Climbers needing support, for north- or east-facing walls

Vitis coignetiae
80ft (24m). Deciduous.

In summer the leaves are dark green on top and brown beneath, covered in down; in autumn they turn yellow, orange, bright red and crimson – a magnificent sight. The plant clings by tendrils to the support provided.

Clematis montana
30ft (9m). Deciduous.

There are several clematis which will grow on north and east walls, but this is the most dependable. The flowers of the species *C. montana* are white and those of the variety 'Elizabeth' are pink and very fragrant. They appear from late winter to late spring. Pruning is done when flowering ends, but if you want to cover a large area little need be done to these two apart from cutting away unwanted shoots. Propagate by cuttings.

Jasminum nudiflorum (Winter-flowering jasmine)
10ft (3m). Deciduous.

A joyful plant to have around on grim winter days. There will be at least some bright yellow flowers on the bare dark green stems throughout the winter but most of them appear in December or January. It is sprawling by nature and will need tying back well if it is not to become a straggly mess. In April cut away the shoots which have flowered during the winter, to encourage the plant to produce more shoots to flower during the following winter. It is hardy, but should not be exposed to much wind. Propagate by cuttings.

Lonicera (Honeysuckle)
Many of those already listed as suitable for south and west walls (see page 100) may be grown on north and east walls in many parts of the country. The two most likely exceptions are *Lonicera brownii* 'Fuchsioides' and *L. tragophylla*.

Shrubs for garden walls and fences

Not all these climbers would be suitable for garden walls or fences; they would soon have gone over the top. The jasmines, clematis and honeysuckles, and the smaller-leaved and slower-growing ivies, can be used and, to widen the choice, there are shrubs which can be trained against a wall, even though they are not naturally climbers. My own preference would be to use a south or sheltered west-facing wall for cordon or other wall-trained fruit trees, and use north- and east-facing walls for non-utilitarian plants. Here are a few possibilities:

Forsythia
    12ft (3.6m). Deciduous.
Magnificent in spring with its clear yellow flowers, but boring the rest of the year. For a spread of colour choose *F. suspensa sieboldii*. After flowering cut back secondary shoots to within two buds of old wood. Propagate by division or cuttings.

Garrya elliptica (Tassel bush)
    12ft (3.6m). Evergreen.
The grey-green early spring catkins are largely the reason why one grows a garrya. The catkins on the male shrubs are often 6in (15cm) long and grey in colour, while those on the female shrubs are shorter and pale green. The leaves, some 3in (7.5cm) long, are dark green on the top surface but grey underneath. Quick-growing and will tolerate a sunless position; is suitable for the seaside.

Euonymus fortunei (Spindle tree)
    10ft (3m). Evergreen.
A trailing shrub which when planted to climb up a wall will cling to it; most convenient. *E.f. (radicans)* 'Silver Queen', with silver variegations, is probably the best plant. The greenish white flowers are not noteworthy.

Chaenomeles speciosa (Japanese quince)
    3–10ft (1–3m) according to variety. Deciduous.
Many varieties and hybrids of this ornamental quince should be satisfactory on a north wall in the warmer parts of the country. The beautiful flowers, which appear in the spring, are mainly red, but *C. speciosa* 'Nivalis' is white. If grown up a wall they should be pruned back hard after flowering. Propagate by cuttings.

Pyracantha (Firethorn)
    15ft (4.6m). Evergreen.
The variety usually planted is the vigorous *P. coccinea* 'Lalandii', which may soon need savage cutting back. *P.* 'Watereri' is better; more compact, it has clusters of white flowers in spring, bronze leaves in summer and brilliant red berries in autumn, which last through to spring. Propagate by cuttings.

The five shrubs already mentioned, as well as the suitably proportioned climbers, can also be grown on south- and west-facing walls if you are not interested in growing fruit, or if you want a little contrast among the fruit trees. Three more very beautiful shrubs can be added for these warmer walls:

Abelia x *grandiflora*
    6ft (1.8m). Semi-evergreen.
    The leaves of this beautiful shrub are a bright green, and trumpet-shaped white flowers tinged with pink appear from mid summer to early autumn. *A. schumanii,* which grows not quite as tall, has rosy pink flowers from early summer until autumn. Both need warm walls.

Ceanothus impressus 'Puget Blue'
    12ft (3.6m). Evergreen.
    In spring ceanothus is one of the showiest wall coverings you can hope for. Unfortunately sometimes, even though they seem to be flourishing, they die on you. *C. impressus* is one of the hardiest species, and the variety 'Puget Blue' the best blue.

Cotoneaster horizontalis
    6ft (1.8m). Deciduous.
    A dramatic plant in autumn when both leaves and berries are scarlet. Not a clinger but grows up the wall without help and without having to be tied back.

Apart from the clinging *Euonymus fortunei* and the well-behaved *Cotoneaster horizontalis* all these plants will have to be given a trellis or wire support.
    And, of course, there are always roses, climbing or rambling. But their flowering period is so short, the unprepossessing period so long, and the potential diseases and pests so numerous, that the alternatives may seem more appealing.

Growing fruit against walls

Fruit has been associated with walls for centuries, perhaps never so extensively as with the walls of the wealthy in the last century. The walls of kitchen gardens were covered with fan-trained trees of peaches, figs and plums, and espalier-trained apples and pears. These forms of fruit trees take up a large amount of room, far beyond that which most modern gardens can provide.
    However, the development of varieties of some fruits which can be grown as cordons has made it possible for many gardeners to cultivate a certain amount of fruit. The cordon is usually a single stem with only short side shoots bearing a mass of fruit spurs. They cannot carry such heavy crops as other forms of tree, but they take up far less room; they need be only 2–3ft (60–90cm) apart. (Some cordons have two or three stems and take up more room, but they produce more fruit.)
    The fruits that can be grown on cordons are apples, pears, gooseberries and red and white currants (but not blackcurrants – they have to be grown as bushes, which take up quite a lot of room).

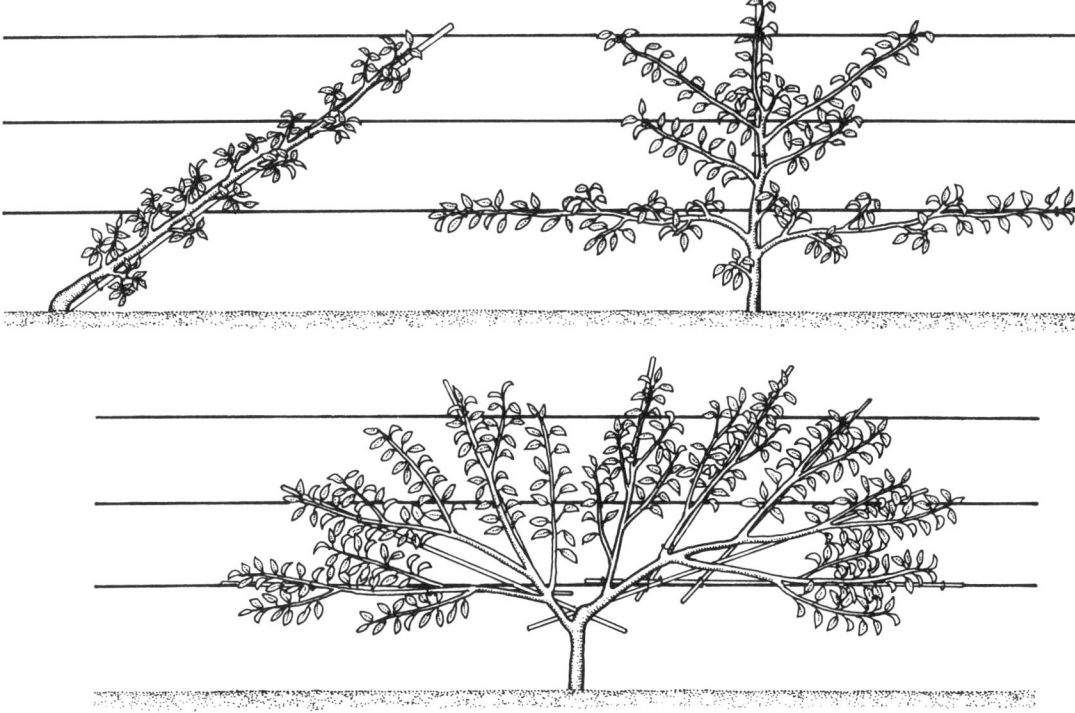

Wall-trained fruit trees. *Top left :* **single cordon.** *Top right :* **espalier.** *Bottom:* **fan-trained**

A row of raspberry canes can also be grown alongside a wall or fence, and takes up comparatively little space.

Blackberries, sensibly the thornless varieties, may be grown up tall walls, if well tied back. Or a chain link fence (which though effective and economical is not beautiful) can be turned into a blackberry hedge. It would be wise to get your neighbour's agreement by pointing out that he will be entitled to the fruit from the canes that stray into his garden.

With a large well-walled garden one can, of course, be more ambitious and grow espalier and fan-trained trees, especially those which will not grow as cordons. Among these are plums and especially gages, which taste better from such a wall-trained tree than when grown any other way. But they will take up to 18ft (5.5m) of wall. Peaches and nectarines, which will ripen only in the warmest parts of the country, must be allowed 24ft (7.3m) of wall space.

Also, for the warmer parts of the country, figs are an attractive wall covering, with the bonus of the fruit, if you like fresh figs. But unless the roots are restricted there will be an awful lot of leaf and very little fruit. Make a sunken brick-lined bed 3ft (90cm) long, 2ft (60cm) wide and 3ft (90cm) deep. Put a 1ft (30cm) deep layer of broken bricks at the bottom of the bed and then fill it with good garden soil. Even when so restricted the fig may still develop a span of 20ft (6m).

Any fruit you grow must be protected against preying birds and children – the losses from both can be stupendous – and straying balls. A simple unobtrusive wooden framework over which a net can be draped for much of the year but removed in winter is better than a permanent frame. In winter there is no fruit to be raided, damage from ball games is less likely, and it is useful to let the birds get to the branches to devour insect pests until the new buds appear.

One vital point to remember whatever you choose to grow against a garden wall is that you are planting it in the driest part of the garden. Watering will probably be necessary in summer, but mulches will help to conserve moisture in the soil.

Annuals and containers to brighten up a wall

Climbers grown from seed, either annuals or treated as annuals, can provide splashes of summer colour. The easiest would be climbing varieties of *Tropaeolum majus*, better known as nasturtiums. *T. peregrinum*, the canary creeper, with less flamboyant yellow flowers, will grow in the shade. The Morning glory (*Ipomoea rubro-caerulea*) is not very hardy, and the sky-blue flowers have a life of only a few hours. But they are so beautiful – and there are new flowers next day to take their place – that in spite of their drawbacks they are worth a try. With greater promise of success there are runner beans, which were originally grown for effect and not for food. The variety Painted Lady has scarlet and white flowers, and Blue Coco has purple flowers and violet pods.

Finally, containers can be used to add a seasonal splash of colour to a drab wall. Securely fix brackets to the wall to support wooden window boxes. Plant them with the kind of brilliantly coloured flowers which you would use for a window box in its more usual place. Trailing plants are particularly effective. This is simply a way of making a show in summer with comparatively few plants. There is also the advantage that they are out of the reach of dogs, cats and young children. Perennial plants are not really satisfactory, because they will inevitably be neglected in winter, and in danger of having their roots frozen to death.

The front garden from a new angle

The secret of making a success of the front garden is thinking about what it looks like from inside the house. Most front gardens, intentionally or not, appear to have been designed for the benefit of people in the street. This shows a notable regard for passing strangers, but you lose out yourself. Since a front garden alongside a road is not the pleasantest place in which to sit the only time you are likely to be there is briefly as you walk from the gate to the door, or vice versa, or when you are gardening. But you probably see it for long periods from indoors, especially when the weather is too cold and wet for spending time outdoors in the back garden. So the place to start planning the front garden is from the upstairs and downstairs windows which look out on it. This will mean planting the tallest plants by the boundary wall and grading them down towards the house.

Planting a tree

On a spring morning getting up to a tree outside your bedroom window and stretching yourself awake rates high as one of the innocent sensual pleasures of life. So plant a tree; the problem is to find the right one and decide on the right place to plant it.

Few of the plants you start with in a garden will survive as long as you do. A tree, however, is a different matter. Not only is it likely to survive you, it will also bear no resemblance to the little sapling you planted. Thirty years later it may well be far too big for the front garden, probably demonstrating that it was planted in the wrong place at the start – too near your house or the house next door, or over-hanging the road. Or it may have had to be cut down because it didn't leave you enough room to park the car.

There are quite a number of trees you can grow in a front garden and many that you should not. Forest trees which might reach 200ft (60m) are obviously not on. Poplars and willows are also out because their roots could dry out the soil in a drought and affect the foundations of your house – or the house next door. Conifers may make the rooms too dark in winter, and look lugubrious as well.

So what we need is a tree which will keep within bounds both above and below ground and will not block out the light. It should also, of course, look good, preferably for as much of the year as possible.

A silver birch is hard to beat, graceful at all ages, fast-growing and hardy. The attractions of the tree in spring are aromatic buds, bright olive green leaves and yellow male catkins; in autumn golden leaves and in winter the remarkable white, black-splashed bark. The small leaves cut off so little light that some flowering plants (notably spring bulbs) can be grown under the spread of the tree as long as the soil is kept moist; birches are thirsty and they have a large root spread. *Betula pendula* 'Fastigiata' is an erect-growing variety, and *B.p.* 'Dalecarlica', the Swedish birch, a particularly graceful drooper. As trees go the silver birch is not long-lived, about fifty years or so, but there are drawbacks to everything.

The rowan or mountain ash (*Sorbus aucuparia*) is another hardy tree of manage-able size, fast-growing and hardy. (Scottish crofters used to plant them to protect themselves from evil.) The feathery-looking leaves are followed in May by great clusters of white flowers, and in early autumn by orange berries (or yellow – 'Xanthocarpa' – or red – 'Beissneri'). You can make the berries into rowan jelly if you get them before the birds do.

The false acacia is not only striking in spring with its yellow leaves but also manages to look interesting in summer when the leaves have turned a light greenish yellow and racemes of creamy white flowers appear. It is hardy, but not the tree for a windy spot. *Robinia pseudoacacia* 'Frisia' is a good choice; its golden yellow leaves give the impression that the sun is always shining on it. The young leaves and seeds of the false acacia are poisonous.

The most brilliant autumn display would be with a Japanese maple (*Acer palmatum*). *A.p.* 'Dissectum' is a good yellow and *A.p. septemlobum* 'Osakazuki' a glorious scarlet, which could look awful against the background of a bright red brick wall.

Among the possible flowering trees are the flowering cherries, but there is no point in growing them when you will see enough, or too many, of them in other people's gardens. Laburnums are lovely, but unwise where children may be tempted to sample the inviting but poisonous pods.

For me that leaves magnolias. Admittedly theirs is a fairly brief moment of glory, but what glory, and all the greater for bursting out so early in the year. An early one is *M. stellata*, flowering around the end of March, with a mass of small white flowers which last for quite a time if frost does not get them. *M. salicifolia* grows into a very graceful tree, but you may have to wait a few years before it begins to produce the mass of flowers which cover the whole tree while the branches are still bare of leaves. *M.* x *soulangiana,* of which there are many varieties, is probably the most widely grown magnolia, but it does not do well in a very limy soil and is an inveterate spreader, 20ft (6m) or more; the flowers appear in April or May. Never dig or fork for some distance around the roots of a magnolia; it is quite likely to die to show its resentment. Spread a mulch instead. The ground surrounding the tree can be used for small early-flowering bulbs.

It may not be easy to decide where to plant the tree. The eventual height and spread of the tree will determine where you cannot put it in a small front garden, as already pointed out: too near the house, too near the house next door or too near the road. In addition avoid planting it where it will overhang the parked family car. Lots of things drop out of trees and not all of them are leaves. When all such practical considerations have been taken into account you will be left with having to decide where it will look well, primarily when seen from the house.

Deciduous trees may be planted at any time between mid autumn and early spring, as long as there is no frost. Evergreens can be planted in early autumn if your soil is light, but otherwise wait until mid spring (when the roots are growing again). Do not plant them during the winter.

Coming down to ground level, because a front garden is usually smaller than the garden at the back of a house it is vital to make a greater impact per square yard (or metre). Simple ways of doing this are by a more sophisticated use of colour or by concentrating on the scents of flowers. Colour and scent are not mutually exclusive, but since many scented plants have modest flowers it is best to consider them separately. So to start with colour, which gives the greater scope.

Planting a one-colour garden

Whatever you plant in your garden – or if you let it run to weed – there will be more green than any other colour. This is fortunate since green is the most tolerable of colours to live with; imagine a magenta countryside.

But green needs some relief, particularly if you smother your garden with ground cover plants. Only a little relief is needed to make a big impact. Fields of growing corn with a few patches of red poppies are one of my most vivid recollections from my childhood. Fields full of nothing but poppies would quickly become an eyesore. Nowadays fields of growing corn from which chemical sprays have driven all poppies are depressing.

In the garden the aim should be to strike a balance between green and other colours, so that the garden does not, on the one hand, suggest a graveyard or, on the other, a Neapolitan ice cream. A small patch of colour in an expanse of green draws your eyes towards it, whereas a whole garden which is a carpet of colour will be too much for your eyes to absorb.

The greatest effect for the least outlay is achieved by using a single colour at any one season of the year. This is done by planting shrubs or perennials of various colours together but so choosing them that only plants of one colour are in bloom at the same time. For example, you could start the year with a white garden with a mixture of the smaller bulbs, followed by a yellow garden in spring and a blue garden in summer, with a few white flowering plants in the autumn as an epilogue for the year. But there are many other combinations.

Planning such a garden needs considerable forethought in order to avoid too much of an overlap between the various colours, since this would lessen the effect. As you would be, in effect, planting several separate gardens in the same area (arranging different shifts, as it were) you would have to be extremely careful where you put plants of different heights. Colour is sometimes a problem, particularly with reds, pinks and blues, for some shades look out of place with other shades. Purples and mauves are especially difficult, and because their overall impact is less than that of other colours I have not included these colours among the lists of suggested plants in the following chapters.

The lists are limited to shrubs, perennial herbaceous plants and bulbs. No annuals or biennials are included, because my aim has been to cut out as much year-after-year work as possible. Many beautiful plants have therefore been excluded, but if you want them by all means plant them; the last thing I want to do is to impose my laziness, likes and prejudices on your garden. For annuals you will need no suggestions from me as to what is available – the gaudy packets of seeds will be staring at you everywhere, or you can spend the winter thumbing through seedsmen's catalogues.

Whether the plants you grow turn out to be the heights I have estimated will depend on many things: which part of the country you live in, the fertility of your garden and the position in which the plant is growing. The only thing I can guarantee is that they will not grow to the same height in different gardens; only rough estimates are possible to give some idea of the size of plants in relation to each other. Note particularly that the heights of different species or varieties of a plant can vary enormously.

There are similar difficulties in trying to put into words the colour of a flower; seed and plant catalogues demonstrate how difficult it is to agree on this. Even when descriptions do agree your flowers might be a rather different colour because of the nature of your soil and the fertilizers you have used. Nor does colour stay constant. The changing quality of the daylight from dawn to dusk alters the colour we see in the flower. Furthermore it may fade with sunlight or as it ages, or become washed out with rain. Thus I excuse myself in advance.

In a large garden given over mainly to ground cover the one-colour impact may be achieved by using only shrubs, or by using also some of the bolder herbaceous plants and bulbs.

In a garden that has been largely paved over, the most reliable way of avoiding any feeling of drabness is certainly to concentrate on one colour, either in raised beds or in containers. The choice of plants would then be limited to lower-growing types – say not more than 2ft (60cm) – so that the flowers do not tower above your head.

The lists, of course, will be an equally useful guide to anyone who wants a good old-fashioned mixed colour border, which when I was younger I both adored and slaved over. Frequent visits to garden centres and gardens open to the public will give you a chance to see what the plants you fancy from the lists actually look like in flower. You can then decide whether you want them after all.

Colour it yellow

Bright yellows have enormous impact and there is a wide choice of flowers for all-yellow gardens at any time from early spring to late summer. Some of the summer flowers spill over into the autumn but otherwise there is a dearth of yellow plants then. The plants are listed in order of flowering.

Shrubs

Winter jasmine is the earliest of the shrubs to flower, but the more dramatic ones, including rhododendrons and brooms, come later.

Hamamelis mollis 'Pallida' (Witch hazel)
   Up to 10ft (3m). Deciduous. Mid winter to early spring.
   Outstanding among winter-flowering plants with its lemon-yellow scented blossom which lasts for weeks, impervious to frost. In autumn the leaves turn yellow. See also page 132.

Jasminum nudiflorum (Winter jasmine)
   8ft (2.4m). Deciduous. Mid-autumn to early spring, but at its best in early
   spring.
   See page 101.

Chimonanthus praecox (Wintersweet)
   5ft (1.5m). Deciduous. Winter.
   Purple-centred yellow flowers with a spicy smell. See also page 131.

Cytisus praecox
   4ft (1.2m). Deciduous. Spring.
   Arching stems carry innumerable creamy yellow sweet pea-shaped flowers; the
   variety 'Allgold' is a deeper yellow. *C.* x *beanii* has golden yellow flowers in late
   spring. They do best in sandy soil and need full sun.

Rhododendron wardii
   10ft (3m). Evergreen. Mid to late spring.
   Clear yellow cup-shaped single flowers with a crimson spot. Needs lime-free
   soil.

Potentilla
   3ft (90cm). Deciduous. Mid spring to early autumn.
   Hardy and extraordinarily long-flowering. The flowers are like miniature single
   roses and there are some good yellows among them. *P. arbuscula* has deep yellow
   flowers and distinctive shaggy branches; *P. fruticosa* 'Primrose Beauty' has grey
   downy leaves and deep cream flowers from early summer to autumn; *P.f.* 'Elizabeth' has brighter green leaves and large canary-yellow flowers; *P.f.* 'Katherine
   Dykes' is primrose yellow. Not fussy about soils, but they need full sun. Will
   thrive by the sea.

Fremontia californica (Tree mallow)
   10ft (3m). Evergreen. Late spring to mid summer.
   Showy, mallow-like flowers, 2in (5cm) or more across, in rich yellow. But it is
   only for warm situations, and best against a wall. Even then it usually has a short
   life in this country.

Piptanthus laburnifolius (Evergreen laburnum)
   8–12ft (2.4–3.7m). Evergreen. Late spring to mid summer.
   Bright yellow laburnum-like flowers in racemes about 3in (7.5cm) long. It will
   do best against a warm wall in any soil except a limy one.

Cytisus scoparius (Common broom)
   Up to 6ft (1.8m). Deciduous. Early summer.
   The variety 'Golden Sunlight' is a strong grower smothered in deep yellow
   flowers. It needs pruning back hard after flowering to prevent its becoming
   straggly. It is not long-lived: eight years is a reasonable expectation of life.

Phlomis fruticosa (Jerusalem sage)
   4ft (1.2m). Evergreen. Early summer.
   Woolly grey foliage and whorls of deep yellow tubular flowers at the end of the
   branches. Only for warm, sunny gardens and better in light, sandy soils.

Genista cineria
    Up to 10ft (3m). Deciduous. Summer.
    Closely related to *Cytisus*, it bears marigold-yellow flowers in profusion on its slender branches. An alternative is the less overpowering *G. lydia* (about 2ft (60cm), which in flower forms a bright yellow hummock. Needs to be grown in the sun. Prune back the flower shoots after flowering.

Senecio laxifolius
    4ft (1.2m). Evergreen. Summer.
    Dense growth of silvery, grey-green, woolly leaves with clusters of single, daisy-like, deep yellow flowers. Uncertain in cold areas. It thrives at the seaside and in limy soils and needs plenty of sun if the foliage is to look its best.

Halimium lasianthum
    2ft (60cm). Evergreen. Summer.
    A showy shrub with silvery foliage and bright yellow flowers 1½in (4cm) across, with a crimson blotch. It likes hot sun, but is reasonably hardy, tolerates limy soil, and thrives near the sea.

Santolina chamaecyparissus
    18in (45cm). Evergreen. Mid summer.
    Small globular heads of deep yellow flowers and silvery grey leaves. It is a plant for hot sunny situations, thriving by the sea; at home in limy soils.

Hypericum elatum 'Elstead'
    4ft (1.2m). Deciduous. Summer.
    The flowers are shining cups formed by five pointed petals, with numerous yellow stamens. These are followed by bright salmon-red, egg-shaped fruits. To keep the shrub bushy prune it hard in early spring.

Bulbs and perennials

There is a wealth of yellow bulbs and perennial herbaceous plants for spring and summer.

Narcissus (miniature types)
    3–8in (7.5–20cm). Bulbs. Early spring.
    These make a change from the 'ordinary' narcissi, and there is an increasing choice of them. *N. cyclamineus* 'Tête à Tête' (8in (20cm)) is early in flower with clear yellow petals and a small orange trumpet. *N. asturiensis*, golden yellow, is another early one, and at 3in (7.5cm) is the smallest yellow trumpet daffodil. Unfortunately slugs also find it attractive. *N. triandrus concolor* (4in (10cm)) carries a number of pendulous golden yellow flowers on each stem. *N. bulbocodium* ranges in size from 2 to 8in (5–20cm). *N.b. vulgaris conspicuus* (5in (12.5cm)), one of the more robust, has deep yellow flowers. It increases quickly, which is an advantage since these miniatures are not cheap. They need well-drained soil.

Euphorbia epithymoides, syn *E. polychroma* (Cushion spurge)
1ft (30cm). Deciduous. Early spring.
Heads of lemon-yellow bracts which later turn green.

Tulip kaufmanniana
8in (20cm). Bulb. Early spring.
The variety 'Cesar Franck' has outstanding deep golden yellow flowers with a band of scarlet on the outside of the petals.

Crocus
5in (12.5cm). Bulb. Early to mid spring.
C. ancyrensis, with numerous small, deep orange-yellow flowers, is very early. Later there are *C. aureus,* deep golden yellow, *C. chrysanthus* 'E.A. Bowles', buttercup yellow, and the large-flowering *C. vernus,* Dutch yellow. Birds are liable to savage yellow crocuses, whereas they leave other colours alone.

Eranthis hyemalis (Winter aconite)
3in (7.5cm). Tuber. Early to mid spring.
Buttercup-like flowers of a vivid yellow, with rosettes of deep green leaves. Will grow in shade under trees.

Alyssum saxatile
1ft (30cm). Evergreen. Spring.
The plant forms a mat of grey-green leaves and the small bright yellow flowers grow in dense clusters. Easily grown, but cut back after flowering or it will become lanky. Needs full sun.

Primulus vulgaris (Primrose)
4in (10cm). Deciduous. Spring.
The beautiful common primrose, creamy yellow with a darker yellow eye. Happy in sun or semi-shade, but prefers a fairly heavy soil.

Erythronium tuolumnense
10in (25cm). Tuber. Spring.
Six pointed petals form a downward-hanging sulphur-yellow star on an erect stem. Hardy and vigorous, it forms clumps, and will grow in the shade of shrubs and trees.

Fritillaria imperialis 'Lutea Maxima' (Crown imperial)
3ft (90cm). Bulb. Spring.
A stately plant with a crown of deep yellow bell-like flowers which hang down below a rosette of leaves. The plant hates to be disturbed and since it dies down by mid summer it is as well to mark where the bulbs are planted. Plant it in full sun.

Doronicum (Leopard's bane)
1ft (30cm). Deciduous. Mid spring to early summer.
Bright yellow daisy-type flowers. *D. cordatum* is a single version and *D. caucasicum* 'Spring Beauty' is fully double.

Trollius europaeus (Globe flower)
18in (45cm). Deciduous. Late spring to early summer.
Globular semi-double buttercup-like flowers of bright yellow. Tolerates sun or partial shade, but must have moisture.

Eremurus bungei (Foxtail lily)
3ft (90cm). Crown. Early summer.
Golden yellow spikes on tall stems rising from sword-like leaves; a spectacular plant, but less overpowering than the 8ft (2.4m) tall *E. robustus* (which has pink or white flowers). Plant in a sunny spot.

Allium moly (Yellow onion)
1ft (30cm). Bulb. Summer.
A dozen or so bright yellow starry flowers grow from the top of the stalk, standing above blue-green lance-like leaves. A vigorous grower, forming large clumps.

Anthemis tinctoria (Ox-eye chamomile)
3ft (90cm). Deciduous. Summer.
Large daisy-like flowers, the bright yellow 'Perry's Variety' having flowers up to 3in (7.5cm) across. It needs a well-drained soil and full sun.

Euryops evansii (or *Euryops acraeus*)
1ft (30cm). Evergreen. Summer.
Small daisy-like plant with bright yellow flowers against a dense background of silvery foliage. It needs sun and thrives at the seaside.

Primula helodoxa (Candelabra primula)
3ft (90cm). Deciduous. Summer.
Two or three whorls of bright yellow flowers on long stems rising from among toothed, tongue-shaped leaves more than 1ft (30cm) long. A graceful, moisture-loving plant.

Lysimachia punctata (Loosestrife)
2ft (60cm). Deciduous. Summer.
Bright yellow, starry, cup-shaped flowers grow in rings among the leaves on the long stems. Will thrive in sun or shade but needs moisture.

Achillea filipendulina (Yarrow)
3ft (90cm). Deciduous. Summer.
'Coronation Gold', which is mustard yellow, is a good variety, but there are many others. The flowers are tiny double daisies jammed together to make a flat head up to 4in (10cm) across. The grey-green ferny leaves have a pungent smell.

Geum chiloense
18in (45cm). Deciduous. Summer.
A graceful plant with brilliantly coloured flowers carried on longish stems rising from dense ground-hugging foliage. 'Lady Stratheden' is the yellow variety, the frilly petals forming semi-double flowers with a cluster of yellow stamens. Likes sun or a little shade.

Senecio przewalski
    4ft (1.2m). Deciduous. Summer.
    Long tapering spikes of orange flowers on tall slender stems. For sun or partial shade.

Oenothera fruticosa (Evening primrose)
    18in (45cm). Deciduous. Summer.
    Numerous deep yellow flowers, 2in (5cm) across, open only in the evenings.

Lilium pyrenaicum (Turks-cap lily)
    3½ft (1m). Bulb. Summer.
    This is one of the easiest lilies to grow. The flowers are lemon-yellow and the scent is strong and bitter. It will grow in sun or shade. The hybrid lily 'Destiny' makes an effective group in the garden with its upward-pointing pale lemon-yellow trumpets, spotted with brown. Likes sun or a little shade.

Coreopsis verticillata 'Grandiflora'
    2ft (60cm). Deciduous. Summer.
    Prolific and long-flowering, the golden yellow starry flowers are carried on wiry stems from a neat-growing bush of yew-like leaves. Plant in full sun.

Helenium autumnale
    3ft (90cm). Deciduous. Summer.
    An easily grown, free-flowering plant with daisy-like flowers more than 1in (2.5cm) across. 'Butterpat' is a clear yellow with a yellow central disc, and 'Wyndley' yellow with a prominent dark brown disc. Needs sun.

Solidago canadensis (Golden rod)
    2–4ft (60cm–1.2m). Deciduous. Summer to early autumn.
    The flowers are tiny and daisy-like, forming fluffy mustard-yellow sprays in 'Crown of Rays' and fluffy yellow heads in 'Golden Thumb'.

Hemerocallis (Day lily)
    2ft (60cm). Deciduous. Summer to early autumn.
    Clusters of lily-like trumpet flowers are carried on stout stems. Although they die quickly they are followed by others over a period of many weeks. The plant is hardy, is not fussy about soil and should be left for years without being disturbed. Hybrids include: 'Dorothy McDade', a clear light yellow, and 'Towhead', a light waxy yellow.

Heliopsis scabra
    3ft (90cm). Deciduous. Summer to autumn.
    Large daisy-like flowers on erect stems. 'Golden Plume' is a double golden yellow and 'Light of Loddon' a single bright yellow. Another sun-lover.

Crocosmia x *crocosmiiflora* (Montbretia)
    18in (45cm). Corm. Late summer.
    The graceful flowers look like flattened arrow heads on arching stems among sword-shaped leaves. 'Citronella' is lemon-yellow and 'Star of the East' is a pale orange-yellow. Montbretias can be grown in sun or semi-shade and increase quickly.

Rudbeckia sullivantii
   2ft (60cm). Deciduous. Summer to autumn.
   Single daisy-like flowers made up of narrow sharply pointed petals. 'Goldsturm' is an orangey yellow with a prominent dark centre; 'Autumn Sun' is a clear lemon-yellow with a greenish centre.

Sternbergia lutea
   6in (15cm). Bulb. Autumn.
   Sternbergia is not a crocus though it looks uncommonly like one. The leaves, which are broader than those of a crocus, appear at the same time as the flowers, which have six stamens instead of three. It is less hardy than the crocus and needs a very warm sunny border.

Colour it white

There is no problem about creating a striking white garden, from the depths of winter to autumn. It will probably look at its most attractive from early spring to early summer; certainly there is the greatest choice at this time of the year. One drawback to white flowers is that they look tatty when turning brown as they die, but dead-heading is not an arduous job.

Shrubs

The white shrubs include some beautifully scented ones, among them lilac, Mexican orange blossom, Mock orange, and skimmia.

Abeliophyllum distichum
   7ft (2m). Deciduous. Late winter to mid spring.
   A slow-growing shrub, best trained up a south- or west-facing wall. It resembles a forsythia, but is more delicate-looking, with sprays of star-shaped pale pink flowers, turning white, with golden stamens and a scent of almond. The leaves appear after the flowers. Needs hard pruning after flowering if it is not to grow straggly.

Ribes laurifolium
   3ft (90cm). Evergreen. Spring.
   One of the smaller flowering currants and slow-growing. It has small, tubular, slightly greenish, white flowers in clusters; the male clusters hang down and the smaller female clusters stand erect.

Exochorda giraldii
   Up to 10ft (3m). Deciduous. Late spring.
   A beautiful shrub with arching branches smothered in single white flowers up to 2in (5cm) across, with yellow stamens. Needs sun.

Syringa vulgaris (Lilac)
 10ft (3m). Deciduous. Late spring.
 'Madame Lemoine' is a double white, good-scented variety, which develops into a broad bush. See also page 133.

Rubus tridel 'Benenden'
 10ft (3m). Deciduous. Late spring to early summer.
 This is a blackberry without thorns. The arching branches are covered in large white flowers with a centre of golden stamens. It will grow in limy soils, in clay, in dry shady places and near the sea.

Choisya ternata (Mexican orange blossom)
 6ft (1.8m). Evergreen. Late spring, early summer.
 Star-like, hawthorn-scented white flowers. See also page 133.

Skimmia japonica
 4ft (1.2m). Evergreen. Early summer.
 Aromatic laurel-like leaves and heads of white, star-shaped, scented flowers. If planted with a male form the female forms will produce scarlet berries, lasting all winter. *S. laureola* (a male form) has oval panicles of white flowers. Will do best in semi-shade; not for limy soils.

Viburnum tomentosum 'Lanarth'
 6ft (1.8m). Deciduous. Early summer.
 Tiers of spreading branches are laden with large clusters of white flowers. The foliage turns crimson in autumn, and there may also be berries. Not too fussy about soil; it tolerates both lime and clay, but prefers loam.

Cistus x *cyprius* (Rock rose)
 6ft (1.8m). Evergreen. Early summer.
 Showy white flowers, resembling wild roses, have a maroon blotch at the base of the petals. This is one of the hardier varieties; it will grow in hot dry situations, in limy soil, and near the sea.

Carpenteria californica
 5ft (1.5m). Evergreen. Summer.
 The white flowers with golden anthers look rather like a white version of the Rose of Sharon. Very free-flowering, but must have sun.

Philadelphus (Mock orange)
 5ft (1.5m). Deciduous. Summer.
 The flowers of 'Beauclerk' are single, about 2in (5cm) across, white flushed with pink at the base and very fragrant. 'Virginal' (10ft (3m)) is the long-popular double white. See also page 134.

Olearia macrodonta (Daisy bush)
 6ft (1.8m). Evergreen. Summer.
 The holly-like grey leaves are smothered under large clusters of small white flowers. Only for mild areas, but it will thrive in town gardens and does especially well by the sea.

Hydrangea paniculata 'Grandiflora'
  5ft (1.5m). Deciduous. Late summer.
  Dense cone-like clusters – 8in (20cm) long and 6in (15cm) across – of white flowers which fade to pink. Prune hard in early spring.

Romneya coulteri (Tree poppy)
  5ft (1.5m). Deciduous. Mid summer to early autumn.
  Pure white very large flowers made up of satiny, crinkly petals with a prominent boss of golden stamens. Sweetly scented. The soft wood growth needs cutting back each spring to hard wood. Only for the warmer parts of the country, and needs sun and shelter.

Bulbs and perennials

Bulbs provide some of the most attractive white flowers – from the snowdrops, snowflakes and anemones of spring, to the tall, dramatic Regal lily of summer.

Helleborus niger (Christmas rose)
  1ft (30cm). Evergreen. Winter to early spring.
  Nodding, saucer-shaped blooms, white often tinged with pink.

Galanthus nivalis (Snowdrop)
  4in (10cm). Bulb. Late winter to early spring.
  The common single snowdrop; the variety *G.n. plenus* is the double version. See also page 132.

Anemone blanda
  4in (10cm). Bulb. Late winter to mid spring.
  Daisy-like flowers of about fifteen petals; in the variety 'White Splendour' they are white, large and long-lasting. *A. nemorosa*, which flowers in spring, is the dainty Wood anemone.

Leucojum (Snowflakes)
  10in (25cm). Bulb. Early spring.
  Bell-shaped flowers rather like snowdrops, with green or yellow tips to their petals. *L. vernum* flowers in early spring after the snowdrops. *L. aestivum* follows in late spring. Plant in sun or a little shade.

Muscari botryoides album (Grape hyacinth)
  6in (15cm). Bulb. Early spring.
  The white variety of the ubiquitous blue.

Ipheion uniflorum (Spring star)
  6in (15cm). Bulb. Early spring to early summer.
  The six-petalled, blue-tinged starry flowers appear over many weeks. The flowers and leaves smell slightly of garlic. Plant in full sun in a sheltered position.

Ornithogalum umbellatum (Star of Bethlehem)
6in (15cm). Bulb. Spring.
Large, white, star-like flowers – when they open, which is from late morning to late afternoon. They spread furiously.

Papaver orientale (Oriental poppy)
2–4ft (60cm–1.2m). Deciduous. Late spring to early summer.
The variety 'Perry's White' has white frilly, silky petals tinged with pale pink with a purple-black blotch at their base. Grow in sun, in well-drained soil.

Paeonia
About 2ft (60cm). Deciduous. Late spring to early summer.
White varieties include the creamy white 'White Wings', single; 'Duchesse de Nemours', a very fragrant, extremely free-flowering double; 'Festiva Maxima', also double, a pure white with a red blotch; and *P. officinalis* 'Alba Plena', a pure white semi-double.

Eremurus robustus
8ft (2.4m). Bulb. Early summer.
A towering plant which needs a fairly large garden to make sense; the poker-like spikes may be 3ft (90cm) long.

Pancratium illyricum
18in (45cm). Bulb. Early summer.
A striking plant with clusters of fragrant starry white flowers. Unfortunately it is tender, and should not be attempted except against a south wall in warm parts of the country.

Anthemis cupaniana (False chamomile)
8in (20cm). Evergreen. Summer.
The long-flowering, daisy-like flowers, with a golden yellow disc, stand up above a mat of silvery grey leaves. The snag is that they may not survive a hard winter; an insurance against that is to take cuttings in the autumn – they root easily.

Lilium regale (Regal lily)
3–4ft (90cm–1.2m). Bulb. Summer.
A very distinguished-looking lily which is nonetheless easy to grow. White trumpet flowers, with yellow-shaded throat and golden anthers; the outsides of the petals are wine-coloured. It also has a strong scent. Will tolerate lime.

Crinum x *powellii* 'Album'
3ft (90cm). Bulb. Summer to early autumn.
Arching strap leaves from which rise stems carrying white trumpet flowers about 3in (7.5cm) across, in clusters of six or more, opening in succession. Needs a warm, sunny position.

Cyclamen neapolitanum album
4in (10cm). Bulb. Autumn.
A beautiful hardy white cyclamen, with silvery leaves, which needs a dry position but is otherwise undemanding. It will seed itself and spread rapidly.

Anemone japonica 'Alba' (Japanese anemone)
   30in (75cm). Deciduous. Autumn.
   Graceful saucer-shaped flowers about 2in (5cm) across, lasting late into autumn. Will grow in sun or shade.

Zephyranthes candida
   6in (15cm). Bulb. Autumn.
   White starry cups, rather crocus-like, with a green centre and golden anthers, appearing among grass-like leaves. It can form large clumps but unhappily will not survive at all except in the warmest parts of the country. Probably best to wait until you get that longed for greenhouse (see pages 167–71).

Colour it blue

A garden of really blue flowers is surprisingly effective, but not easy to achieve because good blues are rarer than purples and mauves, which have less impact. Early to late spring is probably the best time for a blue garden, and autumn almost impossible.

Shrubs

Syringa vulgaris (Lilac)
   6ft (1.8m). Deciduous. Early spring.
   The problem with lilacs is to find a good blue. The early-flowering single 'Firmament', though a purplish mauve in bud, opens to sky-blue, and it has a good scent. Among the doubles 'Michel Buchner' is about the best you can manage. See also page 133.

Rosmarinus officinalis (Rosemary)
   4ft (1.2m). Evergreen. Spring.
   Not particularly showy flowers but for all that attractive against the aromatic grey-green leaves. Not for cold parts of the country, otherwise good for the seaside; prefers light soils.

Ceanothus (Californian lilac)
   6ft (1.8m). Evergreen. Spring, early summer.
   Beautiful shrubs bearing numerous rounded clusters of minute flowers. Unfortunately many of the species are tender. *C. impressus* 'Puget Blue', a fairly hardy deep blue, makes an excellent wall plant, flowering in early summer. *C. thyrsiflorus,*

also reasonably hardy, has bright blue flowers in early summer. The spring-flowering *C. arboreus* is tender, but the variety 'Trewithen Blue' is the least tender and the best blue.

Vinca major
  1ft (30cm). Evergreen. Late spring to early autumn.
  Excellent not only for ground cover (see page 149) but for spreading its clear violet-blue flowers over such a long period. The attractive variegated varieties are less vigorous. Does best in at least some shade, but is not fussy about soil.

Hydrangea macrophylla
  4ft (1.2m). Deciduous. Summer.
  This is the Hortensia or common hydrangea, and you either like or detest the massive mopheads of flowers. To get them blue the soil must be acid, and for a really genuine blue a blueing powder should be applied to the soil weekly or fortnightly during the growing season. When so treated 'Général Vicomtesse de Vibraye' is the best blue, but if left to itself it will be rose.

Lavandula spica (Lavender)
  3ft (90cm). Evergreen. Summer.
  Long spikes of pale greyish blue flowers stand on long stems above the grey aromatic leaves. Clip the plants after flowering to prevent them from growing straggly. But the most striking variety is dwarf and compact, around 8in (20cm). It is 'Nana Atropurpurea' (alias 'Hidcote'), which has very deep purplish blue flowers and silvery leaves.

Hebe 'Autumn Glory'
  1ft (30cm). Evergreen. Mid summer to mid autumn.
  This is a notable shrub: shining, slightly purplish leaves, silvery buds, violet-blue spikes of flowers on erect stems appearing continuously over several months. The snag: it is somewhat tender and needs to be planted in full sun.
  Hebe 'Midsummer Beauty' (3ft (90cm)), summer-flowering, is hardier than 'Autumn Glory' and taller. Bottle brush-like lavender-coloured flowers throughout the summer.

Hibiscus syriacus
  5ft (1.5m). Deciduous. Mid summer to mid autumn.
  'Blue Bird' is the best blue, the flowers rather like those of the hollyhock, and up to 3in (7.5cm) across. It likes a well-drained and alkaline soil, in full sun.

Caryopteris x *clandonensis* (Blue spiraea)
  3ft (90cm). Deciduous. Late summer and autumn.
  Dense clusters of deep violet-blue flowers, which continue from late summer well into autumn – although there will be few other blue flowers then to keep them company.

Bulbs and perennials

Most of the blue flowers of spring are those of small bulbs, whereas those of summer will be found among the tall-growing herbaceous plants. Apart from Michaelmas daisies, which I have little liking for, the autumn garden is short on blue.

Iris histrioides 'Major'
5in (12.5cm). Bulb. Winter.
Rush-like leaves. Royal blue flowers which are marked with white and gold on the falls (these are the three lower petals of iris flowers). Remarkably hardy.

Scilla sibirica
4in (10cm). Bulb. Late winter to mid spring.
Six-petalled open, nodding bells, of gentian blue or darker. *S. bifolia* has flowers of an exceptionally bright royal blue in early spring.

Chionodoxa luciliae (Glory of the snow)
4in (10cm). Bulb. Spring.
Bright green leaves and pale blue flowers like open stars, $\frac{3}{4}$in (2cm) across, up to ten on a stem. *C. sardensis* is a brighter blue.

Muscari armeniacum (Grape hyacinth)
6in (15cm). Bulb. Spring.
Narrow dark green leaves and spikes of fragrant bead-like flowers. 'Heavenly Blue' is a gentian blue, and 'Blue Spike' a double pale blue.

Pulmonaria augustifolia
6in (15cm). Deciduous. Spring.
The funnel-shaped flowers borne in clusters are an intensely vivid blue. They are often seen in rockeries, growing in shade or partial shade.

Endymion hispanicus or *Scilla hispanicus* (Bluebell)
15in (38cm). Bulb. Late spring.
This is like a large bluebell, but is almost scentless. 'Excelsior' is deep blue, 'King of the Blues' deep sky-blue, and 'Myosotis' sky-blue.

Mertensia virginica (Virginian cowslip)
2ft (60cm). Deciduous. Late spring.
Not showy, but graceful, with clusters of cornet-shaped flowers of a rather purplish blue.

Anchusa azurea
About 3ft (90cm). Deciduous. Spring to mid summer.
Forms a mass of brilliant blue flowers over a long period. 'Loddon Royalist' (30in (75cm)) is the most intense and 'Opal' ($3\frac{1}{2}$ft (1m)) is sky-blue. They need a sunny position.

Ajuga reptans (Common bugle)
9in (23cm). Almost evergreen. Late spring to mid summer.
Spikes of deep blue flowers with leaves which are a dark green or purple in the variety 'Atropurpurea', bronze in 'Multicolor', and cream with grey-green in 'Variegata'.

Nepeta x *faassenii* (Catmint)
1ft (30cm). Evergreen. Late spring to summer.
Spikes of small lavender flowers appear throughout the summer. The aroma of the grey-green leaves is found exciting by some cats. It thrives in limy soil, given a dry, sunny position, and is suitable for town gardens.

Iris (bearded)
3ft (90cm). Deciduous. Early summer.
There are innumerable varieties in shades of blue from light violet to blue-black. A good choice for town gardens.

Linum narbonense (Blue flax)
18in (45cm). Evergreen. Summer.
Small erect leaves and deep sky-blue flowers on arching stems. Grow in the sun.

Echinops ritro (Globe thistle)
3ft (90cm). Deciduous. Summer.
A distinguished plant with grey-green foliage and spherical heads of flowers. 'Veitch's Blue' is a bright, deep blue.

Aconitum carmichaelii (Monkshood)
30in (75cm). Deciduous. Summer.
Tall spikes of helmet-shaped flowers of deep purplish blue. Monkshood will grow in sun or shade. The roots are poisonous.

Delphinium
Up to 6ft (1.8m). Deciduous. Summer.
One of the most dramatic and beautiful of summer border plants; there is scarcely a shade of blue that cannot be found among the large-flowered hybrids. They need a sunny position in well-manured soil. Tiresomely, they will probably need staking and protection from slugs.

Camassia quamash (Common camass)
2ft (60cm). Bulb. Summer.
Six pointed petals make up a flower, and up to a dozen of these flowers make up a spike on top of a long stem of this unusually attractive plant – even though it is known as the Common camass. The colour is usually a bright violet-blue, but it does vary.

Meconopsis betonicifolia (Himalayan blue poppy)
3ft (90cm). Deciduous. Summer.
Beautiful, but temperamental; it could live for a decade or die within a year, especially if it is allowed to flower in its first year. It is, however, easily replaced

from seed. It should be grown in partial shade in rich, moisture-holding soil. The almost circular flowers are about 2in (5cm) across and a rich sky-blue, with prominent golden stamens; they will be a paler blue if the poppy is grown in limy soil.

Eryngium oliverianum (Sea holly)
   30in (75cm). Evergreen. Summer.
   Large thimble-like heads of rich blue flowers stand out above rosettes of jagged-edged, glaucous, grey-green leaves. The blue colouring extends down the stems.

Scabiosa caucasica
   18in (45cm). Deciduous. Summer to mid autumn.
   In the variety 'Clive Greaves' very elegant large mauve flowers with crimped petals and a centre like a pincushion are carried on long slender stems.

Agapanthus campanulatus (Africa lily)
   2ft (60cm). Evergreen. Late summer.
   A very impressive plant with strap-shaped arching leaves with a rounded head of flowers on a stiffly erect tall stalk. 'Isis' is a good intense blue but there are many Headbourne hybrids which are hardier and have larger flower heads. Needs a sunny position, and protection from frosts. Highly suitable for growing in tubs.

Colour it red

Apart from the rhododendrons and azaleas of spring there are few shrubs suitable for a red garden – and rhododendrons and azaleas are out of the question for gardens with limy soil. To some extent herbaceous plants make up for the lack of shrubs, not so much in numbers as by the excellence of their colours.

Shrubs

Chaenomeles (Ornamental quince, or Japonica)
   3ft (90cm). Deciduous. Early spring.
   The best known is *C. japonica,* but some of the best reds are among the *superba* hybrids. Two with spreading habits of growth are 'Firedance', which is signal red, and 'Rowallane', bright crimson. 'Knaphill Scarlet' has large translucent flowers, a deeper shade on the inside than on the outside.

Ribes sanguineum
   6ft (1.8m). Deciduous. Spring.
   Some flowering currants are a washy pink, but the variety 'Pulborough Scarlet' has good crimson-red flowers in large racemes. Will grow well in sun or semi-shade, in windy gardens and by the sea.

Paeonia delavayi (Delavay's tree peony)
   4ft (1.2m). Deciduous. Spring.
   The foliage is attractive all through the summer and the flowers, which last for

a fortnight or so, are a magnificent deep crimson with golden stamens. Grow in sun or partial shade, and to be on the safe side give protection from spring frosts.

Paeonia suffruticosa
    3½ft (1m). Deciduous. Spring.
    A fine shrub with large flowers in striking colours. 'Souvenir de Ducher' has reddish purple double flowers.

Rhododendron
    The number of rhododendrons and azaleas to choose from (if your soil is lime-free) is mind-boggling. There are more than 500 species and countless hybrids of both those rhododendrons which are known as rhododendrons and those known as azaleas. Only a few suggestions can be given unless the rest of the book is to be filled with them. Among the rhododendron evergreen hardy hybrids good reds are: 'Britannia' (4ft (1.2m)), scarlet crimson; 'Cynthia' 5ft (1.5m)), rosy carmine; 'Doncaster' (4ft (1.2m)), scarlet. The evergreen azaleas are only about 2ft (60cm) tall, with a spreading habit. Among the reds are 'Addy Wery', a brilliant vermilion; and 'Vuyk's Rosy Red' and 'Vuyk's Scarlet', both with large flowers. A striking deciduous azalea, growing about 6ft (1.8m) tall, is 'Satan', which is a deep scarlet. But there are scores of other possibles to be found in nurserymen's catalogues, or in the R.H.S. Wisley handbook No. 2 on rhododendrons.

Salvia grahamii
    4ft (1.2m). Deciduous. Late summer to mid autumn.
    This aromatic sage produces its long racemes of scarlet-crimson flowers when other reds are scarce, but unfortunately it is tender and often a victim to English winters. It is worth trying against a south-facing wall in warm parts of the country.

Bulbs and perennials

Anemone fulgens
    9in (23cm). Tuber. Spring.
    The single, 2in (5cm) diameter flowers, scarlet with the striking contrast of a white centre and black stamens, are carried on strong stems above the lacy leaves. Grow in full sun.

Tulip
    4in–3ft (10–90cm). Bulb. Spring.
    There are nearly 4,000 varieties to choose from, and many of them are red. They are usually grouped in fifteen main divisions, and this is the rough order of flowering of the most popular. Single early; double early; *fosteriana*; *kaufmanniana* and *greigii* hybrids; lily-flowered; cottage; parrot; Darwin. Some varieties in each group will be earlier or later than the others so give yourself plenty of time in early autumn to browse through the bulb catalogues. Tulips need well-drained soil and sun.

Papaver orientale (Oriental poppy)
    30in (75cm). Deciduous. Summer.
    Flamboyant, brilliantly coloured large flowers, against a background of large,

grey-green, deeply cut, hairy leaves. 'Marcus Perry' is orange-scarlet with a black blotch. Needs well-drained soil and plenty of sun.

Pelargonium

These are such an obvious choice that they tend to be overdone. In large beds they may fit in with Buckingham Palace, but in an ordinary garden they are far more striking if used in containers or window boxes, or even in a small raised bed. They have the disadvantage of being tender and in need of constant renewing by cuttings.

Potentilla atrosanguinea (Cinquefoil)

1ft (30cm). Deciduous. Summer.

This is pretty rather than showy, flowering over a long period. The leaves are strawberry-like and the small saucer-shaped flowers are borne in loose clusters. 'Gibson's Scarlet' is a single brilliant scarlet. Potentillas will grow even in poorish soil as long as it is well-drained, and in sun or partial shade.

Lychnis chalcedonica (Campion; Maltese Cross)

2ft (60cm). Deciduous. Summer.

The petals of each flower form a five-armed cross and together they make a rounded head. Bright scarlet.

Kniphofia uvaria (Red hot poker)

3ft (90cm). Deciduous. Summer.

The poker-like heads of flowers stand erect on thick stems from the clumps of narrow leaves. The typical colour is coral red, becoming orange, but there are hybrids with other colours. It needs sun.

Lobelia cardinalis or L. fulgens (Cardinal flower)

2ft (60cm). Deciduous. Summer.

Not at all like the little blue annual that consorts with alyssum and geraniums. The Cardinal flower bears tall spikes of brilliant red flowers. 'Red Flame', 'Will Scarlet' and 'Queen Victoria' are scarlet and 'Cherry Ripe' is cerise. The plant is not particularly hardy and needs winter protection from wet as well as frost.

Monarda didyma (Bergamot)

2ft (60cm). Deciduous. Summer.

The very aromatic leaves are carried on erect stems, and the variety 'Cambridge Scarlet' produces rounded heads of brilliant scarlet flowers. Grow in moist soil in sun or partial shade.

Polygonum amplexicaule

3ft (90cm). Deciduous. Late summer to early autumn.

The narrow leaves form a dense clump from which rise tall stems carrying slender spikes, reminiscent of lavender, but crimson in the variety 'Atrosanguineum' and bright red in 'Firetail'. It will grow in sun or partial shade.

Colour it pink

You could have a pink garden pretty well all the year round just by growing the various heaths and heathers – *erica, calluna* and *daboecia* – but it would be deadly boring. *Erica carnea* is the one to choose for winter colour, and this species has the advantage of being at least lime-tolerant, whereas the others need a lime-free soil.

A pink garden would probably be easiest to achieve in summer, with either shrubs or herbaceous plants, or both.

Shrubs

Erica carnea
   8in (20cm). Evergreen. Winter to early spring.
   The bell-shaped flowers grow in dense downward-pointing clusters, providing delightful bloom in the dead of winter and into early spring. Pink varieties include: 'December Red', large, bright, rose-pink flowers on long sprays, early; 'King George', also early, a deep pink; 'Springwood Pink', with dense trailing growth and rose-pink flowers from the beginning of the year; and 'Aurea', with bright pink flowers and golden foliage. These heathers will tolerate lime, but it does help if you add some peat to the soil when planting. Grow in full sun or partial shade.

Camellia japonica
   4ft (1.2m) and up. Evergreen. Late winter to mid spring.
   Exotic-looking plants which are far hardier than they appear. 'Elegans', a broad bush, has salmon-pink flowers with an outer row of large petals and a centre of small petals and stamens; 'Gloire de Nantes' is an early-flowering, semi-double clear rose, and very reliable; 'Lady Clare', a rather floppy-growing bush, has large, soft pink, semi-double flowers. Camellias should be protected from north and east winds and planted only in sunny, sheltered spots in colder parts of the country.

Prunus triloba 'Multiplex'
   5ft (1.5m). Deciduous. Early spring.
   There are many species of prunus; this is a flowering apricot bush with rosette-like double pink flowers which appear before the leaves. Good on limy soils.

Skimmia rubella
   3ft (90cm). Evergreen. Spring.
   The pink version of skimmia (see *S. japonica*, page 116).

Kalmia latifolia
   6ft (1.8m). Evergreen. Late spring to early summer.
   Glossy leaves and large clusters of rose-coloured flowers. Needs a lime-free soil.

Kolkwitzia amabilis (Beauty bush)
 6 ft (1.8m). Deciduous. Early summer.
 Graceful bush with 3in (7.5cm) clusters of small flowers which resemble those of foxgloves – pure pink with a yellow throat.

Gaultheria shallon
 5ft (1.5m). Evergreen. Early summer.
 Sprays of pink bells followed by dark purple fruits. See also page 81.

Spiraea japonica 'Alpina'
 1ft (30cm). Deciduous. Early summer.
 Flat heads of small rose-pink flowers. Not fussy about soil.

Vaccinium vitis-idaea (Cowberry or Mountain cranberry)
 6in (15cm). Evergreen. Summer.
 A carpeting plant with pale pink bell-like flowers in profusion, bright red berries which are edible, and small, smooth green leaves tinged with bronze in winter. It needs an acid soil, will grow in dry shade, and does well by the sea.

Escallonia
 4–5ft (1.2–1.5m). Semi-evergreen. Summer.
 Showy, free-flowering shrub, with small leaves and star-like flowers. It is likely to suffer in bad winters. The variety 'Peach Blossom' has peach-pink flowers, while 'Apple Blossom' is pink and white; 'Donard Star' is rose-pink, 'Donard Gem' a sweetly scented clear pink, and 'Glory of Donard' bright pink. Will grow in sun or a little shade, but it is a plant for warm areas. It is very good near the sea, and prefers limy soils.

Cistus 'Silver Pink'
 18in (45cm). Evergreen. Summer.
 Papery-looking petals of silvery pink with a boss of golden stamens. Does well in a sunny, dry position.

Erica cinerea (Scotch heath)
 1ft (30cm). Evergreen. Early summer to early autumn.
 The variety 'C.D. Eason' is glowing pink. Grow in full sun in a lime-free soil.

Hydrangea macrophylla hortensia 'Hamburg'
 4ft (1.2m). Deciduous. Summer.
 Large heads (up to 1ft (30cm) across) of deep rose florets – but only if the soil is alkaline; if it is acid the flowers will be deep blue. See also page 120.

Clerodendron bungei
 3ft (90cm). Evergreen. Late summer.
 Tender shrub with small, deep pink, fragrant flowers carried in dense rounded heads.

Calluna vulgaris (Ling)
 1–2ft (30–60cm). Evergreen. Late summer to autumn.
 This is also known as the Scottish heather. The tiny flowers are carried in branching sprays. Good pink varieties include: 'County Wicklow', free-flowering,

double, shell pink; 'H. E. Beale', double pink; 'Peter Sparkes', long sprays of double purplish pink; 'J. H. Hamilton', double rose-pink. Grow in lime-free soil, and preferably in sun, though it will tolerate partial shade.

Bulbs and perennials

Border pinks and Border phlox are among the best of the summer pink flowers.

Scilla campanulata or *Endymion hispanicus* (Spanish bluebell)
   1ft (30cm). Bulb. Spring.
   Looks like a bluebell, but the flowers of the variety 'Queen of the Pinks' are deep rose-pink (and scentless).

Papaver orientale (Oriental poppy)
   30in (75cm). Deciduous. Late spring to early summer.
   There are pink as well as red and white varieties: 'Mrs Perry' is a soft salmon-pink. See also page 118.

Pyrethrum roseum
   18in (45cm). Deciduous. Early summer.
   Popular daisy-like flowers with a yellow centre carried on tough stems; dark green lacy leaves. 'Eileen May Robinson' is salmon-pink; 'Kelway's Glorious' dark pink, 'Brenda' cerise-pink. They need to be grown in sun.

Geranium (Cranesbill)
   18in (45cm). Deciduous. Summer.
   G. endressii 'Wargrave Pink' is salmon-pink. *G. sanguineum lancastriense* 'Splendens' is a dwarf-growing rose-pink. Plant in sun or shade. Likes limy soils and tolerates clay. Good for seaside or town gardens. Propagate by division.

Filipendula palmata (Pink meadowsweet)
   2ft (60cm). Deciduous. Summer.
   Fluffy heads of flowers, pink but fading, on branching stems above the maple-like leaves. Needs a moist soil in part shade.

Heuchera (Coral bells)
   18in (45cm). Evergreen. Summer.
   Small bell-like flowers grow along tall erect stems from ground-hugging leaves. The Bressingham hybrids include shades of pink.

Dianthus x *allwoodii* (Border pinks)
   8in (20cm). Deciduous. Summer.
   'Doris' is an outstanding variety – fragrant, long-flowering, a delicate shrimp pink with a deep pink eye. See page 134 for cultivation.

Helianthemum 'Wisley Pink'
   1ft (30cm). Evergreen. Summer.
   Grey foliage and shell-pink flowers, with a central boss of yellow stamens. Needs sun and shelter.

Erigeron
18in (45cm). Deciduous. Summer.
Masses of daisy-like flowers with yellow centres. 'Charity' is a clear light pink; 'Foerster's Liebling' a large, semi-double, deep pink.

Dimorphotheca barberiae (Cape marigold)
1ft (30cm). Deciduous. Summer to early autumn.
Daisy-like flowers of purplish pink, with yellow centres, on tall stems, appearing over a long period. Needs a warm sunny position.

Phlox paniculata (Border phlox)
30in (75cm). Deciduous. Summer to early autumn.
Large heads of flat, five-petalled flowers. Among the pink varieties are: 'Annie Laurie', salmon-pink; 'Firefly', peach-pink with a crimson eye; 'Sandringham', cyclamen-pink with a darker eye. Best in partial shade.

Polygonum bistorta 'Superbum'
3ft (90cm). Deciduous. Summer to autumn.
Clear pink flowers form a poker-like spike on the end of a tall stem. Will grow in sun or partial shade, but likes moisture.

Colour for autumn

Autumn is not the most satisfying season in the garden. In late winter and early spring even a few flowers and scents are exciting, but after we have been spoilt by the prodigal show of late spring and summer the autumn flower garden looks subdued. Moreover, our enthusiasm for gardening wanes with the dying of the year and the garden soon takes on an air of neglect and tattiness.

Gardening writers go on a lot about the brilliance of foliage in autumn, but this is something of a snare. New England in the fall is impossible to reproduce on a small scale in this country. So much depends on the vagaries of the weather; the leaves may fall before they have properly turned yellow, gold or crimson, and when they have turned they may be whipped off in a gale overnight. They also change colour at different times and one or two isolated shrubs hardly make a spectacle. However, here are some possibles for those who want to stare out of windows, front or back, at some brilliantly coloured autumn foliage.

Aesculus parviflora (Chestnut)
4ft (1.2m). Deciduous.
This is a bushy horse chestnut which can be kept within reasonable bounds.

The white spikes of flowers appear in summer and the leaves turn a typically chestnut gold in autumn.

Amelanchier lamarckii
    7ft (2m). Deciduous.
    The bush form of a taller tree. In spring there are clusters of white flowers, in summer purplish black berries (adored by birds), and in autumn the leaves may turn yellow or red. Sometimes sold as *A. canadensis*. Needs a lime-free soil.

Berberis thunbergii 'Atropurpurea'
    4ft (1.2m). Deciduous.
    Pale straw-coloured flowers in spring, purplish leaves in summer and bright red leaves and berries in autumn.

Callicarpa bodinieri 'Profusion'
    7ft (2m). Deciduous.
    Pinkish mauve flowers in late summer, violet berries and violet-tinged leaves in autumn.

Cotinus americanus (Smoke tree)
    10ft (3m). Deciduous.
    Clusters of small pinky grey flowers in spring and a riot of crimson and scarlet leaves in autumn; most brilliant when grown in sandy, poor soils.

Fothergilla major
    5ft (1.5m). Deciduous.
    White, scented, bottle brush-shaped flowers in spring and startling orange and scarlet leaves in autumn. Must have lime-free soil.

Lindera benzoin (Spice bush)
    10ft (3m). Deciduous.
    Sulphur-yellow flowers in early spring, red berries in summer and deep yellow leaves in autumn. Must have lime-free soil and sun.

Rhus typhina (Stag's horn sumach)
    9ft (2.7m). Deciduous.
    Striking, easily grown, large shrub (or small tree) with fernlike pinnate leaves, about 2ft (60cm) long, made up of about a dozen leaflets. Brilliant orange and scarlet colouring in the autumn. Does well in town gardens, but is given to suckering.

Ribes aureum (Flowering currant)
    7ft (2m). Deciduous.
    Spicy-smelling yellow flowers in spring, followed by black berries and brilliant autumn foliage.

Viburnum opulus and *Viburnum tomentosum* 'Lanarth'
    6ft (1.8m). Deciduous.
    Clusters of white flowers in spring, followed by crimson leaves in autumn. See also page 116.

The scented garden

The great virtue of scented flowers in a front garden is that you do not have to sit outdoors amongst them to be aware of their presence; the scents will float indoors with even slightly open windows (counteracting the stench from passing traffic).

Even if you concentrate on colour there is one area of the front garden which could be devoted to scent. This is the blind area just along the front of the house, which you do not see from inside unless you have French windows. You could, of course, grow tall plants there with their tops peeping in at you through the glass, but they would both look absurd and partly block the view of the garden beyond. A better way to use this space is to fill it with low growing plants which you can smell even if you do not see them.

Winter, spring and summer have their fair share of scented flowers; autumn has fewer, but some linger on from late summer. Here are some to choose from, mainly shrubs. They are listed, as far as possible, in order of flowering.

Scents of winter

Viburnum fragrans (or *V. farreri*)
Up to 10ft (3m). Deciduous shrub.
Clusters of small white flowers smelling of almonds may begin to appear in autumn before the leaves fall, but most of them open from winter – they are frost-resistant – through to spring, followed by scarlet berries. It is a fast grower. Propagate by cuttings.

Mahonia japonica
6ft (1.8m). Evergreen shrub.
This shrub often starts flowering before Christmas and continues well into the spring. The long racemes of yellow bell-shaped flowers, which are not damaged by frost, smell richly of Lilies-of-the-valley. At home by the sea. Propagate by layering. See also page 81.

Daphne odora
3ft (90cm). Evergreen shrub.
White, spicy-smelling flowers appear in clusters from mid winter to early spring. *D.o.* 'Aureomarginata', which has yellow-edged leaves, is the hardiest variety. Needs a sunny, sheltered position; best grown against a wall.

Chimonanthus praecox (*C. fragrans*) (Wintersweet)
5ft (1.5m). Deciduous shrub.
The purple-centred yellow flowers which appear on the bare branches in winter have a spicy smell. Unfortunately, it may be six or seven years before the young plants come into flower. Needs shelter.

Azara microphylla
   5ft (1.5m). Evergreen shrub.
   The yellow bell-like flowers appearing at the end of winter or in early spring tend to be hidden by the small but dense leaves, but the strong vanilla smell comes through. The shrub should be planted only in a mild area, preferably against the shelter of a wall.

Hamamelis mollis (Chinese witch hazel)
   10ft (3m). Deciduous shrub.
   The golden flowers make this one of the best of the winter-blooming shrubs, and the sweet scent is a bonus. *H.m.* 'Pallida', a pale yellow, is one of the best of many varieties; all are hardy. They prefer lime-free soil. Propagate by layering.

Galanthus nivalis (Snowdrop)
   6in (15cm). Bulb.
   One of the sweetest smelling varieties is *G.n.* 'S. Arnott', with large single flowers. Even if the honeyish smell is not overwhelming in the garden it is very pleasant to be able to stick one's nose into a little bowl of snowdrops in the house. They spread quickly.

Iris reticulata
   About 6in (15cm). Hardy bulb.
   Violet, gold-marked flowers, smelling of violets; they appear in late winter and early spring. They need a sunny position.

Scents of spring

x *Osmarea burkwoodii*
   6ft (1.8m). Evergreen shrub.
   Heavily scented tubular white flowers appear in profusion in early spring. This hybrid is sturdier and hardier than its parent *Osmanthus delavayi*, which, however, has more attractive small, leathery leaves and flowers just as fragrant.

Berberis x *stenophylla*
   8ft (2.4m). Evergreen shrub.
   The barberries are not overpoweringly scented but this hybrid is one of the sweetest. The small yellow flowers appear in early spring and the shrub should be pruned after flowering. Suitable for seaside planting.

Viola odorata
   4in (10cm). Herbaceous.
   This is the sweet violet, which has not lost its fragrance. 'Princess of Wales' is a bright violet, and 'Coeur d'Alsace' is pink.

Viburnum carlesii and *V.* x *burkwoodii*
   6ft (1.8m) or less. Deciduous shrubs.
   These are viburnums to provide an almond smell in spring, following *V. fragrans* in winter. Both have pink buds opening to white flowers, but *V.* x *burkwoodii*, which has a spreading habit, grows far more vigorously than the bushy *V. carlesii*.

Syringa vulgaris (Lilac)

Up to 10ft (3m). Deciduous shrub or tree.

There are endless varieties, producing in late spring panicles of flowers, single or double, in colours from white to red to purple. Two heavily scented varieties are the old favourite 'Souvenir de Louis Spath' (deep wine-red, single) and 'Madame Lemoine' (white, double). Lilacs are not fussy about soil, but seem particularly satisfied with chalky clay.

Bulbs provide some of the loveliest scents of spring; the most fragrant are narcissus and hyacinths. To these should be added Lily-of-the-valley, especially if the rhizomes can be allowed to spread in partial shade to form large clumps. 'Fortin's Giant' has large white flowers; 'Rosea' is pink; 'Variegata' has variegated leaves.

There is no richer scent than that of wallflowers, as velvety as the flowers themselves; a bed of them on a still, warm spring day is intoxicating, without fear of hangover. Spring-flowering Brompton stocks also have a rich, individual scent. These are biennial, and the wallflower, though a perennial, is best treated as a biennial.

Scents of summer

Choisya ternata (Mexican orange blossom)

6ft (1.8m). Evergreen shrub.

The scent is rather like that of hawthorn. The clusters of star-like white flowers appear in spring and early summer against a background of shiny aromatic leaves. The shrub needs shelter from wind, but otherwise tolerates seaside conditions. Propagate by cuttings.

Daphne x *burkwoodii*

3ft (90cm). Semi-evergreen shrub.

The white or pale pink flowers give off a sweet spicy smell in early summer. This hybrid grows fairly quickly and has a higher expectation of life than most daphnes.

Spartium junceum (Spanish broom)

10ft (3m). Deciduous shrub.

Smothered in summer in deep yellow pea-like flowers, smelling of honey. The shrub needs sun, and to keep it from becoming straggly new growth must be pruned after flowering. Flourishes near the sea.

Cytisus battandieri

8ft (2.4m). Deciduous shrub.

The scent, quite strong, is of pineapple. Yellow flowers appear in racemes 3in (7.5cm) long in summer, among silvery leaves – each leaf attractively divided into three leaflets. A choice only for warm parts of the country, and best against the shelter of a wall. Suitable for the seaside.

Philadelphus (Mock orange)

Average 5ft (1.5m). Deciduous shrub.

Many species and hybrids have a strong orangey smell, so your choice largely depends on whether you prefer single or double flowers and how large a shrub you want. Among the most fragrant are 'Beauclerk', about 5ft (1.5m), with large single white flowers flushed with pink; the ever-popular 'Virginal', 10ft (3m), which has large panicles of semi-double pure white flowers; and *P. microphyllus*, less than 3ft (90cm), which has dainty leaves and single white flowers. Not demanding about soil or position.

Magnolia grandiflora 'Exmouth' (Laurel magnolia)

15ft (4.5m). Evergreen shrub or tree.

A must if you have a stately home, but overwhelming in a small garden. The creamy white flowers (summer to early autumn) are up to 10in (25cm) across and have a sweet lemony scent. A related shrub, *Michelia figo*, would be more manageable, but needs a warm garden. The yellowy green flowers, marked with purple, are very fragrant, smelling of bananas.

To add to this wide range of sweet-smelling summer shrubs there are also scented lilies, pinks and border carnations and a few annuals.

Lilium

Various heights. Bulbs.

Not all lilies are fragrant, but those which are include:

Lilium auratum, white and gold, flowering late summer, up to 7ft (2m); it likes partial shade and hates lime.

Bellingham hybrids, orange and red, flowering mid summer, up to 7ft (2m), likes partial shade.

L. candidum (Madonna lily), white flowers with gold stamens, early to mid summer, up to 4ft (1.2m), tolerates lime.

L. hansonii, golden yellow flowers in early summer, up to 5ft (1.5m), likes partial shade.

L. henryi, orange flowers in late summer, up to 8ft (2.4m), likes partial shade, does well on lime.

L. regale, white with yellow throat and maroon on the outside, flowers mid summer, up to 4ft (1.2m), prefers sun, tolerates lime.

Dianthus (Border pinks and carnations)

Up to 1ft (30cm). Perennial.

The most heavily clove-scented border carnations are 'Candy Clove', white marked with red; 'Cherry Clove', light cherry coloured; 'Robin Thain', white striped with red; 'Imperial Clove', mauve.

The most fragrant old-fashioned pinks are: 'Mrs Sinkins', double white; 'Pink Mrs Sinkins', double pink; and 'Sam Barlow', double white, with a dark eye.

Both garden pinks and border carnations need sun, a well-drained soil, and a little lime. They may last for three or four years, but each year take cuttings of side shoots in summer so that you have a constant supply of young stock to replace the deteriorating older generation.

Four annuals give distinctive old-fashioned scents. The honey-scented *Alyssum maritimum*, a dwarf carpeter, has white or blue or pink flowers in summer and autumn. The flowers of mignonette (*Reseda odorata*), appearing summer to mid autumn, are not much to look at, but the warm smell which belongs to mignonette alone is heavy with nostalgia. *Mathiola bicornis* (Night-scented stock) is also un-impressive-looking, but the scent through an open window on a summer night is unforgettable. The tobacco plant (*Nicotiana alata*), flowering from summer to mid autumn, is also most fragrant at night, though there are now varieties which do at least keep their flowers open during the day. This annual is only half-hardy so must be sown in warmth and planted out in late spring (or plants can then be bought from garden centres).

Scents of autumn

Elaeagnus pungens
   8ft (2.4m). Evergreen shrub.
   The sweetly scented flowers are inconspicuous, but their fragrance and the attractiveness of the leaves make up for that. There are three excellent smaller variegated varieties: *E.p.* 'Dicksonii' has green and yellow leaves; *E.p.* 'Maculata' has yellow leaves edged with green; 'Variegata' has green leaves splashed with gold. Ruthlessly cut out all shoots which do not bear yellow leaves or the whole shrub may revert to green. Propagate by cuttings.

Clerodendron trichotomum
   10ft (3m). Deciduous shrub.
   The clusters of white star-shaped flowers have a fragrance which is very perva-sive, but it is as well not to brush against the shrub for the leaves then smell most unpleasantly. Turquoise berries follow the flowers.

In addition a scented wall can be created up the front of the house. Two climbing plants, a *Clematis montana* (see page 99) and *Jasminum officinale* 'Affine' (see page 99), could be paired to frame a large window or indeed several, for they are very vigorous-growing, and may have to be hacked back from time to time. The sweet-smelling clematis will flower in early summer and with luck may continue until the jasmine takes over, producing at least some flowers well into the autumn.
   Of course scented plants smell just as good in the back garden.

Warning: planting can seriously damage your health

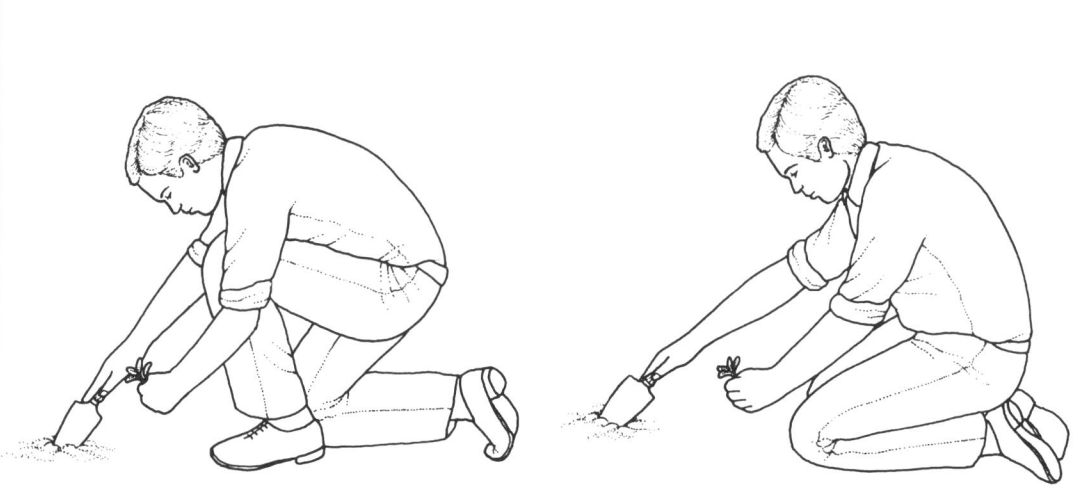

Right and wrong ways of planting

When planting at ground level do not kneel on both knees; this is a position which may induce sciatica. Just as for hand weeding, kneel on one knee, bending the other leg but keeping the foot flat on the ground. This is not only a more comfortable position to stay in but an easier one to get out of.

Back to ferns

In my youth I disliked ferns and managed to kill most of those in my father's garden. But since then they have grown on me, if I can put it that way, and I make no apology for dragging them in here. I now appreciate their outstanding grace and I am fascinated by the fact of their survival as a very primitive form of plant life. Perhaps it is this which helps some of them to thrive in parts of the garden which many other plants would find uncongenial to the point of death. Most of them do best in partial shade in a north-facing position, but sheltered from wind, and in soil with plenty of humus, moist but well-drained. They need little looking after: a mulch in early spring, with the removal of dead fronds, and another mulch in autumn. The best time for planting is early spring.

Here are some of the many hardy ferns available – although there are now far fewer than the thousand or so British ferns one could choose from in Victorian times.

Adiantum pedatum (Hardy maidenhair)
    2ft (60cm). Deciduous.
    This maidenhair from North America is much hardier than the British *A. capillus-veneris*. The delicate-looking fronds, made up of pale green kidney-shaped leaves, are carried on black wiry stems which grow from creeping rhizomes. *A. venustum* is smaller (6in (15cm)) and even more graceful.

Asplenium scolopendrium (Hartstongue)
    18in (45cm). Evergreen.
    An easily grown fern which will tolerate both dry and moist conditions and sun or shade. The broad solid fronds are a shiny rich green. If closely planted these ferns can be used as ground cover. (Often listed as *Phyllitis scolopendrium*.)

Athyrium filix-femina (Common lady fern)
    3–4ft (90cm–1.2m). Deciduous.
    Feathery pale green arching fronds. This fern does best in a moist position in partial shade, but tolerates sunlight. After a few years the crown will push its way above soil level and should be lifted and replanted.

Blechnum spicant
    18in (45cm). Semi-evergreen.
    The narrow leaves are dark green and leathery. It should be chosen only for lime-free soil and for a moist position.

Ceterach officinarum (Rusty back fern)
    8in (20cm). Evergreen.
    A fast grower with narrow, lance-shaped, leathery fronds. It gets its common name from the scales on the back of the leaves which are silvery at first but turn

rusty brown. Likes lime and must have a well-drained position; it is often found growing in the lime mortar of old walls.

Cryptogramma crispa (Parsley fern)

6in (15cm). Deciduous.

At home only on really acid soils, but there it is an attractive, almost emerald-green fern, particularly striking in spring. The deeply divided fronds explain the comparison with parsley.

Cystopteris fragilis (Bladder fern)

6in (15cm). Deciduous.

This fern does best in a limy soil. The fronds are as fragile as the name suggests, but even if you clumsily break one off another will grow in its place.

Dryopteris filix-mas (Male fern)

4ft (1.2m). Deciduous.

The commonest British fern, growing vigorously to form large clumps, which can be overpowering in a small garden. Though it does best in moist soil in part shade it will put up a reasonably good show in dry, sunny positions in poor soil. *D. pseudomas* (syn. *D. borreri*), the Golden-scaled male fern, is probably a better choice, especially in the variety 'Cristata the King'. It is semi-evergreen, and the young fronds, a golden green, grow into symmetrical arching fronds up to 3ft (90cm) long. The stems are covered with golden scales.

Gymnocarpium dryopteris (Oak fern)

10in (25cm). Deciduous.

One of the loveliest ferns, with soft, fresh, green fronds on long stems, growing from spreading underground rhizomes to make a dense carpet. Needs a rather acid soil.

Matteuccia germanica (Ostrich feather fern)

3ft (90cm). Deciduous.

The rhizomes creep underground and at intervals throw up a group of graceful, light green fronds, arranged like a shuttlecock (another common name for this fern). Does best in damp places with some shade, since sunlight browns the fronds.

Onoclea sensibilis (Sensitive fern)

18in (45cm). Deciduous.

This is a runner and no clumper, throwing up single elegant fronds at intervals from underground rhizomes. Sensitive because the fronds turn brown at a touch of frost, the rhizomes are nevertheless thoroughly hardy. Needs moist, rich soil in sun or light shade.

Phegopteris connectilis (Beech fern)

10in (25cm). Deciduous.

A vigorously spreading little fern with fronds of tiny, triangular, fresh green leaves rising from a mass of creeping rhizomes. Useful as a carpeter in the shade of trees, given acid soil with plenty of humus in it. (Another renamed fern; formerly it was *Thelypteris phegopteris*.)

Polypodium vulgare (Common polypodium)

1ft (30cm). Basically evergreen.

The fronds, growing from rhizomes creeping along the surface of the soil, are lance-shaped, and sharply cut. The great virtues of this fern are that it will grow in most conditions and stay a brilliant green throughout the winter, so it can be excused the brief dull period from spring to early summer between the fading of the old frond and the appearance of the new.

Polystichum setiferum (Soft shield fern)

3ft (90cm). Evergreen.

An exceedingly beautiful fern, especially when grown in moist situations. The deep green fronds are finely divided, forming great lacy plumes.

Insect life

Plants and human beings are not the only living things in a garden; innumerable others fly in or creep about. Some of them may be more welcome than others, but we should get out of the way of looking at them indiscriminately with suspicion or dread. There are reckoned to be more than 20,000 kinds of insects in the British Isles, but only a few hundred of these can properly be regarded as pests – because of the harm they inflict on plants, animals or humans.

Bees should be particularly welcome in the garden, not only because you depend so much on them for good fruit crops through pollination of blossom, but because they are fascinating to watch, whether collecting pollen or nectar. It is as pleasant and relaxing a way of loafing away a summer's day as you can wish for.

I have not suggested bee-keeping as one aspect of having a family garden largely because of the amount of work bees can involve, but if you do not mind that I can heartily recommend a hive (which unless disaster strikes will invariably increase to several). In my first post-marriage garden there were several hives as well as young children and the garden itself was near the centre of Manchester. (Nowadays town bees may be far less at risk from death from insecticides than their country cousins, who are massacred in large numbers by agricultural spraying.)

But you do not have to keep bees to be able to watch them. You can encourage them to visit your garden by choosing plants they love. Bulbs will bring them along in spring – winter aconite, snowdrop, crocus, narcissus and hyacinth. Shrubs which attract them include berberis, cotoneaster, fuchsia, genista, heather, holly, simphoricarpus (snowberry) and veronica. The blossom of gooseberries, raspberries and blackberries is especially popular. Most climbing honeysuckles and the blue buddleias defeat the honey bees because the nectar is out of reach of their comparatively short tongues, though it is available to the long-tongued species of bumble bees and to butterflies; honey bees can cope only with the globular yellow buddleia.

Double flowers are also useless, so this excludes most roses, dahlias and chrysanthemums. Among the workable flowers are alyssum, arabis, aster, aubretia, campanula, catmint, helenium, hollyhock (single), lavender, mignonette, poppy, salvia and wallflower. Bees work hard in a herb garden, which thus provides food for man and bee. A bee/herb garden would include borage, chives, mint, rosemary, sage, winter and summer savory, and thyme.

The butterfly population is sadly diminishing, and needs encouragement. Admittedly butterflies produce caterpillars, but the fact is that in general they prefer to lay their eggs on wild flowers. Among flowers which butterflies visit for nectar are:

Spring: *Alyssum saxatile* (the yellow alyssum), arabis, aubretia and wallflowers.

Summer: *Buddleia davidii,* catmint, French marigolds, heliotrope, phlox, valerian and verbena.

Autumn: Michaelmas daisies.

Having thus enticed bees and butterflies it would, of course, be dastardly if you sprayed a blanket of death over the whole garden.

The garden
in middle age

Arbor Ground Raised
cover shrubs Pool Enlarged
Patio

House

Magnolia
Tree

Raised beds enlarged

Summer
House

Garage

Concrete
Drive

Compost
bins

Time for change

What parents do with the garden once the children have finally flown depends on how much enthusiasm they have for gardening. The choices are the same as those which faced non-family gardeners when first faced with a garden.

One is to pretend that the garden is not there and let it run wild. This is the most labour-saving garden of all; if the neighbours are difficult and complain about pernicious weeds invading their garden all you have to do is spray everything to death from time to time. This may be satisfying if you have a full social life and your home and garden are nowhere near the centre of your life, but you will find a neglected garden a very depressing sight as you get old and spend more time at home.

The totally opposite choice is to devote time and energy to the garden to the exclusion of everything else – the gardening counterpart of the houseproud housewife. The result may well be aphidless rose beds and weedless, newly mown lawns that you feel you should take your shoes off to walk on, but it also often means a gardener who has little time left from his labours to enjoy the result.

The golden mean between these two extremes is a garden in which the gardener does have time to take his shoes off and put his feet up; a garden which is so planned that there is some leisure time left to spend in it and not too much work to do. This is not a lazy gardener's garden, but a sensible gardener's garden.

The dedicated plantsman may spurn this solution, and he will be helped with advice from endless gardening books on anything from roses to rhubarb. But the time comes when even the most enthusiastic gardener has to come to terms with diminished vigour. If he or she is not to fight a losing battle against the garden in old age a gradual changeover to a more labour-saving garden is essential. This will have to be done while there is still the physical energy left to do it.

Gardeners who from the start – or from the post-children start – plump for a labour-saving garden will at the same time be establishing the basic pattern of an old-age garden, even though old age may be a long way off. The raised beds and the raised pool are an investment for life, and so is the summerhouse. Once the children have gone and you get possession of it you can clear out the fittings and junk you don't want and decorate it and furnish it to your own taste.

There you will be able to do your swotting for the Open University in peace; practise your hobbies; write a book or just read one; opt out of T.V. watching so that you can listen to Stockhausen; escape from people who call; get out of the way of the vacuum cleaner or moments of domestic friction. (Who wants a converted loft?)

But there are other changes to make to fit the garden for the future: the lawn, for instance. A lawn, to give it its courtesy title, which has been punished by children for a decade or more is unlikely to be in the best of trim. The choice is either to improve it or to dig it up and plant something else.

There is much to be said for a beautiful lawn as long as you enjoy looking after it; if not, there is little to be said for it. One undoubted thing in its favour is that it is the cheapest way of colouring a piece of ground a beautiful green – even though keeping it that way is the most laborious (and I write as one who used to enjoy mowing almost more than any other gardening job).

It takes only as much time to mow a good lawn as a bad one, so if you think a lawn is worth mowing it is worth improving. This can be done gradually, or by returfing or reseeding, all fully explained on pages 28–39.

Or you can dig up the lawn – or part of it. If you have an overwhelming urge to grow roses or pot leeks, or have a bent for formal bedding-out plants, a mixed herbaceous border or other exacting forms of gardening, this is the best time of life to get such urges out of your system. After that you will be ready to make a start on achieving the ultimate aim of a garden that as far as possible looks after itself.

However, if you want to start straightaway with a gradual approach to such a garden, you can profitably begin by cutting down the space given over to grass, planting instead less demanding, ground-covering, weed-smothering plants. Some might be herbaceous, but most would be longer-living shrubs.

A ground cover garden is expensive to establish, far more expensive than a lawn unless you buy the finest turf, but by making a modest start you not only spread the cost, but reduce it. You can do this by dividing the original plants when they grow too large and by taking cuttings and growing them in a small nursery bed. In these ways you can without cost expand the area under ground cover and renew ageing plants. Further spending would only be to add variety to the collection.

Even a gradual approach must be thoroughly planned ahead, to avoid future upheavals. Draw a plan of how you wish the garden to finish up – where there will be ground cover, where paved areas, where, perhaps, more raised beds, where a greenhouse, if you want one, and so on. Time may show that you have made some awful mistakes, and if so better to change them than to go on living with them. That apart, try to stick to your plan.

A pick of the plants for ground cover

Successful ground cover gardening depends on two factors. The first is the correct choice of shrubs and perennials. Only those which are of dense growth *at ground level* are effective in smothering weeds. Furthermore, they must be of a kind which within a few years will spread enough to cover all the ground, smothering all weeds and so making the tedious job of hoeing unnecessary. The second essential is regular mulching with such vegetable matter as garden compost, leaves, peat, forest bark, chopped straw and (in limited quantities) lawn mowings and sawdust.

Mulching has two purposes. It helps to smother weeds, especially while the clumps of plants have not yet joined up with each other. It also adds fertility to the soil, as manure does, but from the top, leaving it to the rain and living organisms in the soil to take it downwards, thus saving us the burden of digging it in.

Once ground cover plants are thoroughly established they can be depended on to suppress almost all the weeds trying to grow around them. However, when newly planted they cannot cope with weeds without your help. A mulch about 3in (7.5cm) deep will keep down most of the weeds (as long as vicious deep-rooting weeds are dug up before the ground is planted). An alternative, at least for a year or so after planting, is to use black plastic sheeting as a mulch, laying it between the plants. This will suppress weeds underneath by depriving them of light; the sheeting must therefore be black since white or clear plastic will let the light through and the weeds will germinate underneath the sheeting. Remove this plastic 'mulch' as the plants spread.

One of the best natural mulches in a ground cover garden is provided by the autumn harvest of leaves falling from the trees. These can be removed and rotted down in a heap, but there is no reason why they should not be laid round the shrubs as they are. The birds may scatter them around during the winter while searching for food, but you can tidy up in the spring. By then many of the leaves will have rotted down and will be carried into the soil by earthworms.

After the shrubs and plants are established, and the chores of digging and hoeing are things of the past, several jobs – besides the regular mulching – cannot be escaped. These involve pruning, dividing up clumps which have grown too big and cutting back the rampant spreaders which threaten to overwhelm the slower-growing plants. You should also start a nursery bed in which to root cuttings. When you want to put more of the garden down to ground cover, or you need to renew the garden as the ageing plants pass their best, you will have the new plants ready without cost and with little effort.

The following three lists suggest some large shrubs, small shrubs and perennial herbaceous plants which can be used as ground cover. These are listed in order of heights, starting with the smallest. Before buying any which are unfamiliar identify them in a garden centre or nursery and then see if you can track them down in public parks – or other people's gardens – to see what they look like when more mature. Shrubs are too expensive to buy on the strength of a necessarily brief description. Not only must they do their ground covering job efficiently; you must also like them.

The figures of heights and spread given in the lists are estimates of a mature plant's needs. Some are rapid growers or spreaders; others are slow. Much also depends on whether they are growing in the colder north or the warmer south and on the condition of the soil. Some will grow taller, even much taller, if allowed to, but at the cost of growing straggly. They will need pruning to be kept bushy.

I have largely chosen evergreens, but there is no need to rely entirely on evergreens; in spring particularly the new leaf growth of deciduous plants will greatly enliven a largely evergreen background.

Methods of propagation, where appropriate, are shown. Many shrubs are easy to propagate. Generally speaking shrubs have a longer expectation of life than herbaceous perennials, but most herbaceous plants are also easily propagated.

Warning: weeding can seriously damage your health.

The right way to weed, by hand and using a hoe

One great advantage of combining ground cover planting with mulching is that it cuts down weeding, which whether done with your fingers or with a hoe can be a dangerous occupation. Many people bend over when hoeing in order to push harder. This is bad for your spine. Use a long-handled hoe and hold it at a low angle, as advised for the lawn mower (page 41). When hoeing stand with one foot in front of the other; when you push the hoe into the soil you will feel that the force is coming from the back leg.

Do not go down on both knees when hand weeding. Go down on one knee, and keep the other leg bent with the foot flat on the ground. If you do both of these weeding operations correctly you are far less likely to develop sciatica.

Small shrubs for ground cover

Shrubs provide long-lasting ground cover. This selection covers those, including a few conifers, ranging in height from 4in to 3ft (10–90cm). To look effective and be effective as ground cover shrubs should be planted in groups of several of the same kind; take care the clumps are not too large in proportion to the size of the garden. Avoid choosing plants that are all of the same height, or of the same leaf texture and colour. On the other hand avoid too many contrasts or the result will be like the proverbial dog's dinner.

Rubus calycinoides
Height 3in (7.5cm), spread 2ft (60cm). Evergreen.

This is a bramble with dark green leaves which spreads fairly rapidly; hardy in most parts of the country. It will succeed in limy soils or in clay, in dry shady places as well as in full sun, and is suitable for the seaside. It needs to be cut back in spring to keep it bushy. Propagate by division, cuttings or layering.

Cotoneaster dammeri
Height 4in (10cm), spread 2ft (60cm). Evergreen.

A rapidly growing carpeter with small glossy leaves, tiny white flowers and red berries. It will grow in limy or clay soils and in sun or shade, but it is not to be relied on under trees. Propagate by cuttings or layering – but the branches will root themselves where they droop on to the soil and thus go on spreading year after year.

Gaultheria procumbens (Spicy wintergreen, Winter berry, Checkerberry)
Height 6in (15cm), spread 18in (45cm). Evergreen.

Dark green, aromatic, glossy, leathery leaves, tiny white bells in late summer, tinged with pink, and scarlet berries if the plant is grown in full sun. Does best in a lime-free soil in the shade, and survives well in dry weather. Propagate by division or layering.

Vinca minor (Lesser periwinkle)
Height 6in (15cm), spread 2ft (60cm). Evergreen.

Small, pointed, dark green leaves, blue or white flowers from late spring onwards. Will grow in limy or clay soils and in shade – even dry shade – and thrives near the sea. A better choice than the larger *Vinca major* (see below). Propagate by division or cuttings.

Cornus canadensis (Dogwood)
Height 6in (15cm), spread 2ft (60cm). Deciduous.

Dull green leaves which turn winy red in autumn; white flowers in late spring and early summer. Spreads rapidly by underground shoots. Needs lime-free soil but given that will grow even in dry shade. Propagate by division.

Juniperus horizontalis (Creeping juniper)
Height 6in (15cm), spread 3ft (90cm). Evergreen conifer.
The blue-green leaves form a dense mat when the shrub is well established; it may then be 18in (45cm) or more tall. Grows in limy soil, likes full, hot sun, and thrives near the sea.

Vaccinium vitis-idaea (Mountain cranberry)
Height 6in (15cm), spread 1ft (30cm). Evergreen.
Small, smooth green leaves tinged with bronze in winter, and pale pink bell-like flowers in summer. Propagate by division, cuttings or layering. See also page 127.

Erica (Heath or heather)
Height 8in (20cm) upwards, spread 18in (45cm). Evergreen.
Erica carnea, about 8in (20cm), flowers from mid winter to early spring – white, pink, red, purple according to variety. (See also page 126.) This erica will tolerate slightly alkaline soil, whereas ericas in general are lime-haters. *Erica tetralix*, up to 18in (45cm), has white or pink flowers from summer to mid winter and *Erica australis,* up to 4ft (1.2m), has white, pink or purple flowers from mid spring to early summer. Heathers do best in full sun. All should be pruned after flowering or they become ungainly. Propagate by cuttings.

Pachysandra terminalis
Height 8in (20cm), spread 2ft (60cm). Evergreen.
Rapidly spreading to give good cover. The dense, glossy, rich green leaves grow in rosettes, with spikes of small yellowy-white scented flowers in spring. Needs a lime-free soil, but will grow in deeper shade than many plants, even beneath trees. Propagate by division or cuttings.

Iberis sempervirens
Height 8in (20cm), spread 18in (45cm) or more. Evergreen.
The dark green leaves are small and narrow but the plant makes good ground cover. In late spring it is covered with heads of brilliantly white flowers. It does best in full sun, but it will grow in shade, though not under trees; does well at the seaside. Propagate by cuttings or layering.

Vinca major (Larger periwinkle)
Height 1ft (30cm), spread 2ft (60cm). Evergreen.
This, not unnaturally, is a larger version of *V. minor*. It grows twice the height, with larger blue flowers in spring, but it takes time to get established. Propagate by division or cuttings. See also page 120.

Hypericum calycinum (Rose of Sharon)
Height 1ft (30cm), spread 3ft (90cm). Evergreen.
A very dependable ground cover plant in any soil and in dense shade or hot sun. The broad leaves are a rich green and the large yellow flowers appear from summer on. To keep it compact and effective as ground cover it must be pruned back hard in early spring. Propagate by cuttings.

Cytisus x *kewensis*

Height 1ft (30cm), spread 4ft (1.2m). Deciduous.

Long, spreading branches are covered with tiny grey-green leaves and small yellow flowers in spring – it is a member of the broom family. It needs full sun and does best in sandy, lime-free soils. Propagate by cuttings.

Halimiocistus sahucii

Height 1ft (30cm), spread 2ft (60cm). Evergreen.

Hummocks of narrow dark green leaves with white flowers in clusters in summer. It is a shrub for warm sunny places, including the seaside; not for cold parts of the country. Propagate by cuttings.

Hebe pinguifolia 'Pagei'

Height 18in (45cm), spread 2ft (60cm). Evergreen.

The hebes, once known as veronicas, are somewhat tender shrubs, but this is one of the rather hardier ones, except in the coldest parts of the country. The small leaves are grey-green and there are spikes of small white flowers in early summer. It will grow in limy soils and near the sea, and though it does best in hot sunny positions it will tolerate a certain amount of shade. Propagate by cuttings or layering.

Salvia officinalis (Common sage)

Height 18in (45cm), spread 2ft (60cm). Evergreen.

Velvety grey-green leaves and small blue flowers in mid summer. It needs full sun and a bad winter may kill it. A light soil, which can be limy, suits it best; it thrives by the sea. Propagate by division, cuttings or layering.

Taxus 'Repandens' (Yew)

Height 18in (45cm), spread 3ft (90cm). Evergreen.

This is a dark green conifer with slow-growing, dense, horizontal branches. Does well in limy soils.

Santolina chamaecyparissus (Lavender cotton)

Height 18in (45cm), spread 2ft (60cm).

This has silvery grey leaves and rich yellow heads of flowers in summer. Propagate by division and cuttings. See also page 111.

Calluna vulgaris (Ling)

Height 18in (45cm), spread 18in (45cm). Evergreen.

The common heathers have white, pink or purple flowers according to variety. 'Alba Plena' is a good double white. See pages 127–8 for the pink varieties. They do best in full sun and need a lime-free soil. Trim back in spring to keep them compact and dense. Propagate by cuttings or layering.

Halimium lasianthum

Height 2ft (60cm), spread 2ft (60cm). Evergreen.

This has silvery leaves, and forms not over-dense hummocks; striking yellow, crimson-blotched flowers appear in summer. Propagate by cuttings. See also page 111.

Daboecia cantabrica (Irish heath)
    Height 2ft (60cm), spread 2ft (60cm). Evergreen.
    Rosy purple or white flowers last through summer and autumn. Like the other heathers this is a lime-hater. Propagate by cuttings or layering.

Viburnum davidii
    Height 2ft (60cm), spread 3ft (90cm). Evergreen.
    Dense and low-growing with small, dark green, deeply veined leaves, white flowers in summer and dark blue berries on the female plants (if a male is planted among them). Will grow in limy soils, and tolerates clay; while it prefers sun it will also grow in shade as long as it is not under trees. Propagate by cuttings or layering.

Genista hispanica (Spanish gorse)
    Height 2ft (60cm), spread 2ft (60cm). Deciduous.
    Tiny leaves, green spines and small, yellow, short-lived flowers in summer. Given a sunny, warm spot it spreads quite rapidly to give dense cover. Propagate by cuttings. See also page 81.

Senecio laxifolius
    Height 3ft (90cm), spread 4ft (1.2m). Evergreen.
    The grey-green woolly leaves, white underneath, make this particularly effective in winter. In early summer it carries brilliant yellow heads of flowers. Propagate by cuttings or layering. See also page 111.

Potentilla fruticosa
    Height 3ft (90cm), spread 4ft (1.2m). Deciduous.
    This makes a dense bush if grown in full sun. The yellow flowers are like miniature single roses. Propagate by cuttings or layering. See also page 110.

Osmanthus delavayi
    Height 3ft (90cm), spread 2ft (60cm). Evergreen.
    Dense and bushy but a fairly slow grower. It is not fussy about soils, but in cold areas needs protection if it is to do well. See page 132.

Tall shrubs for ground cover

In small gardens low-growing shrubs and carpeters may provide all the ground cover needed, but in a large garden the effect could be boring. By planting a few taller shrubs monotony is avoided. Not all large shrubs are suitable as ground cover. Whatever their other attractions they must satisfy the main requirement: that they should have fairly dense or spreading growth near ground level in order to suppress weeds. Here are a few possibles.

Aucuba japonica
   Height 5ft (1.5m), spread 5ft (1.5m). Evergreen.
   The leaves are dark green, shiny and leathery, but there are variegated forms. The female shrubs will produce long-lasting scarlet berries, but only if a male shrub is planted along with them. It will put up with conditions under which most shrubs would die: clay soils, as well as the limy soils it prefers, impoverished town garden soils, dry shady places, even under trees; it is also useful for seaside gardens. Of course it will do better if it does not have to cope with all these problems.

Phillyrea decora
   Height 5ft (1.5m), spread 5ft (1.5m). Evergreen.
   A densely growing shrub with dark green leathery leaves – a rather stiff-looking habit. The small, creamy, sweetly scented flowers in spring are followed on the female shrubs by purplish blue berries. It will tolerate clay and survives even under trees.

Viburnum tomentosum 'Lanarth'
   Height 6ft (1.8m), spread 7ft (2m). Deciduous.
   Even though it is not evergreen there is much to be said for this shrub as ground cover, since the branches grow horizontally in tiers right down to the ground. The large tooth-edged leaves turn crimson in autumn. See also page 116.

Garrya elliptica
   Height 6ft (1.8m), spread 5ft (1.5m). Evergreen.
   Particularly attractive for the catkins which appear in late winter and early spring. Although generally hardy it will do best in cold areas if grown against a wall. See also page 102.

Mahonia japonica
   Height 6ft (1.8m), spread 4ft (1.2m). Evergreen.
   Dense-spreading, though a slow grower, this can survive in shade even under trees, but deserves to be planted where its scent can be appreciated. See also page 81.

Escallonia hybrids
   Height 4–5ft (1.2–1.5m), spread 5ft (1.5m). Semi-evergreen, but evergreen in mild areas.
   Dense shrubs with gracefully spreading branches, small leaves and star-like flowers in mid summer. See also page 127.

Choisya ternata
   Height 6ft (1.8m), spread 6ft (1.8m). Evergreen.
   A quick-growing shrub, which can be planted in shade (but not under trees) or in a sunny, dry position. See also page 133.

Elaeagnus x *ebbi ebbingei*
   Height 9ft (2.7m), spread 6ft (1.8m). Evergreen.
   A trouble-free, fast-growing shrub with shiny mid-green leaves and small

scented flowers in autumn. It withstands wind if not too cold; it will grow by the sea, and in dry soil in the sun.

Perennials for ground cover

There is no point in deliberately restricting ground cover to shrubs, however attractive they may be. Herbaceous plants can be used to provide a variety of foliage and a wider range of flowers. Low-growing herbaceous plants are particularly useful, if only because there are more to choose from than there are really low-growing shrubs (a shrub has woody branches – but not a trunk, like a tree – whereas a herbaceous plant does not have a woody stem). The heights given for low-growing plants are those of the leaf growth: in flower they are taller.

Oxalis inops
Height 2in (5cm), spread 18in (45cm). Deciduous.
Shamrock-like leaves and short-stemmed pink flowers throughout late spring and summer. Needs sun, and will grow in dry positions. All right for the seaside. Propagate by division.

Lysimachia nummularia (Creeping Jenny)
Height 2in (5cm), spread 2ft (60cm). Evergreen.
This is a densely growing carpeter for shady moist places, with small, smooth, bright green leaves and bright yellow flowers in summer. Propagate by division.

Acaena buchananii
Height 3in (7.5cm), spread 2ft (60cm). Deciduous.
A carpeter with pale green leaves and inconspicuous petal-less flowers. Thrives in limy soil and hot dry places, including the seaside. Propagate by division.

Dianthus (Alpine pinks)
Height 3in (7.5cm), spread 1ft (30cm). Evergreen.
A loose mat of grass-like leaves covered with heavily scented pink or white flowers in summer. Propagate by cuttings or division. See also page 26.

Stachys lanata (Lamb's tongue)
Height 4in (10cm), spread 18in (45cm). Evergreen.
Forms a carpet of woolly, silvery leaves. There are small mauve flowers in summer but they are of no great note. Likes lime, needs full sun and will grow near the sea. Propagate by division.

Saxifraga umbrosa (London pride)
Height 4in (10cm), spread 1ft (30cm). Evergreen.
A long-time favourite; the dark green rather formal rosettes make a dense mat. Sprays of small pinkish white flowers on 10in (25cm) or so stems in late spring. Grows well in shade; at home in town gardens and by the sea. Propagate by division.

Asperula odorata (Sweet woodruff)
Height 4in (10cm), spread 3ft (90cm). Deciduous.
A rampant spreader with small rich green leaves and white starry flowers in spring. Among its virtues is that it is a good town and seaside plant and will grow in dry shade. Propagate by division.

Tiarella cordifolia (Foam flower)
Height 4in (10cm), spread 2ft (60cm). Evergreen.
This makes a dense carpet, with masses of fluffy white flowers in spring. The hairy green leaves turn bronze in winter. It does best in the shade in soil with plenty of humus. Propagate by division.

Polygonum affine
Height 4in (10cm), spread 2ft (60cm). Deciduous.
Forms a dense carpet of narrow bright green leaves which turn coppery in autumn and often last well into winter. The spikes of flowers appear from summer onwards; on the variety 'Darjeeling Red' they are a striking crimson. The plants will thrive in town and seaside gardens, in limy soil, and in moist partial shade. Propagate by division.

Phlox subulata
Height 4in (10cm), spread 2ft (60cm). Deciduous.
Large mats of small narrow leaves with magenta or lavender-blue flowers in spring. Propagate by division or cuttings. See also page 24.

Aubretia deltoidea
Height 4in (10cm), spread 18in (45cm). Evergreen.
Smothered in spring with pink, red or purple flowers. Propagate by cuttings or division. See also page 24.

Campanula portenschlagiana
Height 4in (10cm), spread 1ft (30cm). Deciduous.
Forms a large mat of dark green leaves covered with lilac bell flowers in summer. Propagate by cuttings and division. See also page 26.

Gypsophila repens 'Rosea'
Height 5in (12.5cm), spread 2ft (60cm). Deciduous.
Grassy grey-green leaves and a mass of tiny pink flowers in mid summer. It will thrive in limy or lime-free soil, in sunny, dry positions and near the sea. Propagate by cuttings.

Arabis albida 'Flore Pleno'
Height 5in (7.5cm), spread 18in (45cm). Evergreen.
Greyish green leaves and great heads of double white flowers in spring. It is an unfussy plant, objecting only to boggy or very clayey soil and to being planted under trees. Propagate by cuttings or division.

Asarum europaeum (European wild ginger)
Height 6in (15cm), spread 18in (45cm). Evergreen.
Glossy dark green leaves and dull brown flowers, hardly visible, in spring. It will tolerate a clayey soil and grows well in shade. Propagate by division.

Omphalodes verna
Height 6in (15cm), spread 2ft (60cm). Deciduous.
A carpeter with rich green broad leaves which will stand a fair amount of shade. The small blue flowers, borne in sprays, appear in spring. Propagate by division.

Pulmonaria saccharata
Height 8in (20cm), spread 2ft (60cm). Evergreen.
Clumps of long dark green leaves with white blotches, early spring flowers which start pink and turn blue. It grows well in limy soils, but needs shade and a cool moist position to cope with hot weather. Propagate by division.

Alchemilla mollis
Height 8in, spread 2ft (60cm). Deciduous.
A very undemanding plant forming a clump of attractive velvety green leaves with masses of greeny yellow star-like flowers in summer. It will grow in sun or partial shade and will thrive in lime; it tolerates not too heavy clay and the often worn out soil of town gardens. It is also a good plant for the seaside. Propagate by division.

Cerastium tomentosum (Snow in summer)
Height 8in (20cm), spread 2ft (60cm). Evergreen.
The danger of this spreading plant with its dense mat of silvery grey leaves is that it will too quickly cover too much ground. In early summer it carries white flowers rather like miniature pinks. It thrives in limy soil and dry sunny situations. Propagate by cuttings and division.

Nepeta x *faassenii* (Catmint)
Height 1ft (30cm), spread 18in (45cm). Evergreen.
Forms a lump of small greyish green woolly leaves with sprays of pale blue flowers throughout summer and autumn. Propagate by division and cuttings. See also page 122.

Sedum spectabile
Height 1ft (30cm), spread 1ft (30cm). Deciduous.
A clump of large, fleshy, greyish green leaves with large heads of small pink flowers in late summer. It loves lime and sun and does well near the sea. Propagate by division and cuttings.

Brunnera macrophylla
Height 1ft (30cm), spread 2ft (60cm). Deciduous.
In summer it makes a dense clump of dark green hairy leaves with small blue forget-me-not-like flowers over many weeks in late spring and early summer. It needs shade, thrives in lime and tolerates a clayey soil. Propagate by division.

Bergenia cordifolia
Height 1ft (30cm), spread 2ft (60cm). Evergreen.
An adaptable carpeter with dark green glossy leaves which turn purplish in winter, and heads of pinky mauve flowers in spring. It will adapt to all except

really sodden soils, but flourishes best in a rather heavy one. It will grow in sun or shade, but avoid planting it under trees. It is suitable for seaside or town gardens. Propagate by division.

Geranium macrorrhizum

Height 1ft (30cm), spread 2ft (60cm). Deciduous.

A fairly fast-growing carpeter with hairy, fragrant, light green leaves which turn to bright colours in autumn. According to variety, the flowers, appearing in late spring, may be pink, bright red or white. See page 128 for cultivation.

Epimedium perralderanum

Height 1ft (30cm), spread 15in (38cm). Evergreen.

Green glossy leaves and sprays of yellow flowers on long stalks in spring. As long as the soil is fertile it does not matter whether it is limy, sandy or clayey. Likes shade and will do well in town gardens. Not a particularly rapid grower. Cut back 4in (10cm) or so in January. Propagate by division.

Helleborus orientalis (Lenten rose)

Height 1ft (30cm), spread 2ft (60cm). Evergreen.

Forms a clump of deep green lobed leaves, flowering in winter and spring in colours ranging from white to plum. It needs soil with plenty of humus, but given that will be happy in either lime or clay soils. Grow in partial or heavier shade. Propagate by division.

Geranium endressii

Height 18in (45cm), spread 3ft (90cm). Deciduous.

Somewhat taller than *Geranium macrorrhizum*. Choice of pink or blue flowers. See page 128 for cultivation.

Hosta

Heights up to 20in (50cm), spread to 2ft (60cm). Deciduous.

The foliage differs in colour according to varieties – blue-grey, yellow turning to green, deep green, creamy variegated. The flowers are usually mauve or white and appear in summer. They require shade and grow better without lime. Propagate by division.

Put out more flags

Besides covering the ground with dense-growing plants there is another way of getting rid of the endless routine of digging, hoeing, mowing, sowing and staking and still having a beautiful garden. This is to pave the garden. If the area is small a totally paved garden is an excellent solution, with only a few plants to provide living relief. Paving is effective also in a large formal garden, French château style. But for those with a taste for more informal gardens, whether in town, suburbs or the country, it would be best to combine ground cover with paved areas brought to life with plants in raised beds, tubs and other containers to provide striking foliage and splashes of brilliant colour.

Earlier in the book paving has been looked at mainly from a utilitarian point of view, but at this stage it is equally important to look at it from the point of view of its effectiveness in the design of the garden. It is there because it is pleasing to look at, without having to be dug, hoed, manured and so on. In parts of the garden it can be used for solely decorative reasons – that is, it is not there even to be trodden on. This makes it possible to use materials which are unpleasant to walk on at any time and impossible when you are old, such as cobbles, pebbly gravel, or large flat pebbles from rivers and the seashore. Avoid wood; it is menacingly slippery when wet, especially if honeydew has fallen on it or algae grown on it.

Bricks have the great virtue of combining well with many other forms of paving, barring marbles and tiles. They are especially effective in relieving the monotony of concrete slabs. The simplest way is to separate the flags from each other with a single row of bricks, the broad bedding face upwards, both for effect and economy's sake.

If using bricks on their own avoid over-elaborate designs; herringbone is one of the most attractive. Avoid mixing designs if they will be seen together. Variety is achieved far better by the discreet use of different materials.

Oval *cobbles* are best set in mortar on a concrete base, 4in (10cm) deep. Use a mix of 1 part cement and 3 parts sand for the mortar, and lay it deep enough – about ¾in (1.5–2cm) – to ensure that the cobbles are bedded just below their plumpest point. Fill a bucket of water with cobbles and take one out at a time as you lay them; this is to keep them as wet as possible so that they do not draw the moisture out of the mortar. Even so, the mortar will set in something over an hour, so deal with only a small section at a time. Lay the cobbles as close as possible to each other. Three hours or so after they have been laid pour a grout (mortar watered down until it is like thick soup) between the cobbles. Before that has finally set wash down the cobbles and brush off surplus mortar.

Loose pebbles and gravel are comparatively cheap materials and easy to lay, but they are unpleasant to walk on. Lay them on a 4in (10cm) layer of hardcore, well stamped down and topped with a thin layer of sand. The gravel itself should be

Suggestions for paving. *Top :* concrete slabs surrounded by bricks.
Centre : bricks laid in herringbone pattern. *Bottom :* another suggestion for laying bricks

up to 1in (2.5cm) thick. It shifts around somewhat with any traffic on it – and often, it seems, with none – so will need raking from time to time to level it out again. The inevitable weeds can be kept down with a weedkiller.

There are many colours of gravel to choose from according to the rocks from which it comes, and there are some beautiful warm colours among them. Avoid marble chippings – graveyard gravel. Large areas of gravel can with advantage be broken up with an occasional single flagstone, or a group of three or four.

Flat pebbles are a little easier to walk on than cobbles, but that is not saying much. One of the best places to lay them is alongside a wall – where one does not walk – leaving small areas clear of them where climbers are growing. Not recommended around cordon fruit trees, which need frequent mulching.

The front garden may be the first place to start paving. Part of it may have to become the parking lot for your car or for the cars of visiting friends, or for your caravan or boat. From a practical point of view this will involve a fair amount of substantial paving on firm foundations (see pages 23–4). From an aesthetic point of view it means that great effort will be needed to make the paving (and any other features which there are room for) as attractive as possible; you may feel that cars, caravans and boats add to your status, but they do absolutely nothing for the appearance of the garden.

Two important features of the front garden – the tree and the climbing plants up the walls – will still be there (unless disaster has befallen) and increasing in size and beauty with every year. But some plant interest will need to be added near ground level if the garden is mainly covered with paving. This is best done with plants in tubs, either dramatic-looking shrubs (the so-called architectural shrubs) or brilliantly colourful annuals.

Cushion plants can be grown in gaps left in the paving (see pages 24–7). Slightly larger areas of soil can also be left unpaved so that larger plants can be grown there. Arrange these mini-beds in sizes that can easily be filled in with matching paving later when any bending down becomes too onerous.

The plants ousted from the front garden will help to furnish the back garden; the smaller herbaceous plants can go in the raised beds. This is a good time to divide those plants which can be divided, replanting the young growth and discarding the old.

Plants for tubs

In a paved garden plants in containers can be used either to provide splashes of colour or for dramatic foliage effect.

For all-the-year-round drama the obvious choice is evergreen shrubs, relying either on the colour of their leaves or on the overall shape of so-called architectural plants. For splashes of colour it is best to turn to annuals, or plants treated as annuals. Although each kind of plant will provide colour for only part of the year a succession of plants can give a long period of bloom. As a simple example, spring bulbs could be followed by pelargoniums, which flower through summer right into late autumn.

Colour splashing should be used with discretion. One fair-sized tub, say $2\frac{1}{2}$–3ft (75–90cm) across, filled with screeching red or yellow, is astonishingly effective, but two such tubs are not twice as effective, but far less so. Above all avoid a Smarties effect. If you plump for colour in a smallish front garden one good-sized container would be enough; you already have a tree there and climbers up the walls, possibly plants among the paving, and a car taking up much of the space for part of the day. However, if there is room add a container or two planted with foliage plants to give some interest when the colour container is resting.

In a large back garden there may be a fair amount of ground cover. This will provide some colour but the overall effect will be green and an additional few splashes of colour will be welcome. On the other hand you have the raised beds, and you can smother these in colour if you wish. Containers might then be used for a few striking architectural plants which would stand out against the background of ground cover. Such plants would deserve beautiful containers, which would in turn contribute to the dramatic effect.

Whatever you read your choice of containers will in the end be decided by your own taste. On aesthetic grounds there is, however, one basic rule: the more compulsive viewing the plant is the simpler the container should be. A container which is a work of art in itself needs only a modest, delicately leaved plant to furnish it: lavender, rosemary or something like that. Container and plant should never be in competition. Unfortunately, attractive containers, whether of wood, terra cotta or stone, are not cheap.

There are practical considerations also in the choice of containers. Whatever else may be said against them plastic containers have at least comparative cheapness in their favour. They can be used for plants such as ivies which will grow over the sides and eventually cover them. Choose the simplest possible shapes.

Large bowl-shaped containers do not provide enough root room for shrubs, but they look well placed on paving, planted with bright annuals – though you will have to kneel to look after them. Shallow containers also dry out quickly. Plastic and glass fibre containers are very light and are easily blown over if planted with tall shrubs.

A selection of tubs and containers

Always use a container with holes in the bottom to allow the water to drain away and so prevent the compost from turning sour. Put a layer of small stones or broken bricks at the bottom of the container and then a layer of fibrous (not fine) peat; this will stop the compost from dribbling away through the stones. Garden soil is unsuitable for containers; from garden centres you will be able to buy a compost based either on a loamy soil or on peat with added fertilizers. The loam composts are probably better for use outdoors, not least because they provide better ballast to prevent the containers from being blown over. Fill the containers to within 2in (5cm) of the rim. Each year replace a little of the top layer of the compost (carefully, to avoid damage to the roots) with new compost. Liquid fertilizer can also be applied during the growing season.

Word of warning: dogs and cats can kill the lower branches of conifers with their urine. If you choose a conifer plant it in a tub which is higher than your dog can cock its leg.

The following list of shrubs suitable for containers consists mainly of evergreens, but there are one or two deciduous shrubs, notably a fuchsia, a natural for a tub. Remember that plants grown in containers are always smaller than when grown in the open ground.

Azalea
2ft (60cm) and upwards. Spread similar. Evergreen.
Dwarf evergreen azaleas (which are a type of rhododendron) provide a gaudy

show of colour in spring. The Kurume and *Obtusum amoenum* varieties are suitable for small tubs, but the *kaempferi* and Vuyk hybrids will need slightly larger containers. Must not have limy soil. (See also rhododendrons, page 164.)

Berberis candidula 'Amstelveen'
Height 30in (75cm), spread 30in (75cm). Evergreen.
Arching branches of glossy bright green leaves, with bluish white undersides. Small yellow flowers in spring, followed by waxy blue-black berries.

Buxus sempervirens (Box)
3ft (90cm). Upright growth. Evergreen.
Can be clipped in the shape of a pyramid if you want a very formal look.

Camellia japonica and *Camellia* x *williamsii*
Height from 4ft (1.2m), spread 3ft (90cm). Evergreen.
Early-flowering (late winter, early spring) evergreen shrubs, hardier than their exotic appearance suggests. There are many cultivars with single, semi-double or double flowers. *C. japonica* cultivars are the most widely grown, but their flowers stay on the bush after they have died and turned brown, while those of *C.* x *williamsii* obligingly drop off. Camellias do well in tubs if planted in a compost of 3 parts peat, 2 parts lime-free loam and 1 part sharp sand. In hard water areas water with rain water. To prune merely shorten straggling shoots in spring. See also page 126.

Ceanothus thyrsiflorus repens
Height 3ft (90cm), spread 5ft (1.5m). Evergreen.
A dense mound of evergreen leaves smothered in pale blue flowers in late spring and early summer. Not for cold gardens, and better in sun. Cut off dead flower stalks.

Chamaecyparis lawsoniana 'Ellwood's Gold'
Height 2ft (60cm). Upright growth. Conifer.
A compact conical Lawson cypress, with a warm golden colour. Other dwarfs suitable for small tubs are *C. obtusa* 'Nana Gracilis', dark green, and *C. pisifera* 'Plumosa Aurea Compacta', more compact than its name, with soft yellow foliage.

Daphne odora 'Aureomarginata'
Height 3ft (90cm), spread 3ft (90cm). Evergreen.
Already suggested as a scented shrub for the front garden, but attractive even when not in flower because of its yellow-margined leaves. See also page 131.

Elaeagnus pungens 'Maculata'
Height 5ft (1.5m), spread 6ft (1.8m). Evergreen.
Another variegated scented shrub, but the leaves of this are yellow in the centre, not round the edges. It is a neat grower, but rather slow – no disadvantage in a container. More tolerant of draughts than most shrubs. See also page 135.

Euonymus fortunei 'Emerald and Gold'
Height 18in (45cm), spread only 18in (45cm). Evergreen.

A striking golden variegated shrub in summer, and even more interesting when the leaves turn bronze, tinged with pink, during winter. Will grow in partial shade.

Fatsia japonica

Height 5ft (1.5m), spread 5ft (1.5m). Evergreen.

There is a somewhat tropical look about this shrub with its shiny, deeply lobed leaves, which may be 1ft (30cm) across. Clusters of creamy white flowers in late autumn. Does well in shade.

Fuchsia 'Tom Thumb'

Height 2ft (60cm), spread only 2ft (60cm). Deciduous.

An outstanding dwarf fuchsia from among the most elegant shrubs there are. The flowers – a combination of violet and carmine – appear over a long period in summer.

Hebe brachysiphon

Height 5ft (1.5m), spread 4ft (1.2m). Evergreen.

A hebe which should survive in all except the coldest areas. It carries long tails of lilac-mauve flowers in summer. If you prefer white there is the more compact *H.b.* 'White Gem' (height 3ft (90cm)), which has short flower spikes from mid summer on.

Hedera helix

Trailing. Evergreen.

This is the English ivy, and a few varieties – some plain green, some variegated – planted together in a tub look most effective. They will form a mound on top of the soil and spill over the side of the container, turning it into a bush. *H.h.* 'Goldheart', though slow-growing at first, is one of the most popular variegated ivies; it has small green leaves with a golden centre on reddish stems, but it tends to lose its variegation in acid soil. There are some erect-growing cultivars, more formal-looking – *H.h.* 'Congesta', *H.h.* 'Erecta' and *H.h.* 'Ruselliannia' – with leathery leaves growing very precisely along the stiffly erect stems, diminishing in size from the base of the stem to the tip.

Hydrangea (hortensia)

Obviously, but keep well watered. (See blue flowers, page 120.)

Ilex aquifolium (Holly)

Height 6ft (1.8m), spread 3ft (90cm).

The variety 'Argentia Marginata' has broad leaves with silver margins and forms a bushy pyramid. Male and female varieties are needed to have any hope of berries; two golden hollies are frequently paired – the 'Golden Queen' (actually male) and the female 'Golden King'. Alternatively choose the green 'J.c. van Tol', a self-berrying hermaphrodite.

Juniperus

Evergreen.

A number of these conifers are suitable for growing in tubs. *Juniperus scopulorum* 'Blue Heaven' (height 5ft (1.5m), spread 3ft (90cm)), makes a neat pyramid of bluish green leaves. *Juniperus virginiana* 'Skyrocket', the well-called Pencil cedar, is a striking columnar shrub, reaching 5ft (1.5m) or more in height though it is only 1ft (30cm) wide. The foliage is bluish green. These will need medium-sized tubs.

Laurus nobilis (Bay)

5ft (1.5m). Evergreen.

The bay is one of the most effective formal shrubs for tub growing. It can be bought as a round-headed standard or as a pyramid; trimming should be done in spring, and the leaves can be dried for use in cooking. It is not entirely hardy, and one advantage of growing it in a tub is that it can be moved under cover in winter. Take care that the soil does not dry out in summer. Suitable for the seaside.

Phormium tenax

Height 4ft (1.2m), spread 2ft (60cm). Evergreen.

Clumps of tough sword-like leaves growing from the base of the plant – a notable architectural shrub. It also bears tall spikes of long-lasting dull red flowers, but these are less striking than the leaves. In the varieties *P.t.* 'Veitchii' and *P.t.* 'Variegatum' they are variegated green and cream, while in *P.t. purpureum* they are a bronzy purple.

Punica granatum 'Nana'

Height 2ft (60cm), spread 2ft (60cm). Deciduous.

This is the pomegranate, but do not expect it to fruit; it will not even survive except in the warmest areas. Even then it might be advisable to move it under cover in winter. The funnel-shaped scarlet flowers appear through summer into autumn. Not suitable for limy soils.

Rhododendron

Evergreen.

There are numerous rhododendron species and hybrids which may be grown in containers. For small tubs the choice can include the species *fastigiatum*, *glomerulatum*, *pemakoense*, *scintillans*, in shades of blue-mauve and purple, the rose-coloured *R. ferrugineum*, the Alpen rose of Switzerland, the pink *R. trichostomum,* the bright yellow *R. megeratum*, and the beautiful white *R. yakushimanum*. Hybrids for small tubs should be restricted to those sold as dwarfs – the official designation is *Pd*. For medium-sized tubs there is a choice of the species *R. glaucophyllum* with aromatic leaves and rose flowers, lemon yellow in the variety *R.g. luteiflorum*. The hybrids should be chosen from among those of medium height, designated *Pm*. They will not tolerate lime.

Rosmarinus officinalis 'Severn Sea'

Height 3ft (90cm), spread 2ft (60cm). Evergreen.

Aromatic grey-green leaves with small lilac flowers in spring. Keep it trimmed into shape. See also page 119.

Yucca filamentosa

Height 30in (75cm), spread 30in (75cm). Evergreen.

Stiff sword-like green leaves with long panicles of creamy white flowers in mid summer make this a dramatic architectural plant. It needs a sunny position and a large container; root growth is strong and capable of bursting open a too small pot.

With an eye to the future

Raised beds

Planning for the future may include building more raised beds. In a small garden, however, there should not be too many or you may feel hemmed in by them (like having too much furniture in a room). Two or three long beds look less fussy than many small beds, so if the lay-out of the garden allows it build an extension to existing beds, especially if water has been piped to them; it should be simple to extend whatever watering system you fitted in the first place.

The more the garden is given over to ground cover and paving the more raised beds will be relied on for colour. The beds need not be confined to flowers. They make excellent herb gardens, as long as you stick to plants of reasonable height – fennel, for example, would tower above you absurdly. Mint is extremely invasive, so if you include it plant it in a container, buried to soil level, so that the roots are kept under control.

The bed can also be used for certain vegetables, but avoid those which would monopolize it for a great part of the year, and stick to quick growers, perhaps concentrating on salad crops to enjoy the luxury of having them fresh. There is no reason why vegetables should not be grown with the flowers.

The success of raised bed gardening largely depends on maintaining the fertility of the soil, and this cannot be done by inorganic fertilizers alone. Year by year the raised beds should have a good share of the compost you make. It is also a good idea during this stage of the gardener's life to rejuvenate the soil in the bed by removing it and mixing in whatever humus-forming material you can lay your hands on – turf which has been removed from the diminishing lawn and rotted down, leaf mould, peat or forest bark, with the addition of a little slow-acting organic fertilizer such as bonemeal.

The raised pool

The pool may begin to give trouble, with tears appearing in the liner and cracks in the concrete. As explained on page 52, the projected lifetime of different materials varies enormously, from perhaps five to fifty years. Once they begin leaks are not easy to cure, although patching over the cracks will add a little to the pool's life (there are many proprietary preparations for whatever kind of material you used in the first place). A time comes, however, when a cheap liner has to be renewed, and it makes sound sense to replace it with a heavy-duty butyl liner, which has an estimated life of half a century. There is no need to rebuild the whole pool. Remove the topping stones surrounding the pool, empty the pool and let everything out. Then place the new liner on top of the old, in the way described on page 57. You should then have no more trouble with the structure of the pool for the rest of your life. The plants and the fish will, of course, always need regular care, and from time to time will have to be renewed. It is worthwhile keeping the pool in first-rate condition, for growing older does not dim the fascination of water.

Adapting the sandpit

Unlike the raised beds and the raised pool you are unlikely to want to retain the sandpit, as such. But it is worth keeping, if only for the investment in the bricks which form the walls and the flags which make the floor. These will be needed if you come to erect a greenhouse. In the meantime they can be put to use to make an arbor or bower – two good old-fashioned words for one good old-fashioned idea. If you prefer think of it as a patio with a pergola on top.

The floor of the sandpit was made to slope to keep in the sand and drain out the water. If you are to sit comfortably in the arbor, either for reading or eating, the floor will have to be levelled. If there is plenty of sand left so much the better. Shovel it out of the way so that you can get at the flags. Lift them out of the way. Replace the sand to get the base of the arbor level. Stamp it down and relay the flags.

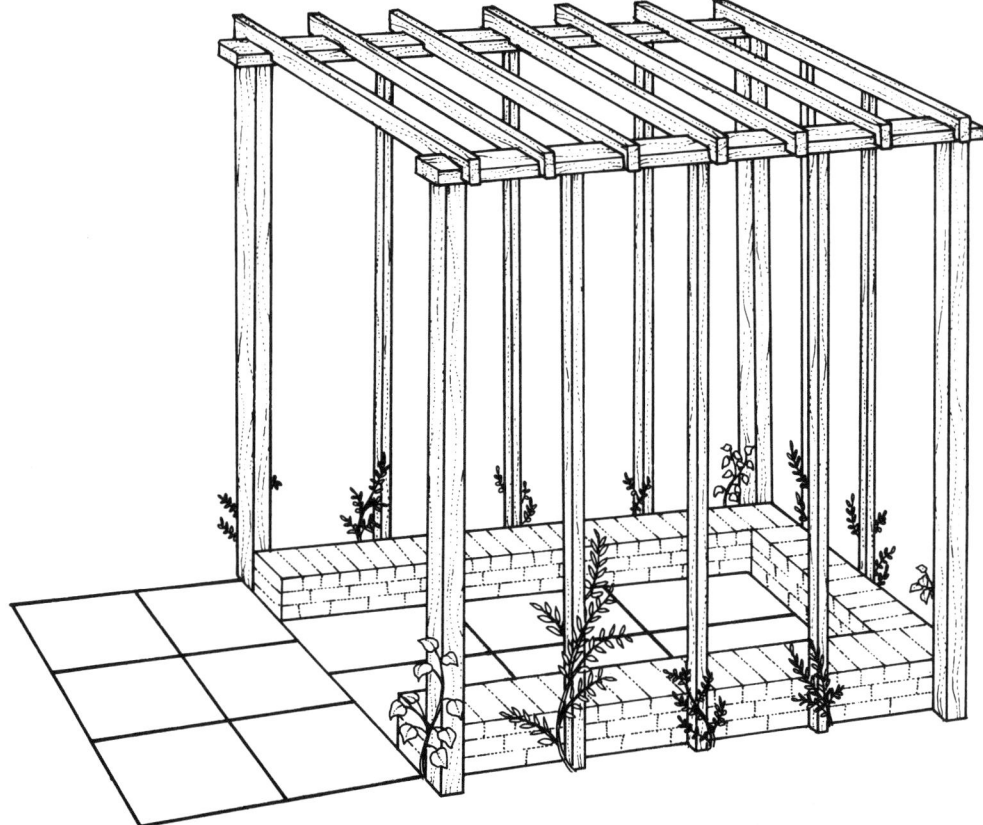

Arbor built on site of former sandpit, making use of sandpit walls

Build the pergola with wooden uprights on the outside of the ex-sandpit walls; this gives you a useful shelf inside the arbor on which to rest your drinks, plates, books or newspapers. The corner posts, 4in × 4in (10cm × 10cm), should be flush against the walls and set in concrete 1ft (30cm) deep. The intervening posts along the sides of the arbor can be set straight into the soil, as long as the timber has been treated with preservative. (If it is intended that the arbor should last a whole life-time bury these in concrete also.) How close to space the intervening posts depends on how many climbers you wish to grow around the arbor. Across the posts at each end of the arbor fix a beam, 4in × 8in (10cm × 20cm), into which are notched the rafters, 2in × 6in (5cm × 15cm), which form the roof.

A vine is very pleasant to sit under in summer, but there are other suitable climbers among those listed on pages 98–101. Here also is a chance to grow climbing or rambling roses, or sweet peas.

Finally, if you decide on a greenhouse, the site of the arbor, or ex-sandpit, can, if it is in a suitable place, be used as the site of the greenhouse. The bricks can be used for the foundations and walls, the flags for the floor of the greenhouse, the sand beneath it for making the mortar, and the timber of the pergola, if it has been regularly treated with preservative, to help build the benches for the plants.

Alternatively, if you do not want an arbor and do not intend to have a green-house, the bricks and concrete slabs can be used to extend the paved areas of the garden.

Investing in a greenhouse

To own a greenhouse is a widespread ambition, and, like many ambitions, it often seems less desirable when it has been achieved. In fact a greenhouse can quickly become a white elephant; gardens throughout the country prove it. The early enthusiasm fades when it is realized how much attention a greenhouse needs if it is to live up to your dreams. A little slackness creeps into the daily routine; the plants wilt through lack of ventilation on hot days, die from lack of water, are killed by frost or consumed by pests. In time the coveted greenhouse turns into a refuge for garden junk, which rots or rusts there when the glass gets broken and is not replaced.

My own feeling is that a young family and a greenhouse are incompatible in an average-sized garden. It will be a constant source of dissension between parents and children, and, as I argued at the start of the book, the garden should be for the children when they are young. When you come into your own again, by all means buy a greenhouse if you are certain you have the enthusiasm, patience and per-sistence to look after it. Bear in mind that while a garden can look after itself for days on end in summer, and for most of the winter, the plants in a greenhouse are totally dependent on you for their *daily* needs, even though you may enlist all kinds of automation to help you. You have to be a madly keen gardener to make a greenhouse worthwhile during your working life if you have other competing leisure interests. On the other hand, when you retire a greenhouse ceases to be time-consuming and becomes both time-filling and time-fulfilling.

Waiting until you are older before buying a greenhouse gives you the pleasure of something to look forward to and it also has several practical advantages. A greenhouse does not last forever, but one bought a few years before you retire should not need replacing. Starting late adds a new dimension to your gardening, at a time when other gardening activities may have to be reduced as they become physically exhausting.

Deciding what use you make of the greenhouse, whenever you buy it, depends in the first place on how much money you are willing to spend on heating it. Consider not only present costs but the heights to which they might rise.

A warm greenhouse with a minimum winter temperature of $55°F$ ($13°C$) would allow you to grow a wide variety of subtropical plants. But heating costs would be heavy, and probably not worthwhile since many of the plants could satisfactorily be grown as houseplants (although they would not do as well in the dry conditions indoors as they would in a humid greenhouse atmosphere).

A cool greenhouse with a minimum winter temperature of about $45°F$ ($7°C$) still leaves a choice of many plants, including the most popular greenhouse plants such as pelargoniums and fuchsias. Aiming at a winter temperature not lower than $40°F$ ($4°C$) you could build up a collection of cacti.

The best results from a totally unheated greenhouse come from growing alpines. There is nothing to beat them in a contemplative and serene old age.

If I have nowhere suggested the idea of building a rockery it is with good cause. I once worked in a garden which had a rockery covering about an acre, and trying to keep the weeds from taking over was a labour which would have made Sisyphus wish himself back in hell, endlessly rolling that stone up the hill. To build a convincing-looking rockery is both laborious and expensive, and when built it would look out of scale in an average garden. On the other hand, a small mound of earth broken up with a few stones is utterly absurd. Further, the British climate, with its generally mild, moist winters, is not the weather in which alpine plants grow in their native mountains, and the soil is usually not free-draining enough, with the result that the plants rot. In any case, to appreciate fully the splendour of these small flowers they must be far nearer eye level than the ground.

An alpine house largely solves these problems, an alpine house being merely a more thoroughly ventilated cold greenhouse. There the alpine plants can be kept cool in winter, but protected from the deadly rain, and in summer they can bake in the sun. An alternative is to give over one or more of the raised beds to growing alpines, covering them in winter with a glass frame – a kind of mini greenhouse – which can be removed in summer. Of course, with a frame you miss the great advantage of a greenhouse – that you too can get out of the wet.

Alpines grown in pots in a greenhouse can be given the individual attention they need: the right size of pot, the right soil, the right feeding, the right watering, for that particular plant. This can take up a lot of your time without demanding much physical work. This is exactly the kind of activity one needs at this time of life, absorbing without being exhausting. Even when there is no work to be done among

Alpine house, with windows opening along its whole length to give adequate ventilation

the plants there is plenty to look at, even at those times of the year when the garden itself is at its most inhospitable. (Remember to wrap up well.)

Having waited for a greenhouse buy the largest that the garden can accommodate and you can afford. It should certainly not be less than 8ft (2.4m) wide and 12ft (3.7m) long. True alpine houses have windows which open along the whole length of the greenhouse on both sides to ensure adequate ventilation. That does not prevent you from using part of such a house for other plants. If it is longer than 12ft (3.7m) it can sensibly be divided by a partition. One part might be heated in winter, with more limited ventilation, but with the benefit of far better ventilation in the height of summer than is usually possible in conventional greenhouses.

In an undivided house room can be found in one corner for an electric propagator if you wish to raise your own plants; it costs far less to heat a propagator than a whole greenhouse. Choose one of a decent size which is thermostatically controlled.

In my lifetime there have been dramatic changes in the design and equipment of greenhouses, and in the lifetime of your garden there will be many more. Some of today's seemingly advanced automation may within a decade seem primitive. But whatever happens to the greenhouse of the future there are some unchanging basic facts to be taken into account in siting and equipping a greenhouse.

Choosing a greenhouse

There is a bewildering choice of designs. Once all greenhouses were made of wood; many still are, but more now have an aluminium framework, which has the great advantage of letting in more light – as well as not needing regular painting. Greenhouses glazed right down to the ground let in far more light than those built on a brick base (usually between 2 and 3 feet (60–90cm) high. This is important if you intend to grow plants at floor level (e.g. tomatoes), but there is no gain if all the plants are to be grown in pots on a staging – as in an alpine house. A greenhouse which is part brick is somewhat warmer. (This is where the bricks which started off as the sandpit might now find a home.)

Whichever type of greenhouse you choose there must be plenty of windows which will open, even though this puts up the cost. Greenhouses are heat traps. This is a good thing in cold weather, but in hot weather it can make them death traps. Short-wave rays from the sun pass through the glass and warm the soil and other surfaces inside. When reflected from them the short waves become long waves and these do not pass back through the glass to the outside. Hence the temperature rises in the greenhouse. In winter the difference between outside and inside may be only a few welcome degrees, but in summer the temperature inside may rise so much that the plants wilt in the heat and even die. Hence the importance of choosing a greenhouse which can be adequately ventilated.

Siting

The greenhouse must be sited so that it gets the best possible light in the dark months of the year. It must not be erected in the shade of the house or under trees. A greenhouse which is sited east to west makes the most of what winter sunlight there is. Only some of the sun which falls on a greenhouse actually enters it; some is reflected from the glass – how much depends on the angle at which the sun's rays fall on the glass. In winter when the sun is low in the sky less than half the available sunlight enters a greenhouse which is sited from north to south. If instead it is sited from east to west about a quarter more sunlight gets through the glass.

Servicing

It is essential to have water laid on.

It is sensible to have electricity laid on, even to a cold greenhouse. It can be used for an electric propagator for raising your own seeds and cuttings (a money saver), and for all the equipment you may eventually feel you must have to cut out as much labour as possible. Gas may be worth laying on for warm greenhouse heating if running costs would make it economic.

Equipping the greenhouse

You can easily spend a fortune on labour-saving equipment, but even if you have a fortune there are priorities. The first is ensuring proper ventilation. Without automatic control of opening and closing of windows you can spend your summer days trundling up and down the garden path to do the job by hand, or risk damage to your plants. Automatic ventilators open the windows when the temperature inside the greenhouse rises above the level you have set, and closes them when the temperature falls. Some need electricity to operate them but others do not. Similarly there are electrically controlled blinds which operate automatically to shade the plants from too fierce sunlight.

There is a wide variety of automatic watering devices, the simplest using capillary action. The pots stand on a moist base and draw up water from below, a controlled supply of water being fed from a tank. The snag is that the system ignores the fact that different plants vary in the amount of water they need. To take account of that no better system has yet been devised than watering each pot by hand, so ensuring that each plant is treated as the individual it is. This is especially important if you are growing a mixed lot of plants, as in an alpine house.

A thermostatically controlled electric propagator for raising seeds and cuttings is a good investment. Even for a cold greenhouse an electric tubular or fan heater, thermostatically controlled, could be bought as an insurance against bitterly cold weather, merely to avoid the plants being killed by frost.

The dedicated greenhouse owner can easily find other gadgets to spend his money on, but the one that should be at the top of any list is one of the cheapest: a maximum and minimum thermometer.

Making a hobby of alpines

The first thing before starting greenhouse gardening is to read a book about it – indeed several books, since I know of no one book which answers all the questions you need answering. Even if you settle, as I suggest, for an alpine house, there is a lot to be learned about alpine plants – though you may be an experienced gardener in other ways. There is no lack of books on alpines to help you. Ask in your local library.

If you intend to develop alpine gardening as a hobby, and have plenty of time to devote to it, there is little point in growing only those plants which will easily succeed out of doors. Happily, there are many beautiful alpines which will be a challenge, although a cold greenhouse will make them less of a challenge.

In drawing up the following list of alpines the temptation – which had to be resisted – was to include too many of the thousands available. Most of those chosen are species rather difficult to grow out of doors, though there are exceptions.

The major appeal of alpines is in their flowers; when they are not in flower most of them are not impressive. Even though the herbaceous perennials among them may die down altogether this is no great matter because it is possible to have something in flower from winter through to autumn.

The following are listed, as far as one can, in order of flowering. Easily grown small bulbs suitable for an alpine house either in spring or autumn are listed separately. Space allows only the briefest of descriptions, but many are illustrated in colour in *The Dictionary of Garden Plants* (by Roy Hay and Patrick M. Synge, published by Ebury Press and Michael Joseph), and detailed instructions for cultivation will be found in specialist alpine books.

Corydalis ambigua yedoensis
  8in (20cm). Winter to early spring.
  Spikes of tubular pale turquoise flowers and fern-like leaves. Stunning but temperamental.

Saxifraga x *jenkinsae*
  1½in (4cm). Winter to early spring.
  There are many saxifrages, but this is one of the best of the Kabschia hybrids. The plant forms a hummocky mat of silvery rosettes which is smothered early in the year with small flowers of the palest pink.

Soldanella montana
  6in (15cm). Late winter, early spring.
  Downward-hanging, starry, violet-coloured flowers in small clusters on erect stems above a flat clump of cyclamen-type leaves. *S. pusilla* (3in (7.5cm)), the Dwarf snowball, carries dainty white bell flowers in late spring to early summer.

Dionysia aretioides
2½in (6cm). Early spring.
Extremely attractive cushion plant with clear yellow primula-like flowers. Do not water from above. The dionysias are certainly not the easiest plants to grow but this is the least difficult species.

Draba rigida
2½in (6cm). Early spring.
A neat tufted plant with heads of golden yellow flowers on slender stems. Do not water from above.

Androsace pyrenaica
1in (2.5cm). Early to late spring.
Forms a cushion of narrow leaves and tiny white primrose-like flowers. Needs good drainage; do not water from above.

Gentiana verna
4in (10cm). Spring.
You can have gentians in flower in spring, summer and autumn. The spring-flowering ones include the Spring gentian, one of the best of alpines, in royal blue, as well as other shades, and white; and *Gentiana acaulis* (4in (10cm)), the Bell gentian, with rich deep blue flowers. However, *G. acaulis* is mysteriously unpredictable about where it will flower and where it will not.

Pleione formosana and *P. limprichtii*
4in (10cm). Spring.
Two magnificent dwarf orchids. *P. formosana* is a delicate pink with a cream frilly lip, brown spots and a yellow throat. 'Alba' is a white form. *P. limprichtii* has bright cerise-pink flowers, with a lip marked with orange and red.

Primula allionii
4in (10cm). Spring.
Dense hummocks are smothered by the flowers, in many shades of pink with a white centre. This is only one of the many suitable primulas, among them *P. auricula*, particularly the yellow hybrids.

Pulsatilla vernalis (Spring anemone)
6in (15cm). Spring.
White cup-shaped flowers up to 2in (5cm) across with a prominent yellow boss of stamens. The underside of the petals has green, pink or purple shading.

Weldenia candida
4in (10cm). Spring.
Exotic-looking white flowers, with three large petals and bright yellow stamens, standing erect above a rosette of glossy leaves.

Ranunculus amplexicaulis
1ft (30cm). Mid to late spring.
Large white buttercup-shaped flowers with yellow centre, two or more to a stem.

Asperula suberosa
   3in (7.5cm). Spring to early summer.
   A mat of hairy silvery leaves with tubular pink flowers opening into stars.

Dryas octopetala
   8in (20cm). Spring to early summer.
   Prostrate shrub with 1½in (4cm) flowers, white with a boss of golden stamens, similar to those of a dog-rose.

Geranium napuligerum
   6in (15cm). Spring to early summer.
   Typical five-petalled geranium flower on a tuft of deeply cut leaves. The colour is lilac pink.

Viola papillonacea
   4in (10cm). Spring to early summer.
   A white 'violet'-type viola, but there are many others. 'Pansy'-type violas include *V. tricolor*, in a wide variety of colours.

Lewisia tweedyi
   8in (20cm). Spring to summer.
   Long-lasting clump of pale apricot or pale pink flowers ('Rosea'), about 2in (5cm) across, with many narrow petals. Outstanding, but difficult because it is so troubled by damp.

Cassiope x 'Bearsden'
   6in (15cm). Late spring to early summer.
   Forms a hummock of dense small leaves covered in small pure white hanging bells. Needs acid peat soil and some shade.

Campanula
   3in (7.5cm). Late spring to early summer.
   Campanulas are a must for the alpine house. *C. cochlearifolia*, one of the most popular, has bell-shaped flowers on slender stems, pale blue or white in 'Alba'. *C. allionii*, with 1½in (4cm) bell flowers, in grey-blue or violet, is trickier. A lime-hater. *C. raineri* is rare and beautiful, with large light blue open bells, facing skywards.

Dianthus alpinus
   2½in (6cm). Late spring, early summer.
   Cushion of small leaves and 1in (2.5cm) flowers, pink spotted with crimson – but only one of many to choose from.

Edraianthus pumilio
   2in (5cm). Late spring, early summer.
   The flowers are striking, both in colour and shape – violet, with open, upward-facing bells with the ends of the petals curved back. They are so profuse that they are likely to cover the cushion of grey-green leaves. *E. serpyllifolius* 'Major' has large rich purple flowers.

Oxalis laciniata
2½in (6cm). Late spring to early summer.
Cup-shaped flowers, 1½in (4cm) across, in variable colours from pink to deep lilac with darker coloured veins.

Phlox nana
6in (15cm). Late spring to early summer.
There are many suitable phlox but this is one of the most desirable. The dainty star-like flowers, shell pink with a white eye, are carried in small clusters.

Leontopodium alpinum (Edelweiss)
6in (15cm). Late spring to summer.
The leaves are grey-green and woolly, the silvery white bracts are star-shaped and look as though they have been made of flannel, and within them are small heads of tiny yellowish flowers.

Roscoea cautleoides
15in (38cm). Late spring to summer.
Pale sulphur-yellow orchid-type flowers. *R. humeana* (8in (20cm)), flowering from summer to early autumn, is an unusual pale purple.

Saponaria ocymoides 'Rubra Compacta'
3in (7.5cm). Early summer.
Mat of narrow leaves covered with star-like deep pink flowers.

Sisyrinchium bermudiana
10in (25cm). Early summer.
Clumps of iris-like leaves and starry violet flowers with yellow centres.

Convolvulus mauritanicus
8in (20cm). Early summer to early autumn.
Long-flowering sprawling plant with small clear violet flowers of typical convolvulus shape.

Leucogenes leontopodium
4in (10cm). Summer.
A mat of silver-leaved rosettes with 1in (2.5cm) clusters of small silvery white flowers.

Campanula zoysii
3in (7.5cm). Summer to early autumn.
A campanula with untypical flask-shaped blue flowers. Also attractive to slugs.

Gentiana septemfida
10in (25cm). Late summer.
This is an easy gentian to grow, providing rich blue flowers in clusters towards the end of the summer. It tolerates lime. *G. farreri* (2½in (6cm)) is another late-flowering species, continuing until mid autumn. The wide-mouthed, funnel-shaped flowers are an unusual Cambridge blue.

Alpine bulbs

The small spring bulbs make a brilliant show in the alpine house very early in the year. Not only do they flower rather earlier than those outside, but they do not get battered about by the weather. And they can be enjoyed in comfort.

In recent years these small bulbs have become more popular and more readily available; many catalogues are full of them. Here are a few ideas:

Galanthus (snowdrop), early spring: *G. elwesii, G. ikariae latifolius, G. plicatus* 'Warham'. See also page 132.

Crocus: *C. ancyrensis,* 2in (5cm), deep orange yellow, and *C. laevigatus fontenayi,* 4in (10cm), soft violet (both mid winter); *C. minimus,* 3in (7.5cm), light violet with purple lines outside, *C. stellaris,* 2in (5cm), deep orange with black lines on the outside, and *C. versicolor pictoratus,* 3in (7.5cm), white with violet stripes on the outside, all flower in late spring.

Narcissus: *N. bulbocodium monophyllus,* 3in (7.5cm), white hoop petticoat, mid winter; *N.b. vulgaris nivalis,* 3in (7.5cm), yellow hoop petticoat, mid winter; *N. cyclamineus,* 5in (12.5cm), yellow long trumpet, petals swept back, early spring; *N. triandrus albus* (Angel's tears), 4in (10cm), creamy white nodding flowers, several to a stem, early spring.

Tulips: *Tulipa pulchella humilis,* 5in (12.5cm), violet-pink with yellow centre, late winter; *T. biflora,* 6in (15cm), two or three small white flowers on one stem, early spring; *T. hageri,* 7in (18cm), red flowers with black and yellow centre, spring; *T. tarda,* 4in (10cm), white with yellow eye, several flowers from each bulb, spring; *T. urumiensis,* 5in (12.5cm), golden yellow, three or more flowers to each stem, spring.

Iris: *Iris vartanii alba,* 4in (10cm), white flowers smelling of almonds, mid winter; *I. danfordiae,* 5in (12.5cm), deep vivid yellow, mid winter; *I. reticulata* 'Harmony', 6in (15cm), sky-blue, late winter; *I.r.* 'J.S. Dijt', 6in (15cm), scented maroon flowers, late winter; *I.r.* 'Violet Beauty', 6in (15cm), violet with orange mark, late winter.

Cyclamen: *C.coum* (or *atkinsii*), 4in (10cm), pink or white, mid winter to mid spring; *C. pseudibericum,* 6in (15cm), crimson carmine, late winter to mid spring; *C. persicum,* 6in (15cm), white or pink, spring; *C. repandum,* 6in (15cm), pink, late spring.

Other small spring-flowering bulbs include:

Chionodoxa (Glory of the snow), 4in (10cm), blues and pinks, winter. See also page 121.

Fritillaria meleagris, 4in (10cm), in many shades, spring.

Ipheion uniflorum, 6in (15cm), white, tinged blue, early spring. See also page 117.

Leucojum vernum (Spring snowflake), 10in (25cm), white, early spring. See also page 117.

Muscari (Grape hyacinth), 6in (15cm), blues or white, spring. See also pages 121 and 117.

Scilla tubergeniana, 4in (10cm), silvery blue, late winter, and *S. bifolia*, 4in (10cm), gentian blue, late winter to early spring.

There are some magnificent small bulbs for autumn flowering. The colchicums in early autumn are followed by the autumn-flowering crocus, which takes us round to the earliest spring crocuses. *Sternbergia lutea*, 6in (15cm), has brilliant yellow crocus-like flowers from mid to late autumn, and is more likely to succeed in the alpine house than outdoors. There is an autumn-flowering Snowflake *(Leucojum autumnale)*, 6in (15cm), and several autumn-flowering cyclamen: *C. cilicium*, 3in (7.5cm), shell pink; *C. cyprium*, 4in (10cm), pink or white and scented; and *C. neapolitanum,* 4in (10cm), pink, or *C.n. album,* the white version, both with particularly beautiful leaves.

The garden in old age

Reducing the drudgery

When you were very young you probably, and naturally, felt resentful because you were not strong enough to do things which older people could do easily. When you are older you should have more sense than to feel resentful that you cannot do the things which younger people can. Eventually all of us have to come to terms with the fact that much of the physical activity involved in gardening has ceased to be a source of satisfaction or pleasure and has become an impossible burden.

On the other hand there is no reason to imagine yourself into the role of doddering old man or frail old lady. Gardening does not have to stop; you merely adjust it to the limit of your physical capacity, but never beyond it.

If your garden has evolved as suggested you will be largely prepared for this stage of diminished physical activity. But unless you have rooted up all your plants and covered the soil with a thick layer of concrete even the most labour-saving garden needs some looking after. Little though it is it may be more than you can manage. Stiff joints and an aching back make bending down difficult and painful; a touch of arthritis may weaken your grip.

There is an increasing number of physical aids to help at this stage. While laying more paving, the use of ground cover and the practice of mulching will have reduced the amount of digging to a minimum, there are times when a spade may still have to be used, e.g. for replanting. A pedal-operated spade saves bending and the strain of lifting a spadeful of soil. The labour of forking is reduced by using a light border fork (once regarded as a lady's fork) with a handle grip fixed to the shaft. There are lightweight hoes with well-designed handles to lessen the misery of weeding. Hand trowels and forks fitted with long handles are the tools to choose for raised beds and containers. Simple grabs cut out the need for bending to pick up leaves or rubbish. The conventional wheelbarrow which feels as though it is pulling your arms out of their sockets should be replaced by a lightweight two-wheeled barrow – a garden version of the ubiquitous shopping basket on wheels. As kneeling becomes more difficult – and undesirable – there are contraptions to make it far easier to kneel when it is absolutely necessary.

Whatever aids you use, at this stage of your gardening life it is more than ever important to use your body as efficiently as possible. Above all, stop whatever job you are doing *before* you feel tired. That way you won't jib at starting it next time.

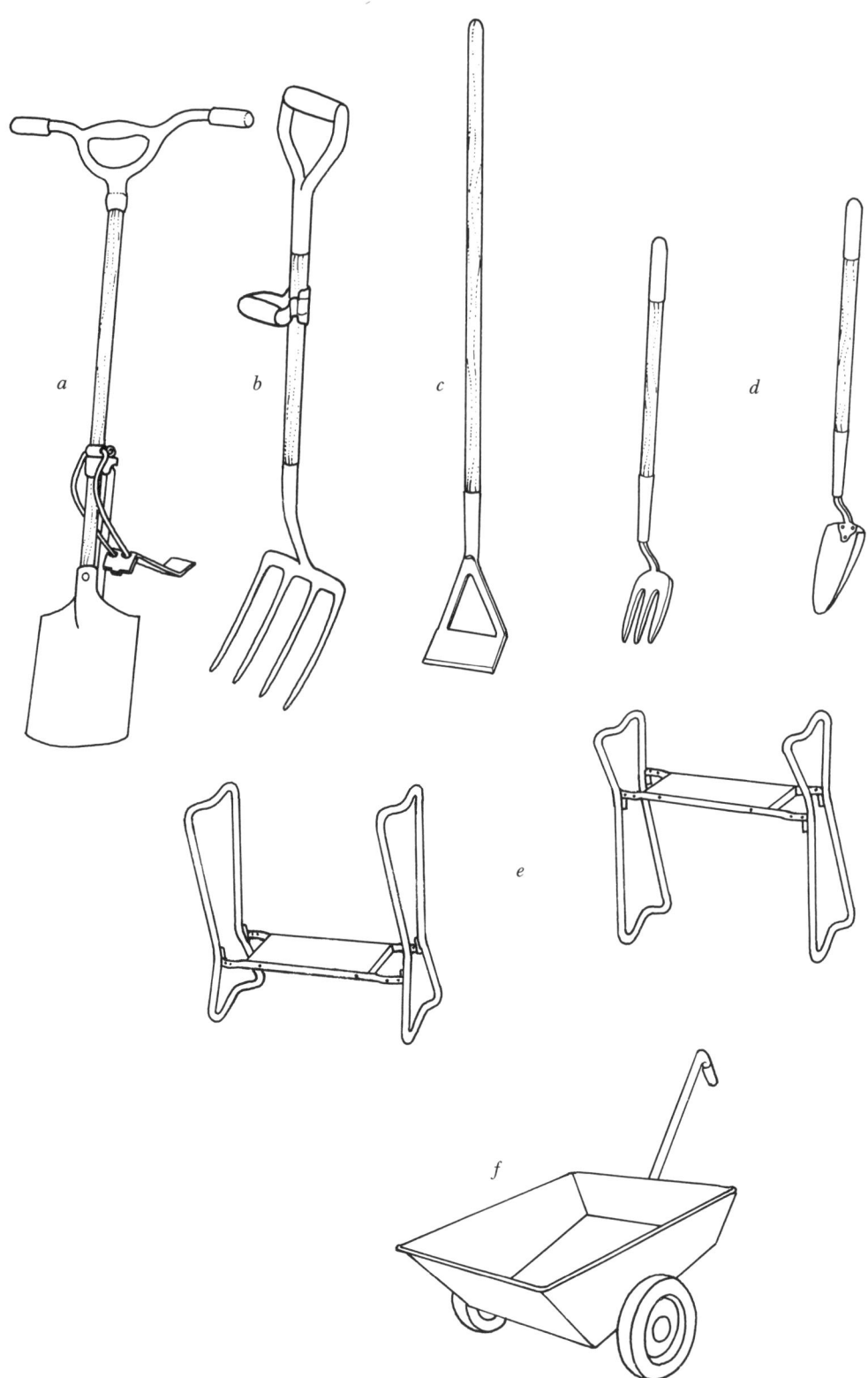

Aids for the elderly. a. pedal-operated spade. b. fork with extra handle grip.
c. lightweight hoe. d. long-handled fork and trowel. e. kneeling aids. f. two-wheeled
barrow

Sitting comfortably

One of the problems the keen gardener has to face when growing older is how to get out of the way of thinking that when you are out in the garden you ought to be *doing* something. Once that might have been necessary to keep the garden under control, but by now you have developed the garden so that there is less to do. There is a chance to enjoy positive idling.

Idling out of doors in pleasant weather is far more enjoyable than doing it indoors. In particular the verandah of your summerhouse is an excellent place for loafing. There, sheltered from the hot sun, sitting comfortably with an unopened book on your knees, you can revel in the attractive garden you have created around you and drop off.

One important ingredient in this idyllic scene is a comfortable chair. This rules out a deck chair – no deck chair has yet been invented which is comfortable to sit in and easy to get out of. A kitchen chair may be easy to stand up from, but for sitting on cannot be endured for long.

What is needed is a well-designed chair which will provide good support for your body, especially your spine. This means that it should be upholstered fairly firmly on the seat and on the back, with padding extended over the front edge of the seat to avoid pressure against the back of your leg, which can hinder circulation. If you want to put your legs up it is far better to have a separate padded stool (on casters) than a chair fitted with a leg extension – these are almost as difficult to get out of as a deck chair. The chair should have seat and arms both at the right height to allow you to lever yourself up easily. If you have difficulty there are spring-operated seats which can be used on many chairs to help you up and down.

Such a chair should be regarded as an essential item of garden equipment at this stage. If it is stored in the summerhouse protect it during the winter under polythene sheeting.

Gardening indoors

For people who must have some gardening to *do* indoor gardening is a good outlet; think of all those who have never had a garden in their life for whom indoor plants are the only solace. With indoor gardening you can control exactly how much time and energy you are going to give to it. Obviously sixty plants scattered all over the house will take up more time than six in one room – and it will be far more than ten times as much. Furthermore, some kinds of plants will need more attention, or more constant attention, than others. Some will need repotting each year, others can stay in the same pot for years. Indoor gardening can occupy a lot of your time if you grow plants from seed or take cuttings. With a propagator you can raise even exotic plants. On the other hand you can cut work to a minimum by growing plants hydroponically: plants are grown in a solution of minerals instead of compost, and the main attention involved is in adding more water every few weeks and more minerals once a year. Or you can grow small plants in a bottle or enclosed case – a so-called terrarium – and after the fiddly job of planting them they can be left to themselves for long periods since they water themselves with the water given off through their leaves and condensed on the side of the bottle. All you will have to do is to remove dead leaves or cut back too vigorously growing plants.

There are hundreds of books on indoor gardening (including mine), and there will doubtless be thousands more as long as the interest in indoor plants lasts. The only advice for which there is room here is to swot up a little before starting indoor gardening and never, ever, to buy a plant on impulse unless you have some idea about the conditions and care it needs. Experience gained from a standing start of total ignorance is both frustrating and costly.

There are other pottering forms of gardening – window boxes, tubs on balconies, miniature gardens indoors and out – and there is no lack of literature about these either.

They are all second best to 'real' gardening. However, if you have adjusted your outdoor garden so that the demands it makes can be kept in balance with your energy there is no doubt that you will spend as much time as you can out of doors – or in the greenhouse – rather than indoors.

Epilogue

It is unfashionable to talk about death, but the simple fact is that our garden will outlive us. Then a new generation will take it over. If you have planned and built well they can in part carry on from where you left off. Some things they may have to renew – the summerhouse, for example, may be showing signs of wear. Other things they will have to change – perhaps bringing back the sandpit and other paraphernalia for a still younger generation.

Some people might find it appropriate for their ashes to be scattered over part of the garden, as a final useful contribution. If you prefer conventional burial a pleasing gesture would be for your children or friends to plant your grave with some of the plants from your own garden, either by division or cuttings. The obvious choice would be the easy-care ground cover plants you grew to make life easier for you. They should be evergreen, low-growing and not so aggressive that they would take up far more room than that allotted to you. Here are a few suggestions to guide your successors.

Waldsteinia ternata
    4in (10cm). Evergreen herbaceous carpeter.
    Forms a thick mat of dark green leaves, and in spring produces a mass of flowers like those of the strawberry, but bright yellow. It will grow in dry or moist soil if well drained, and in sun or shade. Propagate by division.

Hypericum rhodopeum
    3–6in (7.5–15cm). Evergreen herbaceous carpeter.
    This is a dwarf St John's wort; it grows better in sun, but tolerates shade. The leaves are a downy grey-green and the rich yellow flowers appear in early summer. Propagate by division or cuttings.

Juniperus procumbens 'Nana'
    5in (12.5cm). Coniferous carpeter.
    The densely growing leaves are a lighter green than most junipers. It can be planted in sun or partial shade. Not a particularly rapid grower, but long-lived.

Gaultheria procumbens (Spicy wintergreen, Winter berry, Checkerberry)
    6in (15cm). Evergreen creeping shrub.
    The leaves are dark green, leathery and aromatic. The tiny bell-like flowers, white tinged with pink, appear in late summer, followed by red berries. See page 148 for cultivation.

Cotoneaster microphyllus cochleatus
    8in (20cm). Evergreen carpet shrub.
    The small, densely growing leaves are deep green. The tiny white flowers, which appear in spring, are followed by sizeable red berries. Propagate by cuttings.

Hedera 'Feastii' or 'Sagittifolia'

8in (20cm). Evergreen carpeting shrubs, rooting as they go.

These small-leaved forms of the common ivy will do well in sun or shade if the position is not too exposed. Both have dark green deeply cut leaves, but there is also a variegated version of 'Sagittifolia'. There are problems, however, with even dwarf ivies, for they are likely to creep up and hide the headstone.

Pachysandra terminalis

About 8in (20cm). Evergreen spreading shrub.

The dark green leaves grow in rosettes and from the centre of these small yellowy white scented flowers appear in spring. *P.t.* 'Variegata' has leaves with white margins and is somewhat, and desirably, less vigorous. See page 149 for cultivation.

Buxus sempervirens 'Suffruticosa'

Up to 2ft (60cm). Evergreen shrub.

This is a dwarf form of the common box and especially appropriate for grave-yards because it was once widely used for funeral sprays. In other ways there is much to be said for it. It will grow in sun and partial shade and will withstand wind. *B.s.* 'Suffruticosa' can be clipped like other box, but if left to itself slowly grows into a more loosely formed bush. Box has been known to survive for several centuries, so something of your beloved garden could long survive as a living memorial.

Index

Abelia x *grandiflora*, 103; *A. schumannii*, 103
Abeliophyllum distichum, 115
Acaena buchananii, 153
Acantholimon glumaceum, 27
Acer palmatum (Japanese maple), 107; 'Dissectum', 107; *A. septemlobum* 'Osakazuki', 107
Achillea filipendulina, 113; 'Coronation Gold', 113
Aconitum carmichaelii (Monkshood), 122
Acorus calamus 'Variegatus', 64
Actinidia kolomikta, 100
Adiantum pedatum, 137; *A. capillus-veneris*, 137; *A. venustum*, 137
Aesculus parviflora, 129–30
Agapanthus campanulatus, 123; 'Isis', 123; Headbourne hybrids, 123
Ajuga reptans, 122; 'Atropurpurea', 122; 'Multicolor', 122; 'Variegata', 122
Alchemilla mollis, 155
Allium moly, 113
Alpine house, 168–70
Alpines, 168–70, 172–7; bulbs, 176–7
Alyssum maritimum, 135; *A. saxatile*, 112
Amelanchier lamarckii (or *A. canadensis*), 130
Anchusa azurea, 121; 'Loddon Royalist', 121; 'Opal', 121
Androsace pyrenaica, 173
Anemone blanda, 117; 'White Splendour', 117; *A. fulgens*, 124; *A. japonica* 'Alba' (Japanese anemone), 119; *A. nemorosa*, 117
Annuals, climbing, 105; for tubs, 159, 160
Anthemis cupaniana, 118; *A. tinctoria* (Ox-eye chamomile), 113; 'Perry's Variety', 113
Aponogeton distachyus, 63
Apples, 103
Arabis albida 'Flore Pleno', 154
Arbor, 166–7
Aristolochia macrophylla, 99
Armeria caespitosa (Thrift), 24; 'Bevan's Variety', 24
Asarum europaeum, 154
Asperula odorata, 154; *A. suberosa*, 174
Asphalt, 20
Asplenium scolopendrium (or *Phyllitis scolopendrium*), 137
Athyrium filix-femina, 137
Aubretia deltoidea, 24, 154

Aucuba japonica, 152
Autumn colour, 129–30
Azalea, 124, 161–2; *Rhododendron* 'Addy Wery', 124; 'Satan', 124; 'Vuyk's Rosey Red', 124; 'Vuyk's Scarlet', 124; for tubs, 162
Azara microphylla, 132

Barrier shrubs, 71, 79–81
Bay, see *Laurus nobilis*
Bees, 139–40
Berberis candidula 'Amstelveen', 162; *Berberis darwinii*, 80; *B. thunbergii* 'Atropurpurea', 130; *B. wilsoniae*, 80; *B.* x *stenophylla*, 132
Bergamot, see *Monarda didyma*
Bergenia cordifolia, 155–6
Betula pendula 'Dalecarlica' (Silver birch), 106; 'Fastigiata', 106
Blackberries, 104
Blackcurrants, 103
Blechnum spicant, 137
Blue shrubs, 119–20; bulbs and perennials, 121–3
Botomus umbellatus, 65
Bower, see Arbor
Brick-laying, 43–8; mortar, 43; tools, 43; stretcher bond, 44; foundations, 45–6; building wall, 46–8; pointing, 47–8; garden wall bond, 55–6
Brick paviors, 21
Bricks, 42; for paving, 20, 21, 157–8; for raised beds, 42; for raised pool, 54
Brompton stocks, 133
Brunnera macrophylla, 155
Bulbs, 107, 160; yellow, 111–15; white, 117–19; blue, 121–3; red, 124–5; pink, 128–9; alpine, 176–7
Butterflies, 140
Buxus sempervirens (Box), 162; 'Suffruticosa', 184

Calla palustris, 64
Callicarpa bodinieri 'Profusion', 130
Calluna vulgaris (Ling), 127–8, 150; 'Alba Plena', 150; 'County Wicklow', 127–8; 'H.E. Beale', 128; 'J.H. Hamilton', 128; 'Peter Sparkes', 128

Caltha palustris, 64; *C.p. alba*, 64; *C.p. plena*, 64
Camassia quamash, 122
Camellia, 126; 'Gloire de Nantes', 126; 'Lady Clare', 126; *C. japonica*, 162; *C. x williamsii*, 162
Campanula allionii, 174; *C. cochlearifolia*, 26, 174; 'Alba', 174; *C. portenschlagiana*, 26, 154; *C. raineri*, 174; *C. zoysii*, 175
Campsis grandiflora (C. chinensis), 99; *C. radicans*, 98, 99
Carpenteria californica, 116
Caryopteris x clandonensis, 120
Cassiope x 'Bearsden', 174
Catmint, see *Nepeta x faassenii*
Cats, 87, 88–90; kittens, 89, 90; neutering, 89; in the garden, 89–90
Ceanothus, 119; *C. arboreus* 'Trewithen Blue', 120; *C. impressus* 'Puget Blue', 103, 119; *C. thyrsiflorus*, 119–20; *C.t. repens*, 162
Cerastium tomentosum, 155
Ceratophyllum demersum, 61
Ceterach officinarum, 137–8
Chaenomeles, 123; 'Firedance', 123; 'Knaphill Scarlet', 123; 'Rowallane', 123; *C. japonica*, 80, 123; 'Crimson and Gold', 80; *C. speciosa*, 103; 'Nivalis', 103
Chair, for garden, 181
Chamaecyparis lawsoniana 'Ellwood's Gold', 162; *C. obtusa* 'Nana Gracilis', 162; *C. pisifera* 'Plumosa Aurea Compacta', 162
Cherry, flowering, 107
Children, 70–71, 92; stages of development, 72–6; own garden, 90–92
Chimonanthus praecox, 110, 131
Chionodoxa, 176; *C. luciliae*, 121; *C. sardensis*, 121
Choisya ternata, 116, 133, 152
Cistus 'Silver Pink', 127; *C. x cyprius*, 116
Clematis, 99, 102; *C. armandii* 'Apple Blossom', 99; 'Snowdrift', 99; *C. flammula*, 99; *C. macropetala* 'Markham's Pink', 99; 'White Moth', 99; *C. montana*, 101, 135; 'Elizabeth', 101; *C.m. grandiflora*, 99; *C.m. rubens*, 99; *C. orientalis*, 99
Clerodendron bungei, 127; *C. trichotomum*, 106
Clethra alnifolia, 80
Climbing plants, 96–101; support for, 97; self-clinging, for south- or west-facing walls, 98; needing support, for south- or west-facing walls, 98–100; self-clinging, for north- or east-facing walls, 100–101; needing support, for north- or east-facing walls, 101; annuals, 105, 167
Cobbles, 20, 157
Compost, 17–19, 32, 88, 165

Compost bin, 17, 18
Concrete, 43; for paving, 20; for raised beds, 42
Concrete slabs or flags, for paving, 20, 21, 157–8; for raised beds, 42, 49–50
Conifers, 106
Containers, see Tubs and Window boxes
Convolvulus mauritanicus, 175
Cordon fruit trees, 102, 103–5, 159
Coreopsis verticillata 'Grandiflora', 114
Cornus alba, 80; 'Sibirica', 80; *C. canadensis*, 148
Corydalis ambigua yedoensis, 172
Cotinus americanus, 130
Cotoneaster conspicuus, 80; 'Decorus', 80; *C. dammeri*, 148; *C. horizontalis*, 103; *C. microphyllus cochleatus*, 183
Cotula squalida, 26
Crazy paving, 20
Creeping grass, 33; *Agrostus stolonifera*, 39
Crinum x powellii 'Album', 118
Crocosmia x crocosmiiflora (Montbretia), 114; 'Citronella', 114; 'Star of the East', 114
Crocus, 112; *C. ancyrensis*, 112, 176; *C. aureus*, 112; *C. chrysanthus* 'E.A. Bowles', 112; *C. laevigatus fontenayi*, 176; *C. minimus*, 176; *C. stellaris*, 176; *C. vernus*, 112; *C. versicolor pictoratus*, 176
Crown imperial, see *Fritillaria imperialis* 'Lutea Maxima'
Cryptogramma crispa, 138
Currant, flowering, see *Ribes*
Currants, red and white, 103
Cushion plants, 24–7, 159
Cyclamen, 177; *C. cilicium*, 177; *C. coum* (or *C. atkinsii*), 176; *C. cyprium*, 177; *C. persicum*, 176; *C. pseudibericum*, 176; *C. neapolitanum*, 177; *C. n. album*, 118, 177; *C. repandum*, 176
Cytisus battandieri, 133; *C. scoparius*, 110; 'Golden Sunlight', 110; *C. x beanii*, 110; *C. x kewensis*, 150; *C. praecox*, 110; 'Allgold', 110
Cystopteris fragilis, 138

Daboecia cantabrica, 151
Daphne odora, 131; 'Aureomarginata', 131, 162; *D. x burkwoodii*, 133
Delphinium, 122
Dianthus, 134; 'Candy Clove', 134; 'Cherry Clove', 134; 'Imperial Clove', 134; 'Mrs Sinkins', 134; 'Pink Mrs Sinkins', 134; 'Robin Thain', 134; 'Sam Barlow', 134; *D. alpinus*, 174; *D. deltoides*, 26; *D. gratianopolitanus (D. caesius)*, 26; *D. x allwoodii*, 128; 'Doris', 128

Digging, 19
Dimorphotheca barberiae, 129
Dionysia aretioides, 173
Dogs, 87–8, 90; in the garden, 88
Doronicum, 112; *D. caucasicum* 'Spring
  Beauty', 112; *D. cordatum*, 112
Draba rigida, 173
Drive, from concrete, 23–4
Dryas octopetala, 174
Dryopteris filix-mas, 138; *D. pseudomas* (syn.
  D. borreri), 138; 'Cristata the King', 138

Echinops ritro (Globe thistle), 122; 'Veitch's
  Blue', 122
Edraianthus pumilio, 175; *E. serpyllifolius*
  'Major', 175
Elaeagnus pungens, 135; 'Dicksonii', 135;
  'Maculata', 135, 162; 'Variegata', 135;
  E. x ebbingei, 152–3
Electricity, laying on, 15–16, 54, 66
Elodea canadensis, 61
Endymion hispanicus, see *Scilla hispanicus*
Eranthis hyemalis (Winter aconite), 112
Eremurus bungei (Foxtail lily), 113;
  E. robustus, 113, 118
Erica, 149; *E. australis*, 149; *E. carnea*, 126,
  149; 'Aurea', 126; 'December Red', 126;
  'King George', 126; 'Springwood Pink',
  126; *E. cinerea*, 127; 'C.D. Eason', 127;
  E. tetralix, 149
Erigeron, 129; 'Charity', 129; 'Foerster's
  Liebling', 129
Eryngium oliverianum (Sea holly), 123
Erythronium tuolumnense, 112
Escallonia, 127, 152; 'Apple Blossom', 127;
  'Donard Gem', 127; 'Donard Star', 127;
  'Glory of Donard', 127; 'Peach Blossom',
  127
Espalier-trained fruit trees, 104
Euonymus fortunei (radicans), 102, 103;
  'Emerald and Gold', 162–3; 'Silver
  Queen', 102
Euryops evansii (or *E. acraeus*), 113
Exochorda giraldii, 115

Fan-trained fruit trees, 104
Fatsia japonica, 163
Fennel, 165
Ferns, 137–9
Fertilizer, for lawns, 31
Figs, 104
Filipendula palmata, 128
Fish, 65–6
Fontinalis antipyretica (Water moss), 61
Forsythia, 102; *F. suspensa sieboldii*, 80, 102
Fothergill major, 130

Foundations, for path, 21; for brick wall,
  45–6
Fountain, 54
Fremontia californica, 110
Fritillaria imperialis 'Lutea Maxima' (Crown
  imperial), 112; *F. meleagris*, 176
Front garden, 71, 105–7, 159
Fruit trees, 103–5
Fuchsia, 161; 'Tom Thumb', 163

Galanthus nivalis (Snowdrop), 117, 132;
  'S. Arnott', 132; *G.n. plenus*, 117;
  G. elwesii, 176; *G. ikariae latifolius*, 176;
  G. plicatus 'Warham', 176
Garrya elliptica, 102, 152
Gaultheria procumbens, 148, 183; *G. shallon*,
  81, 127
Genista cineria, 111; *G. hispanica*, 81, 151;
  G. lydia, 111
Gentiana acaulis, 173; *G. parseri*, 175;
  G. septemfida, 175; *G. verna*, 173
Geranium, 128; *G. endressii*, 156; 'Wargrave
  Pink', 128; *G. macrorrhizum*, 156;
  G. napuligerum, 174; *G. sanguineum
  lancastriense* 'Splendens', 128
Gerbils, 85
Geum chiloense, 113; 'Lady Stratheden', 113
Glyceria spectabilis variegata, 65
Golden orfe *(Idus idus)*, 65
Goldfish *(Carassius aurata)*, 65, 87
Gooseberry bushes, 103
Grass cuttings, 17–18
Grass seed, 33–4; sowing, 37–8; for hard-
  wearing lawn, 38; for posh lawn, 38–9
Grassy mound, 78
Grave, plants for, 183–4
Gravel, 20, 157–9
Greenhouse, 15, 16, 166, 167–71; warm, cool
  or unheated, 168; choosing, 170; siting,
  170–1; servicing, 171; labour-saving
  devices, 171
Ground cover garden, 109, 145–56
Guinea pigs, 85
Gymnocarpium dryopteris, 138
Gypsophila repens 'Rosea', 154

Halimiocistus sahucii, 150
Halimium lasianthum, 111, 150
Hamamelis mollis (Chinese witch hazel), 132;
  'Pallida', 109, 132
Hamsters, 85
Hebe 'Autumn Glory', 120; 'Midsummer
  Beauty', 120; *H. brachysiphon*, 163; 'White
  Gem', 163; *H. pinguefolia* 'Pagei', 150
Hedera (Ivy), 100–101, 102, 160, 163;
  H. canariensis 'Gloire de Marengo', 101;

H. colchica 'Dentata', 101; *H. helix*
'Buttercup', 101; 'Congesta', 163;
'Discolor', 101; 'Erecta', 163; 'Feastii',
184; 'Goldheart', 101, 163; 'Russelliannia',
163; Sagittifolia, 100, 184
Helenium autumnale, 114; 'Butterpat', 114;
'Wyndley', 114
Helianthemum 'Wisley Pink', 128
Heliopsis scabra, 114; 'Golden Plume', 114;
'Light of Loddon', 114
Helleborus niger (Christmas rose), 117
Hemerocallis (Day lily), 114
Herbs, 165
Heuchera, 128
Hibiscus syriacus, 120; 'Blue Bird', 120
Hiding places, see Barrier shrubs
Holly, see *Ilex aquifolium*
Honeysuckle, see *Lonicera*
Hosta, 156
Hottonia palustris, 61
Humus, 17
Hydrangea, 163; *H. macrophylla*, 120;
'Général Vicomtesse de Vibraye', 120;
H.m. hortensia 'Hamburg', 127;
H. paniculata 'Grandiflora', 117;
H. petiolaris, 100
Hypericum calycinum (Rose of Sharon), 149;
H. elatum 'Elstead', 111; *H. reptans*, 27;
H. rhodopeum, 183

Iberis sempervirens, 149
Ilex aquifolium, 163; 'Argentia Marginata',
163; 'Golden King', 163; 'Golden Queen',
163; 'J.C. van Tol', 163
Indoor gardening, 182
Ipheion uniflorum, 117, 176
Ipomoea rubro-caerulea, 105
Iris, bearded, 122; *I. danfordiae*, 176;
I. histrioides 'Major', 121; *Iris laevigata*,
64; *I. reticulata*, 132; 'Harmony', 176;
'J.S. Dijt', 176; 'Violet Beauty', 176;
I. vartanii alba, 176
Ivy, see Hedera

Jasminum nudiflorum (Winter jasmine), 101,
102, 109, 110; *J. officinale*, 99, 102;
'Affine', 135
Juniperus, 163–4; *J. horizontalis*, 149;
J. procumbens 'Nana', 183; *J. scopulorum*
'Blue Heaven', 163–4; *J. virginiana*
'Skyrocket' (Pencil cedar), 164; *J. x media*,
81; 'Pfitzeriana', 81

Kalmia latifolia, 126
Kolkwitzia amabilis, 127
Koi carp, 65

Kniphofia uvaria (Red hot poker), 125

Labour-saving devices, for greenhouse, 171;
for old people, 179, 180
Laburnum, 107
Lagarosyphon major, 61
Laurus nobilis (Bay), 164
Lavandula spica (Lavender), 120, 160; 'Nana
Atropurpurea' (alias 'Hidcote'), 120
Lawns, 28–41, 144–5; improving, 28–33;
initial cutting, 29; scratching, 29; spiking,
29; dressing, 30, 33; levelling, 30, 33; feeding,
31, 33; reseeding, 31; applying weedkiller,
31–2; mowing, 32, 33; making a new lawn,
33–9; turf or seed, 33–4; preparing ground,
34–5; laying turf, 35–7; sowing seed, 37–8;
seed mixtures, 38–9; looking after, 39–40;
see also Turf, Grass seed, Lawn mowers,
Mowing
Lawn mowers, cylinder, 29, 39; rotary, 29,
39; hover, 40; hand or motor, 40
Leontopodium alpinum (Edelweiss), 175
Leucogenes leontopodium, 176
Leucojum (Snowflakes), 117; *L. aestivum*,
117; *L. autumnale*, 177; *L. vernum*, 117,
176
Lewisia tweedyi, 174; 'Rosea', 174
Lifting, 25
Lilac, see *Syringa vulgaris*
Lilium, 134; *L. auratum*, 134; Bellingham
hybrids, 134; *L. candidum* (Madonna lily),
134; *L. hansonii*, 134; *L. henryi*, 134;
L. pyrenaicum (Turk's cap lily), 114;
L. regale (Regal lily), 118, 134
Lily-of-the-valley, 133; 'Fortin's Giant', 133;
'Rosea', 133; 'Variegata', 133
Lindera benzoin, 130
Linum narbonense, 122
Lithospermum diffusum, 26, 27
Lobelia cardinalis or *L. fulgens*, 125; 'Cherry
Ripe', 125; 'Queen Victoria', 125; 'Red
Flame', 125; 'Will Scarlet', 125
Lonicera (Honeysuckle), 100, 101, 102;
L. americana, 100; *L. brownii* 'Fuchsioides',
100, 101; *L. japonica*, 100; *L. periclymenum*
'Belgica', 100; 'Serotina', 100;
L. tragophylla, 100, 101
Lychnis chalcedonica, 125
Lysimachia nummularia (Creeping Jenny),
153; *L. punctata* (Loosestrife), 113

Magnolia, 107; *M. grandiflora* 'Exmouth',
134; *M. salicifolia*, 107; *M. stellata*, 107;
M. x soulangiana, 107
Mahonia japonica, 81, 131, 152;
M. aquifolium, 81

Marble, for paving, 20
Mathiola bicornis (Night-scented stock), 135
Matteuccia germanica, 138
Meconopsis betonicifolia (Blue Himalayan poppy), 122–3
Mentha requienii, 26
Mertensia virginica, 121
Michelia figo, 111
Mignonette, see *Reseda odorata*
Mimulus luteus, 64; 'Canary Bird', 64; 'Red Emperor', 64; 'Whitecroft Scarlet', 64; *M. guttatas*, 64
Minuartia (Arenaria) verna caespitosa 'Aurea', 24
Mint, 165
Monarda didyma (Bergamot), 125; 'Cambridge Scarlet', 125
Montbretia, see *Crocosmia* x *crocosmiiflora*
Mortar, 43, 46, 47
Moss, 32
Mowers, see Lawn mowers
Mowing, 32, 33, 39–40, 41
Mulching, 19, 145–6
Muscari (Grape hyacinth), 177; *M. armeniacum*, 121; 'Blue Spike', 121; 'Heavenly Blue', 121; *M. botryoides album*, 117

Narcissus, miniature types, 111, 176; *N. asturiensis*, 111; *N. bulbocodium*, 111; *N.b. monophyllus*, 176; *N.b. vulgaris conspicuus*, 111; *N. b.v. nivalis*, 176; *N. cyclamineus*, 176; 'Tête à Tête', 111; *N. triandrus albus*, 176; *N.t. concolor*, 111
Nasturtium, see *Tropaeolum majus*
Nectarines, 104
Nepeta x *faassenii* (Catmint), 122, 155
Nicotiana alata (Tobacco plant), 135
Night-scented stock, see *Mathiola bicornis*
Nymphaea (Water lily), 62–3; 'Froebelii', 62; 'Graziella', 62; 'James Brydon', 62; 'Paul Hariot', 62; 'Rose Arey', 62; 'Sioux', 62; *N. candida*, 62; *N. caroliniana nivea*, 62; *N. laydekeri* 'Purpurata', 62; *N. odorata turiensis*, 62; *N. pygmaea alba*, 62; *N.p.* 'Helvola', 62
Nymphoides peltata 'Bennettii', syn. *Villarsia bennettii*, 63

Oenothera fruticosa (Evening primrose), 114
Olearia macrodonta, 116
Omphalodes verna, 155
Onoclea sensibilis, 138
Ornithogalum umbellatum, 118
Orontium aquaticum, 63
Osmanthus delavayi, 132, 151

Osmarea burkwoodii, 132
Oxalis inops, 153; *O. laciniata*, 175
Oxygenating plants, 61

Pachysandra terminalis, 149, 184
Paeonia, 118; 'Duchesse de Nemours', 118; 'Festiva Maxima', 118; 'White Wings', 118; *P. delavayi*, 123; *P. officinalis* 'Alba Plena', 118; *P. suffruticosa*, 124; 'Souvenir de Ducher', 124
Pancratium illyricum, 118
Papaver orientale 'Marcus Perry' (Oriental poppy), 124–5; 'Mrs Perry', 128; 'Perry's White', 118
Parthenocissus (Virginia creeper), 98; *P. henryana*, 101; *P. quinquefolia*, 98; *P. tricuspidata* 'Veitchii', 98
Passiflora caerulea (Passion flower), 99
Paths, 14, 20–3, 24, 25; from brick, flags or concrete slabs, 21; from concrete, 21–3
Patios, see Paved areas
Paved areas, 14, 20–21, 24
Paved gardens, 20, 24, 109, 157–9
Paving materials, 20, 157–9
Peach trees, 104
Pear trees, 103
Pebbles, 157–9
Pelargonium, 125, 160
Perennial herbaceous plants, yellow, 111–15; white, 117–19; blue, 121–3; red, 124–5; pink, 128–9; for ground cover, 153–6
Perennial weeds, 18
Pergola, see Arbor
Pernettya mucronata, 81; 'Bell's Seedling', 81; Davis's hybrids, 81
Pets, 83–90; children's relationship with, 84, 87, 90
Phegopteris connectilis (Thelypteris phegopteris), 138
Philadelphus (Mock orange), 116, 134; 'Beauclerk', 116, 134; 'Virginal', 116, 134; *P. microphyllus*, 134
Phillyrea decora, 152
Phlomis fruticosa, 110
Phlox nana, 175; *P. paniculata*, 129; 'Annie Laurie', 129; 'Firefly', 129; 'Sandringham', 129; *P. subulata*, 24, 154; 'Temiscaming', 24; 'G.F. Wilson', 24
Phormium tenax, 164; 'Veitchii', 164; 'Variegatum', 164; *P.t. purpureum*, 164
Phyllitis scolopendrium, see *Asplenium scolopendrium*
Pileostagia viburnoides, 100
Pink shrubs, 126–8; bulbs and perennials, 128–9
Piptanthus laburnifolius, 110

Planting, 136
Plants, 16; to enliven paths, 23, 24–7; for a
    small pool, 61–5; to cover walls, 96–105;
    yellow, 109–15; white, 115–19; blue,
    119–23; red, 123–5; pink, 126–9; scented,
    131–5; for ground cover, 145–56; for tubs,
    160–4
Play equipment, 74–6; for water, 73
Pleione formosana, 174; 'Alba', 174;
    P. limprichtii, 174
Pointing, 47–8
Polystichum setiferum, 139
Polygonum affine, 154; 'Darjeeling Red', 154;
    P. amplexicaule, 125; 'Atrosanguineum',
    125; 'Firetail', 125; *P. aubertii* (Russian
    vine), 98; *P. bistorta* 'Superbum', 129
Polypodium vulgare, 139
Pontederia cordata, 63
Poplars, 106
Poppy, see *Papaver orientale*, *Meconopsis
    betonicifolia*; tree, see *Romneya coulteri*
Potentilla, 110; *P. arbuscula*, 110;
    P. atrosanguinea, 125; 'Gibson's Scarlet',
    125; *P. fruticosa*, 151; 'Elizabeth', 110;
    'Katherine Dykes', 110; 'Primrose Beauty',
    110
Primula allionii, 173; *P. auricula*, 174;
    P. helodoxa, 113
Primulus vulgaris (Primrose), 112
Propagator, 170, 171, 182
Prunus triloba 'Multiplex', 126
Pulmonaria augustifolia, 121; *P. saccharata*,
    155
Pulsatilla vernalis, 173
Punica granatum 'Nana', 164
Pyracantha (Firethorn), 102; 'Watereri', 102;
    P. coccinea 'Lalandi', 102
Pyrethrum roseum, 128; 'Brenda', 128;
    'Eileen May Robinson', 128; 'Kelway's
    Glorious', 128

Quarry tiles, 21

Rabbit hutch, 84, 85, 86
Rabbits, 84–5
Raised beds, 14–15, 19, 42–51, 157, 165, 168;
    from brick, 42–8; dimensions, 44;
    watering, 44; foundations, 45–6; building
    walls, 46–8; filling, 48; making seat, 48–9;
    from concrete flags, 49–50
Raised pools, 14, 15, 52–60, 165–6;
    dimensions, 52; materials, 52; formal or
    informal, 52, 53, 54; fountain, 54;
    waterfall, 54; formal pool from brick,
    54–7; planting, 57; informal pool with
    stone walls, 58–60
Ranunculus amplexicaulis, 173; *R. aquatilis*, 61

Red hot poker, see *Kniphofia uvaria*
Red shrubs, 123–4; bulbs and perennials,
    124–5
Reseda odorata (Mignonette), 135
Rhododendron, 124, 164; 'Britannia', 124;
    'Cynthia', 124; 'Doncaster', 124;
    R. fastigiatum, 164; *R. ferrugineum*, 164;
    R. glaucophyllum, 164; *R.g. luteiflorum*,
    164; *R. glomerulatum*, 164; *R. megeratum*,
    164; *R. pemakoense*, 164; *R. scintillans*, 164;
    R. trichostomum, 164; *R. wardii*, 110;
    R. yakushimanum, 164; see also Azaleas
Rhus typhina, 130
Ribes aureum (Flowering currant), 130;
    R. laurifolium, 115; *R. sanguineum*, 123;
    'Pulborough Scarlet', 123
Robinia pseudoacacia 'Frisia', 107
Rockery, 168
Romneya coulteri, 117
Rosa rugosa, 81; 'Blanc Double de Coubert',
    81; 'Fru Dagmar Hastrup', 81; 'Roseraie
    de l'Hay', 81; *R. x* 'Macrantha', 81;
    R. x paulii, 81
Roscoea caulteoides, 175; *R. humeana*, 175
Rose, rambling, 167
Rosmarinus officinalis, 119, 160; 'Severn Sea',
    164
Rowan or mountain ash, see *Sorbus aucuparia*
Rubus calycinoides, 148; *R. tridel* 'Benenden',
    116
Rudbeckia sullivantii, 115; 'Goldsturm', 115;
    'Autumn Sun', 115
Runner beans, 105; Painted Lady, 105; Blue
    Coco, 105
Russian vine, see *Polygonum aubertii*

Sagittaria sagittifolia, 63
Salad crops, 165
Salvia grahamii, 124; *S. officinalis*, 150
Sand play, 73, 76, 77
Sandpit, 73, 76, 77–9; adapting, 166–7
Santolina chamaecyparissus, 111, 150
Saponaria ocymoides 'Rubra Compacta', 175
Saxifraga paniculata (S. aizoon), 26;
    S. umbrosa (London pride), 153; *Saxifraga
    x jenkinsae*, 173
Scabiosa caucasica, 123; 'Clive Greaves', 123
Scented plants, 131–5; for winter, 131–2; for
    spring, 132–3; for summer, 133–5; for
    autumn, 135
Schizophragma integrifolia, 100
Scilla bifolia, 121, 177; *S. campanulata*
    'Queen of the Pinks', 128; *S. hispanicus*,
    121; 'Excelsior', 121; 'King of the Blues',
    121; 'Myosotis', 121; *S. tubergeniana*, 177
Scirpus albescens, 64; *S. tabernaemontani*
    'Zebrinus', 64

Sedum acre, 26; *S. anglicum*, 26; *S. spectabile*, 155
Senecio laxifolius, 111, 151; *S. przewalski*, 114
Services, 15–16
Shrubs, for barriers, 79–81; for garden walls and fences, 102–3; yellow, 109–11; white, 115–7; blue, 119–20; red, 123–4; pink, 126–8; small, for ground cover, 148–51; tall, for ground cover, 151–3; architectural, 159, 160; for tubs, 161–4
Shubunkins, 65
Silver birch, see *Betula pendula*
Sisyrinchium bermudiana, 175
Skimmia japonica, 116; *S. laureola*, 116; *S. rubella*, 126
Slate, for paving, 20
Snails, water, 65
Snowdrop, see *Galanthus*
Solanum crispum 'Glasnevin', 100; *S. jasminoides album*, 99
Soldanella montana, 172
Solidago canadensis (Golden rod), 120
Sorbus aucuparia (Rowan or Mountain ash), 106; 'Xanthocarpa', 106; 'Beissneri', 106
Spartium junceum, 133
Spiraea japonica 'Alpina', 127
Stachys lanata (Lamb's tongue), 153
Sternbergia lutea, 115, 177
Stone, for paving, 20; flags, second-hand, for paving, 20; for raised beds, 42; random rubble, for informal pool, 54, 58; building stone wall, 59
Straight edge, 34
Summerhouse, 14, 15, 16, 66, 72, 82–3, 92, 144
Sweet peas, 167
Syringa vulgaris (Lilac), 116, 119, 133; 'Firmament', 119; 'Madame Lemoine', 116, 133; 'Michel Buchner', 119; 'Souvenir de Louis Spath', 133

Tarmac, 20
Taxus 'Repandens', 150
Thermometer, maximum and minimum, 171
Thrift, see *Armeria caespitosa*
Thymus serpyllum, 26
Tiarella cordifolia, 154
Tobacco plant, see *Nicotiana alata*
Tree, for front garden, 106–7
Trellis, 97
Trollius europaeus, 113
Tropaeolum majus (Nasturtium), 105; *T. peregrinum*, 105
Tubs, 157, 159, 160–4; filling, 161; shrubs for, 161–4
Tulip, 124; *T. biflora*, 176; cottage, 124;

Darwin, 124; double early, 124; *T. fosteriana*, 124; *greigii* hybrids, 124; *T. hageri*, 176; *T. kaufmanniana*, 112, 124; lily-flowered, 124; *T. pulchella humilis*, 176; single early, 124; *T. tarda*, 176; *T. urumiensis*, 176
Turf, 33–4, 35; meadow, 33; parkland, 33; Cumberland sea-washed, 33; in rolls, 33–4; laying, 35–7

Vaccinium vitis-idaea, 127, 149
Ventilator, automatic, for greenhouse, 171
Veronica prostrata (*V. rupestris*), 26; 'Mrs Holt', 26
Viburnum carlesii, 132; *V. davidii*, 151; *V. fragrans* (*V. farreri*), 131; *V. opulus*, 130; *V. tomentosum* 'Lanarth', 116, 130, 152; *V.* x *burkwoodii*, 132
Vinca major, 120, 148, 149; *V. minor*, 148
Vine, 167
Vine eyes, 97
Viola odorata, 132; 'Coeur d'Alsace', 132; 'Princess of Wales', 132; *V. papillonacea*, 174; *V. tricolor*, 174
Virginia creeper, see *Parthenocissus*
Vitis coignetiae, 101

Waldsteinia ternata, 183
Wallflower, 133
Walls, building, 25; plants for, 96–105
Water, laying on, 15, 165, 171
Water lily, see *Nymphaea*
Water moss, see *Fontinalis antipyretica*
Water play, 73
Waterfall, 54
Watering devices, automatic, 171
Weeding, 147
Weedkiller, for lawns, 18, 31–2, 34
Weldenia candida, 173
White shrubs, 115–17; bulbs and perennials, 117–19
Willows, 106
Window boxes, 105
Winter aconite, see *Eranthis hyemalis*
Wisteria floribunda, 98; 'Alba', 98; 'Macrobotrys', 98; *W. sinensis*, 98; 'Alba', 98
Wood, for paving, 20, 157
Worms, 19

Yellow shrubs, 109–11; bulbs and perennials, 111–15
Yucca filamentosa, 164

Zephyranthes candida, 119